Deleuze: A Philosophy of the Event

p 56 - 57 for truth.

Being is Pure
constitutes a fidelity, a way of
to its complexity, a way of
being in the closed
nonetheless a fragmented which
or in its very room
room for
for disruption

creates

Plateaus – New Directions in Deleuze Studies

'It's not a matter of bringing all sorts of things together under a single concept but rather of relating each concept to variables that explain its mutations.'
Gilles Deleuze, *Negotiations*

Series Editors

Ian Buchanan, Cardiff University
Claire Colebrook, Penn State University

Editorial Advisory Board

Titles available in the series

Dorothea Olkowski, *The Universal (In the Realm of the Sensible): Beyond Continental Philosophy*
Christian Kerslake, *Immanence and the Vertigo of Philosophy: From Kant to Deleuze*
Jean-Clet Martin, *Variations: The Philosophy of Gilles Deleuze*, translated by Constantin V. Boundas and Susan Dyrkton
Simone Bignall, *Postcolonial Agency: Critique and Constructivism*
Miguel de Beistegui, *Immanence: Deleuze and Philosophy*
Jean-Jacques Lecercle, *Badiou and Deleuze Read Literature*
Ronald Bogue, *Deleuzian Fabulation and the Scars of History*
Sean Bowden, *The Priority of Events: Deleuze's Logic of Sense*
Craig Lundy, *History and Becoming: Deleuze's Philosophy of Creativity*
Aidan Tynan, *Deleuze's Literary Clinic: Criticism and the Politics of Symptoms*
Thomas Nail, *Returning to Revolution: Deleuze Guattari and Zapatismo*
François Zourabichvili, *Deleuze: A Philosophy of the Event* with *The Vocabulary of Deleuze* edited by Gregg Lambert and Daniel W. Smith, translated by Kieran Aarons

Visit the Plateaus website at www.euppublishing.com/series/plat

DELEUZE: A PHILOSOPHY OF THE EVENT
together with The Vocabulary of Deleuze

François Zourabichvili

TRANSLATED BY KIERAN AARONS
EDITED BY GREGG LAMBERT AND DANIEL W. SMITH

EDINBURGH
University Press

Deleuze. Une philosophie de l'événement by François Zourabichvili © Presses Universitaires de France, 1994, 108, boulevard Saint-Germain, 75006 Paris

Le Vocabulaire de Deleuze by François Zourabichvili © Ellipses Édition Marketing S.A., 2003, www.editions-ellipses.fr, 32, rue Bargue 75740 Paris cedex 15.

Edinburgh University Press Ltd
22 George Square, Edinburgh EH8 9LF

www.euppublishing.com

Typeset in Sabon
by Servis Filmsetting Ltd, Stockport, Cheshire, and
printed and bound in Great Britain by
CPI Group (UK) Ltd, Croydon CR0 4YY

A CIP record for this book is available from the British Library

ISBN 978 0 7486 4562 6 (hardback)
ISBN 978 0 7486 4585 5 (paperback)
ISBN 978 0 7486 4563 3 (webready PDF)
ISBN 978 0 7486 6831 1 (epub)
ISBN 978 0 7486 6832 8 (Amazon ebook)

Contents

List of Abbreviations

ABC   *L'abécédaire de Gilles Deleuze*, 3 DVD's, éd. Montparnasse, 1996.

AO   *Anti-Oedipus* (written with Félix Guattari), trans. R. Hurley, M. Seem, and H. R. Lane (Minneapolis: University of Minnesota Press, 1983).

ATP   *A Thousand Plateaus* (written with Félix Guattari), trans. B. Massumi (Minneapolis: University of Minnesota Press, 1987).

B   *Bergsonism*, trans. H. Tomlinson and B. Habberjam (New York: Zone Books, 1988).

BS   "Balance-Sheet for Desiring Machines" (written with Félix Guattari), trans. R. Hurley in Félix Guattari, *Chaosophy*, ed. S. Lotringer (New York: Semiotext(e), 1995), pp. 90–115.

C1   *Cinema 1: The Movement-Image*, trans. H. Tomlinson and B. Habberjam (London: Athlone Press, 1986).

C2   *Cinema 2: The Time-Image*, trans. H. Tomlinson and R. Galeta (London: Athlone Press, 1997).

CC   *Essays Critical and Clinical*, trans. D. W. Smith (Minnesota: University of Minnesota Press, 1997).

D   *Dialogues II*, trans. H. Tomlinson and B. Habberjam, rev. edn (New York: Columbia University Press, 2007).

DI   *Desert Islands and Other Texts (1953–1974)*, trans. M. Taormina (New York: Semiotext(e), 2002).

DR   *Difference and Repetition*, trans. P. Patton (London: Athlone Press, 1984).

EPS   *Expressionism in Philosophy: Spinoza*, trans. M. Joughin (New York: Zone Books, 1992).

ES   *Empiricism and Subjectivity. An Essay on Hume's Theory of Human Nature*, trans. C. V. Boundas (New York: Columbia University Press, 1991).

F   *Foucault*, trans. S. Hand (London: Athlone Press, 1988).

FB   *Francis Bacon: The Logic of Sensation*, trans. D. W. Smith (New York: Continuum, 2003).

List of Abbreviations

K   *Kafka: Toward a Minor Literature* (written with Félix Guattari), trans. D. Polan (Minneapolis: University of Minnesota Press, 1986).

L   *The Fold: Leibniz and the Baroque*, trans. T. Conley (London: Athlone Press, 1993).

LS   *Logic of Sense*, trans. M. Lester with C. Stivale, ed. C. V. Boundas (London: Athlone Press, 1990).

M   *Masochism: Coldness and Cruelty*, trans. J McNeil (New York: Zone Books, 1991).

N   *Negotiations, 1972–1990*, trans. M. Joughin (New York: Columbia University Press, 1995).

NP   *Nietzsche and Philosophy*, trans. H. Tomlinson (London: Athlone Press, 1983).

PI   *Pure Immanence: Essays on a Life*, trans. A Boyman (New York: Zone Books, 2001).

PS   *Proust and Signs, The Complete Text*, trans. R. Howard (Minneapolis: Minnesota University Press, 2000).

S   *Superpositions* (with Carmelo Bene) (Paris: Minuit, 1991).

SPP   *Spinoza: Practical Philosophy*, trans. R. Hurley (San Francisco: City Lights Books, 1988).

TR   *Two Regimes of Madness: Texts and Interviews 1975–1995*, trans. A. Hodges and M. Taormina (New York: Semiotext(e), 2007).

WP   *What is Philosophy?* (written with Félix Guattari), trans. G. Burchell and H. Tomlinson (New York: Columbia University Press, 1994).

Translator's Acknowledgments

A fellowship from the Social Sciences and Humanities Research Council of Canada was indispensible in completing this translation.

This translation would also not have been possible without the generous and patient aid of several friends and colleagues. Elizabeth Rottenberg looked over early drafts and encouraged me to undertake the project. I am immensely grateful to Grégoire Chamayou, who made innumerable suggestions without which this project would not be what it is today. As editors, Dan Smith reviewed the final manuscripts, and offered many useful suggestions, while Gregg Lambert was instrumental in securing the rights and permissions to combine both original French volumes into one translated edition. My thanks go to both. All remaining errors and imperfections are naturally no one's responsibility but my own.—K.A.

The Involuntarist Image of Thought

Kieran Aarons

> Tell me the affections of which you are capable
> and I'll tell you who you are.
>
> Deleuze, January 14, 1974

Over the past two decades the discourse treating Deleuze as an "ontologist" has become normalized, accepted wisdom. Against such a background, François Zourabichvili's claim that "there is no 'ontology of Deleuze'" will undoubtedly appear alien, as either uninformed or at best a scruple over words. It is therefore worth pointing out that this accusation of ontology is in many respects a consequence of a more pressing question, mainly whether philosophers after Deleuze have sufficiently weighed the stringency of his "involuntarism."[1] The latter entails not only a critique of the subject who wants the truth, but a critique of a mode of truth as merely "possible," one that could exist by default or "once and for all," as well as the vision of practical engagement and political action that this subject and this mode of truth imply. It is a question, in short, of critically dismantling the voluntarist philosophy of truth—a question of critique. The injunction against ontology is inseparable from Zourabichvili's conviction that for Deleuze, a critical philosophy of experience implies an involuntarist image of thought, and vice versa. It is this claim that I would like briefly to unpack in what follows.

The Self-Immolation of Ontology

The general problematic of Deleuze's thought, Zourabichvili argues, is not Being but *experience*. The use Deleuze makes of Nietzsche, Spinoza, and Bergson must accordingly be understood from this critical or transcendental perspective.[2] However, Zourabichvili insists, in Deleuze's thought this opposition between ontological and transcendental problems is not static, but is rather the consequence of a kind of self-immolation immanently affecting ontology itself, a

1

logical undertow that draws us *through* ontology toward a thought of experience that outstrips it.

Those who read Deleuze as an ontologist typically point to his notion of the "univocity of being" as a positive ontological doctrine, as if the notion signified a name—metaphysical or otherwise—for an ultimate truth or principle of reality. However, Zourabichvili argues, this misses the significance of this concept. As readers of Deleuze are aware, the thesis of the univocity of being states that "being is said in a single sense of everything of which it is said [this is the classical doctrine, drawn from Duns Scotus], but [Deleuze adds], it is said of difference" (DR 35–42). This position is doctrinally contrasted with an analogical or equivocal conception, according to which being is said in many ways or according to a set of fixed categories, e.g. generic and specific differences. So far the issue remains uninteresting, and in the strict sense that Deleuze gives to this word: the state of thought detached from a problem. What does Deleuze want with this notion? To which problem does it respond?

On Zourabichvili's reading, the significance of the concept of univocity lies not in a knowledge about reality but in a quest for a "pure logic of sense."[3] In a lecture course from 1974 Deleuze says of the difference between equivocity and univocity, "I'm not even interested in knowing if it's an ontological problem; it's just as much a problem of statements."[4] That is to say, rather than a metaphysical thesis or name of being, the truth of which one may either affirm or deny, the affirmation of univocity addresses the relation between the objects of experience and the expression of sense (hence the emphasis on *saying*, on how the sense of existence is *said*).[5] For Deleuze, the key point is that this relation can no longer legitimately be confined to categories that remain *general* or *external* to the experience in question:

> Categories ... are strictly inseparable from an analogical conception; one calls categories the concepts which are said of every possible object of experience, or what amounts strictly to the same thing: the different senses of the word "being." And the categories in Aristotle are presented as the different senses of the word "being," exactly as in Kant the categories are defined as the concepts which are said of every possible object of experience. Therefore there's no question of a thought proceeding by categories if it does not have, as background, the idea that being is analogical, which is to say that being is said of what is in an analogical manner.[6]

Rather than categories or conditions of possibility in general, which ensure a structural supervision of experience in advance by the subject, the thought of univocity signifies that "beings are not distinguished by their form, their genus, their species, that's secondary; everything which is refers to a degree of power."[7] This critique of representational forms of judgment hurls thought into a problematic of *evaluation* or appraisal. If being is said in a single sense of everything of which it is said, and it is said only of difference, the consequence is that differences can only be parsed affectively, through the actualization and counter-effectuation of the given (and not in advance of it), as the outcome of an appraisal that can only be decided case-by-case, and as a function of the assemblage into which this experience is inserted: "To each degree of power corresponds a certain power of being affected . . . The affect is the manner in which a degree of power is necessarily effectuated as a function of the assemblages into which the individual or the thing enters."[8]

When the thesis of the univocity of being is taken to its final conclusion, it has two major consequences. First, if differences can only be parsed affectively, the name "being" ceases to have any conceptual pertinence, since it cannot aid in the description of the conditions of real experience (it picks nothing out). As Zourabichvili writes, "the vocabulary of being has ceased to be pertinent in the universe of the disjunctive synthesis, owing to what it still preserves from the fixed and identitarian horizon."[9] Since the affective logic of univocal being holds that a given being, itself a pure difference, can test or measure itself against others only by first encountering its own specific thresholds and limits,[10] and this "test" of univocal difference eschews *a priori* categories, it inherently becomes a thought of experience.

Second, because affective evaluations involve the encounter with an immanent as opposed to an extrinsic limit, the critical thought *of* experience is itself contingent *upon* an experience, and a special sort of experience: that of the higher or "active" deployment of the faculties or powers that compose us.[11]

In short, the supreme ontological thesis becomes the supreme critical injunction against ontology. The logic of the univocity of being, when deployed to its full consequences, leads to a critical or transcendental problematic of experience, the principal concern of which is no longer the knowledge of or meaning of Being but the relation between a determinate regime of disjunctive syntheses or differences and their description in accordance with the empiricist doctrine of the faculties. The moment ontology arrives at an immanent formulation it effaces itself qua ontology, leaving only one problem: the construction of logical objects that respond to the fluctuating conditions of "real" experience.

As a result—and contrary to popular opinion—Deleuze is not an ontologist, but a logician. The orientation of his thought is critical and transcendental, and can best be described as a ruthless construction of vital logics.[12] If this transcendental logic eschews a search for conditions of possibility *in general*, this is for two principal reasons. First, as we have seen, his immanent perversion or "overthrow" (ATP 25) of ontology implies that a being can only be defined by the singular declination of its affects. This topples ontology into a problematic of experience. However, this displacement remains incomplete on its own, for it does not explain how it is that the relationship between experience and sense gives rise to a *need* of truth. For this, a critique of truth, of the *possibility* of truth, and of the voluntarist will-to-truth itself is necessary.

Irrationalism, Not Illogicism

What Deleuze calls an "image of thought" is an image of what it means to think, an image of the conditions of an act of thinking, of the conditions under which thought enters into a relation with truth. An image is deemed to be dogmatic when it reveals itself to be founded on a pre-philosophical or moral *doxa*, an unchecked empirical prejudice or conventional view. In other words, one is guilty of dogmatism whenever one imports into the realm of the transcendental principles that are merely extrapolations from empirical facts or opinions. To evaluate an image of thought is to engage in a critique of the conditions under which the faculty of thought attains a necessity, or manages to distinguish itself from its arbitrary exercise under the forms of convention or of opinion.

What defines philosophy's dogmatic image of thought is the assumption, from the outset, of an *a priori* affinity between the thinker and what they are seeking. For once such an affinity is presupposed, the thinker need only exercise their good will in order to find themselves already on the path of the true.[13] In short, where thought possesses a rightful access to truth in advance of setting out after it, a possession that awaits its activation by a "decision" or a "willful act" on the part of its seeker, we may refer to a *voluntarist* conception of truth. Voluntarism of this sort is found through-

4

out the history of philosophy. Whether we look to Descartes or to Heidegger, we see a similar situation of *prior* possession, a possession by default. It matters little whether this possession is formal in nature (guaranteed by God), or established existentially through a structure like Heidegger's "pre-ontological understanding" by means of which "the subject appears to itself already preceded by an instance that opens the possibility of such an appearing."[14] For as Deleuze writes,

> If it is a question of rediscovering at the end what was there in the beginning, if it is a question of recognizing, of bringing to light or into the conceptual or the explicit, what was simply known implicitly without concepts—whatever the complexity of this process, whatever the differences between the procedures of this or that author—the fact remains that all this is still too simple, and that this circle is truly not tortuous enough. (DR 129)

Deleuze's critique of the voluntarist image of truth is transcendental because it concerns the conditions under which thought relates to truth. It is a matter of describing the conditions under which a truth comes to distinguish itself from an abstract possibility or an indifferent concept. The critical question *par excellence* concerns the *necessary*: "not the necessity of thinking, but how to arrive at a necessary thought," which is to say, a thought that solicits a need of truth in us.[15] It is insufficient for critique to point to conditions of possible experience in general, which remain untouched by the fluctuations of concrete events. Instead, it must concern itself with the *conditions under which something is recognized as possible*. Once the question is posed in this way, critique will by the same token be able to describe how it is that mutations or aberrations in our capacity to recognize the possible can occur. In other words, a theory of the conditions of "possibilization" (the genesis of representational forms) will at the same time allow us to account for how it is that the possible can potentially become impossible, how the available alternatives of a situation can suddenly become unlivable, intolerable. It is for this same reason that the critique of the voluntarist image of truth has, as we shall see, important political implications as well.

In place of a default affinity between thought and that which it has yet to think, Deleuze insists that a critical philosophy of truth can only be a philosophy of the event, a philosophy of the encounter: "There is always the violence of a sign that forces us into the search, that robs us of peace ... Truth is never the product of a predisposed good will but the result of a violence in thought" (PS 15–16).

Thought does not *want* the true innately, but must first be *spurred* to seek it out by encountering a sign whose development or explication the thinker jealously pursues. Something must force us. Thought is entirely reliant on contingent encounters, which is to say, on events. Its necessity lies in its being forced by an event, which is to say by an *encounter* with the world, with something that does not depend upon us. Thought always implies a *forced movement*, which occurs when we are made the patient of a sign that threatens to throw the coherency of what had up till then functioned into crisis. "The act of thought is engendered in a *passive synthesis*,"[16] through which an encounter bears down on us, giving rise to a difference.

Zourabichvili highlights the important way in which this involuntarist primacy of the event re-orients a perennial question governing thought, namely the opposition between necessity and chance. For if necessity is only ever the necessity of an encounter, and of a relation that this encounter gives rise to within us, a relation whose nature cannot be known prior to the forced movement it induces, then we must reconsider the meaning of the *arbitrary*. The concern of critical philosophy cannot be bound up with evaluating truth from a position of relative or extrinsic indifference (the judgment of natural light, or else a reasoned consensus established by convention).[17] When truths are separated from the necessity of an encounter they become abstract, which is to say, they are reduced to being merely possible or hypothetical. No longer compromising us, no longer demanding more than we can give, they remain mute and stupid, their recognition has become entirely voluntary. "The explicit and conventional significations are never profound; the only profound meaning is the one that is enveloped, implicated in an external sign" (PS 16).

As a result, the critical question must be: on the basis of which signs are we compelled to seek the truth? And at the same time: under what conditions does what is *arbitrary*—the pre-given possibilities of a situation—all of a sudden become insufficient, provoking a failure in our ability to recognize? In other words, the critical question lies at the event horizon, the site at which the arbitrary provides the occasion for a *necessary encounter*.

This insistence on the encounter may at first blush appear to clash with Zourabichvili's emphasis on the role of logic in Deleuze's thought. After all, what is the meaning of "logic" for a thought that has done away with general categories, one whose critique of the dogmatic image of representational thought hinges on the refusal to grant philosophy any "formal" participation in a general element of the true, and on the abandonment of any pre-established affinity with the very object of its thought? Even if we were to concede the argument regarding the immanent destruction of ontology (as distinct from an external rejection of it), it is by no means clear how the call for a new logic will not lead us back to a "vulgar metaphysical" discourse making pronouncements about the fundamental elements of all reality.[18] And if it doesn't, from whence does the "bar" against metaphysics come, if not from a subjectivistic restriction of thought within the policed boundaries of an egological finitude? In short, if this logic is neither metaphysical nor ontological, yet is no less confined within the "supervision of a subject," then what kind of logic is it?

To grasp the singularity of the Deleuzian approach to logic we must attend to a distinction that Zourabichvili returns to several times throughout his commentaries: "Deleuze vehemently protests against the confusion of irrationalism and illogicism."[19] The distinction appears already in the 1994 study: "Insistent on the difference between irrationalism and illogicism, Deleuze draws the consequences of his critique of the dogmatic image: thought refers to a logic of the outside, necessarily irrational, that challenges us to affirm chance."[20] We must reject the forced choice between a self-grounding panlogicism (a logic sheltered from the encounter) and an irrationalist pre-critical vitalism (an encounter lacking transcendental consequences). What we find in Deleuze is the quest for "a 'new logic, definitely a logic, but one that . . . does not lead back to reason,' an 'extreme and nonrational logic,' an 'irrational logic.'"[21] By denying thought any *de jure* power to circumscribe the outside, the critical sanction placed on philosophy requires it to affirm the entrance of chance into its relationship to necessity.[22] The outcome of Deleuze's critical destruction of dogmatic thought is in this respect an irrationalism: if reason is no longer master of itself, it must consequently abandon any objective *de jure* ground of knowledge. In fact, to know the world is no longer an adequate characterization of the orientation of thought at all, for there are important differences between this classical ambition and Deleuze's "explication" of signs.[23] Yet this must not be confused with a rejection of objectivity as such. Indeed, this point cannot be overemphasized: the undermining of the foundations of knowledge in Deleuze's thought does not take place through a problematic of skepticism—nothing is more foreign to Deleuze's thought.[24] On the contrary, only in this way is the *exteriority* of objectivity finally taken seriously. Thought draws its necessity only at the moment it is dethroned, plunged into a field of exteriority. Not exteriority *to a subject*, but exteriority as the disjunctive synthesis of forces/points of view ("immediate synthesis of the multiple"):[25]

> They are not called "forces of the outside" because they come from outside, but because they put thought in a state of exteriority, hurling it into a field where points of view enter into relation, where homogeneous combinations and significations yield to relations of forces within sense itself.[26]

Involuntarism in Philosophy and Politics

Where it attacks the dogmatic presupposition of the will, the involuntarist critique of truth not only affects the orientation of philosophy toward the world, it also has important implications for political action. In this respect, the significance of Deleuze's logic of sense—the key concepts of which are the *sign*, the *problem/form of life*, and the *possible world*—is that it provides a positive and *determinate* account of the emergence of the will within the given, while rejecting as dogmatic or imaginary any appeal to action that cannot do the same. This genetic conception of the will implies an important logical reversal of the relation between the possible and the event. In what space remains, I would like to briefly explicate this connection between the concept of sense and the emergence of the will.

From a transcendental point of view, necessary truths are to be distinguished not from errors, but from stupidities. "Stupidity" [*bêtise*] is defined as the state of thought when nothing forces it to think, where we possess the simple *possibility* of thought, but do not yet think. In such a condition, we negotiate the milieu of actual or existing objects: we navigate pre-existing possibilities, and the relative truths and falsities that came to be inscribed within them as a result of the event that brought them into being, and which continue to present themselves despite the fact that the event itself on the basis of which they are ordered often appears to have long-since dried up and sedimented itself, like a strata or geological formation gradually settled into homogeneous layers.

Truth and falsity are immanent to the distribution of sense, the genetic element of which lies not at the level of the relations between propositions, but at the level of problems themselves (DR 159). It is by virtue of a certain problematic that a given set of truths or propositions comes to have a sense (Deleuze contra the positivists). Hence, when the encounter with a sign forces us to think, it is not a question of suddenly being released from error and pointed toward a previously concealed truth. Rather, the relation between the true and the false is itself redistributed under the influence of the problem that the sign envelops. Every problem carries within it a (re)distribution of the important and the unimportant, the interesting and the uninteresting, the possible and the impossible, the alluring and the repugnant: in this sense, a problem is already an evaluation—it is the selection of a form of life that affirms itself within the given. When thought becomes the patient of a sign, the nature of the difference that jars us is a distribution of this sort. The relations that comprise the problem are crucial because (as we shall see) they make it possible to provide a determinate account of mutations that affect the apparatus of recognition. It is the distributive difference between these affirmations, these differential criteria marking out a form of life enveloped within the matrix of a problematic that puts our thinking in crisis, that spurs us to think otherwise, that makes something that was previously possible impossible or insufficient.

Considered in themselves problems are always determinate. What is and must remain undetermined is the outcome of their interaction. To encounter the sign is to be spurred to decipher its sense, which is to say, the *problematic form of life* it envelops, and which brings its singularities into relation.[27] "Sense" refers to the resonance of these differences between problems or forms of life. The difference between problems, the difference *of* a problem, constitutes the difference *internal* to truth itself, its multiplicity. *Transcendental empiricism* is this evaluation of the sense of problems, which measures the distance between these distinct distributions of truth and falsity, pleasure and pain, good and bad, important and unimportant, etc.[28] The "object" of Deleuze's empiricism is therefore strictly speaking not an "object" at all, or at least not in the classical sense. By regarding the phenomenon as a sign through which the force of a way of living and thinking affirms itself, the thinker attempts by means of an appraisal of the forces encountered to introduce a new evaluative criterion into them, to *pose a new problem*, where the only suitable "criteria of criteria" lies in the efficacy of the intervention vis-à-vis the field of forces in question.

What consequences does the involuntarist critique of truth have for the question of political transformation?

We must dispense with the notion that there is anything like an innate or default will to political change that resides in all of us. There is no natural disposition toward the political good, any more than there is an upright nature of thought on which philosophy can rely. Something must *force* us. Beginning from this critical postulate, the challenge is to conceptualize the conditions of political *commencement* on non-dogmatic grounds. Involuntarism in politics refers to the emergence or inauguration, through rupture, of politicized sensibilities, along with the possible worlds in relation to which they draw their urgency. What is at issue, in short, is a transcendental empiricism of the will: "the will no longer precedes the event."[29]

The Deleuzian critique of truth thinks the *problematic distribution* in accordance with which something is recognized as possible. As we have seen, this implies a theory of affect, since the differential relations that fill out the sense of the problem—un/important; in/tolerable; un/thinkable; im/possible—make the composition of our faculties affective in nature, modulating our capacity both to affect and to be affected, making us sensitive to this or that set of signs. Hence it is these relationships—above all that of the tolerable and the intolerable—that must be put in crisis if a political event or transformation is to occur, if a becoming-revolutionary is to emerge from the rubble of recognitional clichés.

The Deleuzian political question is not, "Which of the available actual alternatives should we hold out for ourselves as an ideal to be realized or brought into being?" It is not a matter of constructing an imaginary double (the plan, the projected possibility), and then debating its formal determination: Do we have a true model of the real, or is our image of it a false claimant? Has our image, our plan, accounted for the innumerable contingencies of the given situation? The latter is an "operation *upon* the real, rather than *of* the real itself."[30] The lack of any impetus *of* the real always confers a certain degree of artificiality on it. As Zourabichvili reminds us, "nothing is more foreign to Deleuze than the enterprise of transforming the world in accordance with a plan, or in relation to an end."[31]

The thought of political transformation is an empty abstraction so long as the affective determinations that *produce a will in us* are not taken into consideration. Militancy of any sort, a will to change, presupposes an encounter with the world that redistributes the relationships between the tolerable and the intolerable, the interesting and the uninteresting, the important and the unimportant, the true and the false. Herein lies the interest of the philosophy of the event for politics. Of the political event of May '68, Deleuze and Guattari write:

> What counts is what amounted to a visionary phenomenon, as if a society suddenly saw what was intolerable in it and also saw the possibility for something else. It is a collective phenomenon in the form of: "Give me the possible, or else I'll suffocate . . ." The possible does not pre-exist, it is created by the event . . . The event creates a new existence, it produces a new subjectivity (new relations with the body, with time, sexuality, the immediate surroundings, with culture, work. . .). (TR 234)

What are the conditions that give rise to this demand, this will drawn from the necessity, this *"or else I'll suffocate"*? It is here that the analysis of the problem, of the affect, and the entire genetic conception of recognition bears out politically. For what is at issue is the reorganization of the conditions of experience—a "disharmonious" reorganization of our faculties around a problem, one which renders the available alternatives of the situation unlivable, generating thereby an urgency, a will to change. In an important passage, Zourabichvili describes the two vectors or dynamisms that constitute a political event or sequence:

> The idea of creating the possible is split in two complementary aspects. On the one hand, the event brings about a new sense of the intolerable (virtual mutation); on the other hand, this new sense of the intolerable calls for an act of creation that responds to the mutation, tracing a new image and literally creating the possible (actualizing mutation). To create the possible is to create a novel collective spatio-temporal assemblage that responds to the new possibility of life created by the event, or which serves as its expression. A genuine modification of the situation does not take place as the realization of a project, for it is a matter of inventing the concrete social forms that correspond to the new sensibility, hence the inspiration can only come from the latter. The new sensibility does not present a concrete image that could be adequate to it: from this point of view, there is only creative action, guided not by an image or a project of future reform but by affective signs which, following the Deleuzian leitmotif, "do not resemble" that which actualizes them.[32]

Since the conceptual couple virtual/actual requires its own complex philosophical unpacking,[33] one that has led to many misunderstandings, for the purposes of explication I would like to pursue another path, one emphasizing the presence of the problem within experience. To this end, I would suggest that the first of these vectors could be called *eviction*, and the second *secession*.

11

What generates this first vector, this event of "eviction"?

We begin within a homogeneous and coded actual milieu, in a state of stupidity or torpor. A sign disturbs us. Yet it is not merely because of a lack of innate affinity with the sign that we can describe it as a heterogeneity. Rather, it is because what we encounter by confronting this new relation of forces is a *point of view* presently incompossible with the relations defining the problematic field we occupy. The rupture begins with the encounter, in the sign, with a form of life or problematic evaluation incommensurable with our own, which brings us to *see the intolerable* of our present situation. We find ourselves incapable of continuing to do what we were doing, yet mute and indeterminate in the face of this impossibility: "[O]ne can no longer tolerate what one had previously tolerated until then, even yesterday. The repartition of desires has changed in us, our relations of speed and slowness have been modified, a new type of anxiety comes to us, also a new serenity" (D 126).

We are evicted from the sensibility that previously held sway over us: "The effect . . . is not only to impugn what Bartleby prefers not to do, but also to render what he was doing impossible, what he was supposed to prefer to continue doing." Eviction is "not a will to nothingness, but the growth of a nothingness of the will" (CC 70) that ejects or evicts us from the *stupefying control* at the very level of the sensible, the "flow of stupidity" that "effects an absorption and a realization, and that ensures the integration of groups and individuals into the system" (AO 235–6). The effect of the event's introduction within a situation is a force of eviction that renders the previously sanctioned reaction to our situation, as Zourabichvili puts it, "not only derisory and inappropriate, but intolerable."[34]

The political starting point is this disaffection with regard to recognized human stakes (determinate actions to realize, the choice of such and such profession, leisure, or the taste for such and such particulars). However, it is not a question of desiring this mutation or not. The "for" or "against" emerges rather after, in a second moment, in which we take up a relation to this event, and assume or don't assume a responsibility toward it, in playing out its consequences, or else obscuring it, acting as if it didn't happen (hence the title of Deleuze and Guattari's article, "May '68 Did Not Happen").[35] When the eviction resulting from this affective mutation is affirmed, it has the potential of becoming a secession. What matters is how the affirmation of this disaffection as a positive force can lead to the construction of new spatio-temporal assemblages that respond to it.

Secession is the affirmation of the encounter with the sign, which occurs when the violence of the sign is converted into a critical aggression and directed against the self that we previously were, against the stupidity from which he have been wrenched.[36] If transcendental empiricism is the evaluation of the sense of problems that measures the *distance* between distinct distributions of truth and falsity, then as the equivalent form of thought in politics, secession occurs when the "de-mobilization" (a failure to recognize . . . a mutation in the conditions of recognition) that has robbed us of peace becomes a critical aggression that exerts itself by measuring the distance between the self we were (the previous distribution of sense) and that which we are becoming. It is a distinct mode of contracting a difference. Since, for Deleuze, subjectivity is always the contraction of a difference, secession is a distinct mode of subjectification. A subjectification such as this may be contrasted with the state of stupidity, in which we contract the difference of the conventional significations only so as to measure their homogeneity or so as to realize a pre-given possibility, by enacting a play of resemblance between what is and what will be. A subject in secession (strictly speaking: a collective assemblage of enunciation "put into flight") is still the contraction of a difference, but instead of canceling this difference out through recognition, it contracts itself as *the measuring of a difference between what we were and what we are becoming*, and directing its aggression against the former. The subject produced through this movement lives time as a caesura, since it is bordered on both sides by irreconcilable dimensions.

If secession is transcendental, the transcendental is inseparable from a process that reorganizes our experience around a new problem, one which envelops a possible world that could be mine or ours if we were to attempt to occupy it—which, in political terms, means if we were to build the corresponding assemblages.

This Deleuzian concept of the possible world has a peculiar modality to it. In place of the possible/actual couple, what characterizes the possible world is the dyad envelopment/development. "Logical" possibilities are explicit, but they are abstract and indifferent. By contrast, enveloped possibilities—*possible worlds*—are not yet explicit. Their mode of being is to be "distinct-obscure": they await development. "Development" should not be confused with "realization." In the case of merely logical possibilities, the actual already contains the dimension that is necessary for its realization (hence the Bergsonian complaint that realization in the actual "adds

13

nothing" to the possible but existence). In the case of the possible world, the dimension necessary for its development is not yet present as actual. It *insists*, it is imbricated or "intagliated" [*en creux*]: its mode of appearance is not explicit, like an object of recognition we can calculate, but neither is it a vague and indeterminately pure "potentiality as such" either. It is as determinate as the event that introduced it, and makes itself known through the determinacy of a *sensed compulsion*, an urgency located not quite *within* the actual but at its surface: the possible world *haunts* the actual, without it being the case that the actual is yet *sufficient* for its emergence.

Secession is the development of a possible world. We must secede from the available to encounter the possible. Yet it remains the case that, where politics is concerned, this cannot be done alone, as it always implies a relation not only to the Outside, to one's own conditions, but taken in their objectivity as an encounter with something that does not depend upon us, these must also become the conditions of others. In politics, the development of a possible world is always something explicating an encounter with a condition connecting us to others: in this sense, it is shared, but not as possessed.

Involuntarism is Deleuze's completion of the critical project. Its significance lies in the fact that it multiplies the conditions under which a given truth takes on a *necessity*, at the same time as it supplies differential criteria that account for this passage from the arbitrary to the necessary, yet without circumscribing in advance the way in which this will come about. The involuntarist priority of the event means that the point of departure for the new must always be the affect, or the redistribution of the interesting and the uninteresting, the tolerable and the intolerable, the important and the unimportant (a sensitivity to certain kinds of signs rather than others). However, "the conditions do not resemble that which they condition." These affects, and the mutation of the sensible they give rise to, and even the secession which affirms this mutation, and aims to draw its consequences, cannot *resemble* the future they make possible: they must be explicated, unfolded, and the corresponding assemblage remains to be invented.

Notes

1. The term is taken from the Zourabichvili's essay, "Deleuze et le possible (de l'involontarisme en politique)," contained in the volume *Deleuze: une vie philosophique* (Paris: Synthélabo, 1998) pp. 335–57.

2. See the entry on "Transcendental Empiricism", in *The Vocabulary of Deleuze*, below p. 210. The claim appears again in the "New Introduction" from 2004; see below p. 37.
3. See Zourabichvili, "New Introduction," below p. 38.
4. "Ça ne m'intéresse même pas de savoir si c'est un problème ontologique; c'est aussi bien le problème des énoncés." Lecture course of January 14, 1974. Transcript available at webdeleuze.com
5. The liberated relation between content and expression we find in *A Thousand Plateaus* should also be understood from this perspective.
6. Lecture course of January 14, 1974. A similar link between conditions of appearance and sense is found in the lecture course of March 14, 1978: "For the disjunctive couple appearance/essence, Kant will substitute the conjunctive couple, what appears/conditions of apparition."
7. Lecture course of January 14, 1974.
8. Ibid. This link between a power of thought that is constituted only *within* the given and an overthrow of the "theoretical" pretensions of philosophy is a consistent refrain in Deleuze's oeuvre. To cite just one more example: it was, it will be remembered, the key thesis of his first book: "If the relation cannot be separated from the circumstances, if the subject cannot be separated from the singular content which is strictly essential to it, it is because subjectivity is essentially *practical* . . . The fact that there is no theoretical subjectivity, and that there cannot be one, becomes the fundamental claim of empiricism. And, if we examine it closely, it is merely another way of saying that the subject is constituted within the given . . . *Relations are not the object of a representation, but the means of an activity* . . . Association does not define a knowing subject; on the contrary, it defines a set of possible means for a practical subject for which all real ends belong to the moral, passional, political, and economic order . . . Philosophy must constitute itself as the theory of what we are doing, not as a theory of what there is" (ES 104, 120, 133).
9. See the entry on "Univocity of Being," below p. 214. A similar claim appears already in the 1994 study: "For Deleuze, difference is not even being, since it merges with *becoming*, and since becoming does not go from one being to another, but is accomplished *between*" (below p. 104).
10. "'To the limit,' it will be argued, still presupposes a limit. Here, limit [*peras*] no longer refers to what maintains the thing under a law, nor to what delimits or separates it from other things. On the contrary, it refers to that on the basis of which it is deployed and deploys all its power" (DR 37).
11. The philosophical gesture of making the thought *of* experience contingent *upon* an experience undoubtedly shares something with the

phenomenologico-Heideggerian problematic. Regardless, it must not be confused with the latter, for the structure of conditioning is strictly distinct in each case. As Zourabichvili makes clear, the relation that (for example) Heidegger's "pre-ontological understanding" has to discourse as an "already" is still a *general* condition, event being understood here as the "Event of presencing" as such. Since, for Deleuze, the subject emerges through the contraction of a distance or difference between forces/points of view, one is on the contrary always dealing with a synthesis of terms that are exclusive from the point of view of their conditioned result or actual solution, yet "distinct but indiscernible" at the level of sense. With this we pass from a thought of being as "Advent" [*Avènement*] to a logic of sense-events as irreducibly multiple: "the event is always at least two" (see Zourabichvili, "New Introduction," below p. 40).

12. This characterization of Deleuze as a "ruthless logician" (*logicien impitoyable*) is taken from David Lapoujade's excellent short article, "Les logiques de la vie" which appeared in *Le Monde des Livres*, November 4, 2005, under the heading: *Gilles Deleuze et les joies du dehors*. Available at <http://quel.monde.free.fr/spip.php?article36> (accessed February 2011).
13. See DR 131–8, and below, Chapter 1.
14. Zourabichvili, "New Introduction," below p. 36.
15. See below p. 44.
16. See below p. 74.
17. Cf. NP 2: "This is Nietzsche's two-fold struggle: against those who remove values from criticism, contenting themselves with producing inventories of existing values . . . but also against those who criticize, or respect, values by deriving them from simple facts, so-called "objective facts" . . . In both cases, philosophy moves in the *indifferent* element of the valuable in itself or the valuable for all . . . Nietzsche substitutes the pathos of difference or distance (the differential element) for both the Kantian principle of universality and the principle of resemblance dear to the utilitarians."
18. There is no question of constructing a straw man here: many of the best, most renowned readers of Deleuze maintain such a view. See, for example, Constantin Boundas' "Introduction" in *Deleuze and Philosophy* (Edinburgh: Edinburgh University Press, 2007), p. 27, fn. 2: "I do hold the vulgar metaphysical position and, therefore, Zourabichvili's reminder reaches me also." Boundas claims that any other attitude would strip the objectivity from concepts such as affect or virtuality, reducing them to "useful fictions." However, as Zourabichvili points out, to make sense "inseparable from an encounter with and the capture of a new force," thereby rendering necessity in thought dependent on the affect, is nonetheless "not a subjective

criterion since (1) the affect, by contrast, involves the subject in becoming where the individuating points of view overlap, distinct but indiscernible; (2) it stimulates, in the subject thus stripped of its mastery, the supreme activity of vital evaluation (the *ethical* activity itself)" (see Zourabichvili, "Six Notes on the Percept," in P. Patton, ed., *Deleuze: A Critical Reader* [Oxford: Blackwell, 1996], p. 214, fn. 8).

19. See the entry on "Disjunctive Synthesis," below p. 170.
20. See below p. 57.
21. See the entry on "Disjunctive Synthesis," below p. 170. The Deleuze citations are from CC 82–3 and FB 83.
22. "Do not count upon thought to ensure the relative necessity of what it thinks. Rather, count upon the contingency of an encounter with that which forces thought to raise up and educate the absolute necessity of an act of thought or a passion to think" (DR 139).
23. On the contrast between judgment and evaluation, see below Chapters 2 and 3: "Sense concerns a will rather than a thing, an affirmation rather than a being, a cleavage rather than a content, a manner of evaluating rather than a signification. Thing, being, content, signification: this is what the phenomenon is reduced to when it is separated from its genesis, from the conditions of its apparition, when it is not longer seized as a sign" (p. 63).
24. As Zourabichvili notes, "Deleuze is not amazed that there are bodies—only the body 'exists,' and it is rather thought that must be explained—but, following Spinoza, he is amazed by what a body can do" (below p. 65).
25. See the entries on "Disjunctive Synthesis" and "Univocity of Being," below pp. 169 and 212.
26. See below p. 73.
27. In place of "form of life," Deleuze and Guattari will also refer to the *expressed* of a concrete assemblage. On this point, see Zourabichvili, "Deleuze et le possible," p. 340.
28. Contrary to most scholarship, which has pegged him as a "non/anti-dialectical" thinker, Deleuze in fact also employed the word "dialectics" to describe precisely this evaluation of the sense of problems. Cf. DR 157, 179: "Dialectic is the art of problems and questions . . . However, dialectic loses its peculiar power when it remains content to trace problems from propositions: thus begins the history of the long perversion which places it under the power of the negative . . . *Problems are always dialectical* . . . every problem is dialectical by nature and there are no non-dialectical problems." Zourabichvili's reluctance to employ the term is no doubt due to the fact that (like many of Deleuze's readers) his view of dialectics is limited to the philosophy of the negative. However, this "long perversion" does not exhaust the value of the term, and Deleuze himself was content to reclaim it, provided the

priority of the problem/sense complex be modified accordingly. (See also DR 159–64, 186–8, 221.)

29. Zourabichvili, "Deleuze et le possible," p. 347.
30. Ibid., pp. 337–8.
31. Ibid., p. 335.
32. Ibid., p. 346.
33. See the entries on "Crystal of Time" and "Virtual," below pp. 156 and 214.
34. Zourabichvili, "Deleuze et le possible," p. 350.
35. See ibid., p. 341.
36. On the difference between this "critical aggression" and the labor of the Negative, see below pp. 76–85.

François Zourabichvili and the Physics of Thought

Daniel W. Smith and Gregg Lambert

This volume presents to the English-speaking world two books by the French philosopher François Zourabichvili (1965–2006): *Deleuze: A Philosophy of the Event* and *The Vocabulary of Deleuze*. These two works were the bookends, as it were, of Zourabichvili's short career, and they are both landmarks in the interpretation of Deleuze's philosophy. *A Philosophy of the Event* was published in 1994, a year before Deleuze's death, and while it was not the first book to be published on Deleuze, it was the first to provide a systematic analysis of Deleuze's work as a whole, and it has remained a touchstone of all subsequent readings of Deleuze. "We assume that philosophy will not emerge from the Deleuzian adventure unscathed," Zourabichvili wrote, "but we know that it is up to us to demonstrate this and to pursue it . . . I have sought above all to extract the logical movements of an oeuvre that seems to me to be one of the most important and most powerful of the twentieth century."[1] The *Vocabulary of Deleuze* appeared nine years later, in 2003, as a volume in the "Vocabulaire de . . ." series directed by Jean-Pierre Zarader—a well-known collection of books that includes similar volumes on Bergson by Frédéric Worms, and on Foucault by Judith Revel. Whereas the first book was oriented around the Deleuzian concept of the event, the second book provided a concise analysis of many of the new concepts Deleuze had created, which are presented in the "dictionary" form that Deleuze himself had utilized in his short books on Nietzsche and Spinoza. "No one has indicated what a 'Vocabulary' should be better than Deleuze," Zourabichvili noted, "not a collection of opinions on general themes, but a series of logical sketches that describe so many complex acts of thought, titled and signed."[2]

By the time the *Vocabulary* appeared in 2003, Zourabichvili had developed a number of theses about Deleuze's work that went beyond mere exegesis, and which have had a decisive influence on later readings. Two of these theses are worth highlighting here. On the one hand, Zourabichvili strongly criticized interpretations that saw in Deleuze's work the development of a new ontology. "There is no 'ontology of Deleuze,'" he starkly claimed, "If there is an orientation of the philosophy of Deleuze, this is it: *the extinction of the term 'being' and therefore of ontology.*"[3] This assertion is all the more surprising in that Deleuze himself wrote, in *The Logic of Sense*, that "philosophy merges with ontology" (LS 179), and readers content with proof-texting are easily content to cite such phrases as definitive. But Zourabichvili points out that the second part of the Deleuze's statement—"but ontology merges with the univocity of being" (LS 179)—essentially "perverts" the appeal to ontology, since the thesis of univocity equates the term "Being" with difference, and replaces ontology with a theory of relations (becomings, multiplicities. . .). The introduction of *A Thousand Plateaus* ends with the admonition to "establish a logic of the AND," and to "overthrow ontology" (ATP 25), and it is this undermining of ontology that Zourabichvili traces out in many of the entries in the *Vocabulary*. Yet this thesis had already been prepared for in the first book. For Zourabichvili, the principal theme of Deleuze's logic, its "abstract motor," is the concept of the *event*. "In all my books," Deleuze said in an interview, "I've tried to discover the nature of events; it's a philosophical concept, the only one capable of ousting the verb 'to be' and attributes" (N 141). This leads Zourabichvili to pose a series of pivotal questions: What are the consequences of Deleuze's elevation of the concept of the event? What problematic regions are thereby invented, and through what original assemblage of concepts? What exactly is a philosophy of the event? Throughout his early book, Zourabichvili attempts to disengage—through its echoes and variations—the logic of one of the most epochal philosophical experiments of the twentieth-century: a non-dialectical logic of becoming, grounded in the articulation of the notions of the outside and the fold, and the emergence of the concepts of multiplicity and singularity.

On the other hand, and perhaps even more importantly, Zourabichvili developed the thesis of the *literality* of Deleuze's philosophical concepts. There exists a common assumption that Deleuze's concepts should be understood as metaphors, and Zourabichvili fought strongly against this misconception. The concept of metaphor depends on a distinction between an originary sense and a figural sense, with the latter resting on its resemblance to the former. But Zourabichvili shows that Deleuze's notion of literality overthrows this distinction between the originary and the figural: the production of sense is itself a matter of *transport* or passage, that is, it implies a plane in which heterogeneous significations encounter each other, contaminate each other, forming lines or connections with each other (becomings), and thereby forming what Deleuze calls "blocks" that are endowed with their own consistency:

> If the line of flight is like a train in motion, it is because one jumps linearly on it, one can finally speak "literally" of anything at all, a blade of grass, a catastrophe or sensation, calmly accepting that which occurs when it is no longer possible for anything to stand for anything else ... "I am speaking literally" because it is not so much a question of defining something as effectively drawing a line ... This is neither one nor the other ... nor is it a resemblance between the two: "I am speaking literally," I am drawing lines, lines of writing, and life passes between the Lines ... Not only does one speak literally, one also lives literally, in other words, following lines, whether connectable or not, even heterogeneous ones. (ATP 198, 200–1)

This is why Deleuze always insisted that his concepts must be understood literally, and in this regard, he can be contrasted with Jacques Derrida, who suggested that philosophy could be seen as a kind of "generalized metaphorics."

Zourabichvili developed this theme of literality in a series of remarkable essays that have recently been published in a posthumous collection entitled *Literality and Other Essays on Art*, which in effect constitutes the third volume of Zourabichvili's trilogy of works on Deleuze.[4] Yet this book goes much further. Although Zourabichvili was known primarily as a brilliant interpreter of Deleuze and Spinoza, the essays collected here reveal the broad range of Zourabichvili's interests. The book includes not only three pivotal essays on Deleuze's concept of literality, but articles on Nietzsche and Chateaubriand, a discussion of revolution, the development of a non-Gadamerian concept of "play" (as an act of inaugurating an always-variable rule), studies of the politics of vision found in various cinematic works (including films by Vertov, Barnet, and Santiago), an investigation into the nature of "interactive" artworks, and several pieces on aspects of Deleuze's aesthetics. Taken together, the essays define a contemporary aesthetic that reveals the full range of Zourabichvili's thought—an oeuvre that goes far beyond his readings of Deleuze, and shows the degree to which Zourabichvili, despite the tragic brevity of his career, must be considered to be one of the more significant French philosophers of the contemporary period.

Zourabichvili was born in 1965, and took his own life on April 19, 2006, at age 41. He came from an aristocratic Russian family of Georgian descent, who had been dispersed throughout Europe after the Russian Revolution, and with whom he maintained complex ties.[5] During his university studies, he regularly attended Deleuze's seminars at the University of Paris–Vincennes at St. Denis. He passed his *agrégation* exam in 1989, and taught at various *lycées* from 1988 until 2001, when he took up a position as *maître de conferences* at the University Paul Valéry in Montpelier. From 1998 to 2004, he served as a *directeur de programme* at the Collège international de philosophie in Paris. He received his doctorate in 1999 with a thesis on Spinoza directed by Étienne Balibar and Dominique Lecourt. Though he is better known for his work on Deleuze, Zourabichvili's work on Spinoza was equally extensive and distinguished. In 2002, Zourabichvili published two substantial works on Spinoza: *Spinoza: A Physics of Thought* and *Spinoza's Paradoxical Conservatism: Childhood and Royalty*. The first book argues that, since for Spinoza ideas belong to Nature as much as bodies, only a special physics—in no way metaphorical—can account for the strange universe that they compose, a physics conceived as a science of *transformations* (a non-cognitivist naturalism) whose scope is as much medical as it is logical. This physics of thought led Spinoza to undertake a clinical study of mental pathologies in third and fourth parts of the *Ethics*, which revealed what Zourabichvili calls a *transformist imaginary* that haunts the human spirit and keeps it in a state of powerlessness, and which the *Ethics* aimed to release us from. The second book continues these themes in the two registers indicated by its subtitle. Spinoza provides a new point of view on the growth and education of children around which ethics must be reorganized, while at the same time pursuing a pitiless critique of absolute monarchy in favor of a popular freedom (the "multitude"), revealing an unexpected relation to war outlined in the *Tractatus*. Both analyses point to Spinoza's "paradoxical conservatism," which is the exact opposite of what is usually meant by the term: whereas ordinary conservatism aims at preserving the existing state of things, Spinoza's paradoxical conservatism instead aims at inventing the conditions for a true conservation of oneself (the neutralization of death and servitude). The result is a "revolutionary" reading of Spinozism that leads to a new concept of conservatism.

Zourabichvili's work on Spinoza thus opens up as many new paths for research as does his work on Deleuze. Indeed, in 2007, a conference entitled *The Physics of Thought in François Zourabichvili* was organized by the Collège international de philosophie and the École normale supérieure under the direction of Bruno Clement and Frédéric Worms, which brought together an international group of scholars to explore these new directions of thought, and included Pierre Macherey, Pierre-François Moreau, Pierre Zaoui, Paula Marrati, Paul Patton, Paolo Godani, and Marie-France Badie. Zourabichvili's last published article, "Kant with Masoch" (which was meant to be contrasted with Lacan's famous article, "Kant with Sade"), was published in the journal *Multitudes*, and examined the ways in which Deleuze reorganized the relations between art, desire, and the Law. All these works exemplify Zourabichvili's own insistence that the Deleuzian revolution in philosophy is not an already accomplished fact, but must be taken up anew by every reader who is affected by Deleuze's thought.

With this all-too-brief overview of Zourabichvili's career in hand, we can return in more detail to the themes found in *A Philosophy of the Event* and *The Vocabulary of Deleuze*. The method (even a "style" as we will define it further down) Zourabichvili chooses to employ in both volumes he calls an *"exposition of concepts."* In the 2004 introduction to *A Philosophy of the Event*, a work that was actually written ten years earlier when the author admits that Deleuze was not yet openly acknowledged as "a major thinker in the twentieth Century," Zourabichvili urgently addresses a new problematic according to which these volumes should be read. Ten years later, although the claim of Deleuze as a "full-fledged thinker" was now possible, since philosophers and non-philosophers alike were laying claim to something like "a Deleuzian event" in their own respective domains, nevertheless the meaning of this event is in danger of being misapprehended under "the pompous name of Ontology." In other words, what Zourabichvili hears at this moment, even despite the excess of monographs on Deleuze that are beginning to appear, is a strangely muted but nevertheless persistent "refusal of the literal," a refusal that even touches upon the sense of actual statements. For example, as he cautions us to listen [*entendre*], "Deleuze spoke clearly [*en toutes lettres*]—and literally [*à la lettre*]—of his program: substitution of IS (*est*) by means of AND (*et*) or, what amounts to the same thing, substitution of becoming for being."[6] Consequently, it is in response to this new danger, which he regards as much more pernicious than mere naivety, that Zourabichvili chooses a purely expository mode as his own method of approaching Deleuze's philosophy, and the genre of a vocabulary or lexicon as "the only guarantee of an *encounter* with a body of thought."[7]

But in what sense do we speak here of *ex-posing* the literal sense of concepts? Of course, concepts are never exposed as singular facts, but are distributed according to a logic that orders the conditions of intelligibility. As Deleuze himself remarks at several points, the sense of concepts is not only to be found at the level of terms (as in a philosophical understanding), but also on the level of percepts and affects that run underneath the surface of a linguistically or syntactically composed order of statements that claim to define the concept *qua* concept (N 165).[8] As one of the four modes of discourse, exposition is defined as an art of expressing ideas clearly, and the order of logic is implied in the very syntax of the sentences employed to render the sense of ideas literally, and not as expressions of opinion, as in the case of persuasion or argument. Although it may employ the other modes (argument, narrative, description) as subjacent movements, the distinguishing feature of exposition as a form of presentation is to offer statements as *matters of fact*, that is, to achieve as closely as possible a "literal" sense of the idea. (Thus, the generic appearance of the glossary or lexicon only gives a vague approximation of the literality that is being sought.) Whereas the goal of a dictionary or glossary is the definition of terms as parts that will serve knowledge, which is always constructed afterwards employing terms or concepts in a patchwork of understanding, the goal of the expository mode is *to position* the unfolding of a concept at the very moment of its intelligibility, which necessarily precedes its comprehension as belonging to a system of philosophy, much less to an already recognized proper territory of an author's work. As Zourabichvili describes this moment, "every concept participates in an act of thinking that displaces the field of intelligibility, modifying the conditions of the problem we pose for ourselves; it thus does not let itself be assigned a place within a common space of comprehension given in advance for pleasant or aggressive debates with its competitors."[9]

In the above statement, Zourabichvili seems to be implying that, to become the literal expression of a unique sense-event, the concept must first be extracted from a common place (or topic) of discussion that has already pre-comprehended its meaning. The most common manner of understanding this event occurs when we regard, either in the manner in which the concept is defined or in the expression itself, the presence of a novelty that displaces or "shifts" the conditions of a previous order of intelligibility. Thus, in the history of philosophy the idea of novelty is often employed to represent the cause of this sudden re-distribution on the level of sense. And yet, according to Zourabichvili, the form of "novelty" appears as the greatest danger, because even though it appears to announce a new distribution of a common space or comprehension, more often than not it merely provides a new metaphor, which has occurred often in the history of ontology around the different senses accorded to the word "being." Of course, the second manner of extracting the concept from a common space of understanding is by means of the negative, and Zourabichvili himself employs this mode in the statement, "there is no ontology in Deleuze," which in some ways prepares for a new exposition of the sense of the event since it clears away the common space of a previous comprehension. At the same time, with regard to this second strategy, there is also the immediate danger that another term will be erected in the place (empiricism or pragmatism, for example), which obstructs the literal sense of the event announced since these terms are equally pre-comprehended as already existing topics of a common space of comprehension, thereby becoming merely yet another occasion for "aggressive discussions and competitions" (or rivalries between those who claim fidelity to the sense of the event), but which only manage to distribute the concept according to an already established logic of sense.

As is well known, Deleuze himself deplored the image of discussion as an adequate conception of the event that causes concepts to become re-distributed at certain moments in the history of philosophy. According to Deleuze and Guattari's last work, the fact that discussion (and, therefore, polemic) has become the dominant image of thought is only the expression of a general movement in contemporary philosophy that has replaced the conditions of critique (i.e., *krisis*, judgment) with the logics of marketing and self-promotion. The academic fields that comprise what Zourabichvili sarcastically calls "Deleuzeology" have not been not been immune to these trends either, and here he discerns the presence of two fallacies that have resulted in the dominant appropriations of Deleuze's philosophy to date. The first error, already addressed above, is the identification of the event of this philosophy as the arrival of a new ontology—"What fun, naive or perfidious, to want by all means to rediscover one in Deleuze!" he says. However, it is the second fallacy that is much more subtle and persistently responsible for instituting across the disciplinary fields that have opened themselves to the event of this philosophy a "congenital form of misrecognition" [*méconnaissance*], which has occurred under the false alternative of an intrinsic and, therefore, "proper" versus extrinsic and "figurative" *ex-position* of concepts.

In the opening entry of the 2003 *Vocabulary*, "*á la lettre*," Zourabichvili addresses this second fallacy most explicitly in the following statement:

> Perhaps philosophy today suffers too often from a false alternative—
> either to explain *or* to use—as well as well as a false problem: the
> impression that a too-precise approach would amount to canonizing a
> current author. Consequently, we are not surprised to occasionally find
> philosophical production divided on the one hand into disincarnated
> exegeses, and on the other into essays which, although ambitious, still
> seize their concepts *from above*. Assuming it is not merely decorative, the
> same applies to the artist, the architect, or the sociologist who at a certain
> moment in their work uses an aspect of Deleuze's thought, for they too
> are eventually led to explain it to themselves.[10]

In this passage, what Zourabichvili exposes as a false alternative might be better understood today under the twin banners of either a purified and properly philosophical Deleuze (one who often appears without the shadow of Guattari), or of an "applied Deleuzism." This alternative continues to distribute in advance the conditions for the intelligibility of the event and the promise of this philosophy according to a metaphorical equivalence in the division [*partage*] of proper and figurative appropriations of Deleuze. However, the literal does not belong to this distribution [*partage*] of sense, and would appear outside the strict alternatives offered by intrinsic versus extrinsic, or properly philosophical versus non-philosophical understanding. In fact, "we need both wings to fly," as Deleuze earlier argued concerning Spinoza, especially given that the sense of concepts does not move only between terms, but also among things and within ourselves (N 165).

In response to this metaphorical economy of "*either* one *or* several Deleuzes" ("just as there is a Beckett before Pim, during Pim, and after Pim—a quite muddled affair, as it should be"[11]), Zourabichvili rejects the alternative, and it is precisely around this point that he claims that a literal "exposition of concepts is the only guarantee of an *encounter* with a body of thought"[12] (5).

How is this so? First, following Deleuze, he affirms the *necessity* of an encounter with thought that is effectuated by what might appear, at first, as "strange" and even "irrational."

The fact that a concept has no sense or necessity without a corresponding "affect" or "percept" does not prevent there being something else in addition: a condensation of logical movements that the mind must effectuate if it wants to philosophize. Otherwise we remain in the initial fascination of words and phrases that we mistake for the irreducible component of intuitive comprehension.[13]

It is here, moreover, that we might we glimpse the manner in which the movement of concepts must be placed into contact with something beyond words and phrases whose sense cannot be foreseen or comprehended beforehand, which first transforms the encounter with thought into a necessary rather than merely a logical association of ideas. Therefore, the ex-position of concepts is first effectuated in the mind through the presence of a "pre-elective affinity," or as Deleuze calls it, "a non-philosophical comprehension" that cannot be known beforehand. "That the heart beats when reading the text is a necessary prelude, or better still an affinity needed in order to comprehend." And yet, as Zourabichvili reminds us, this initial encounter is only half of comprehension and still does not guarantee a re-distribution of the previous conditions of intelligibility according to a new logic of sense. "It is true that this part deserves to be insisted upon," he writes, "since the practice of philosophy in the university excludes it almost methodically, while a dilettantism believing itself to be cultivated confuses it with a *doxa* of the times."[14] As Deleuze and Guattari also argue, although absolutely necessary, a non-philosophical comprehension is not enough in the same measure that the initial fascination and intoxication with the novelty of thought is not enough to change what it means to think.[15] What is required in addition is another kind of affection; as Zourabichvili writes, "We wouldn't need Deleuze if we didn't sense in his oeuvre something that has never been thought, something capable of affecting philosophy in still inestimable ways—which is a result of our *letting ourselves be affected philosophically by it.*[16] We would propose to call this third form of affection simply a "style."

Everything we have said up to this point concerning the exposition of concepts really comes down to a question of "style," as well as to our acknowledgment of Zourabichvili as a great philosophical stylist. Of course, it might seem odd to talk of "style" with regard to these volumes that, on first glance, appear in the form of a glossary or philosophical vocabulary, a genre that one might presume to be a *degree zero* of style. And yet, as Zourabichvili also reminds us, Deleuze himself often employed the form of a lexicon in his earliest works on

Nietzsche and Spinoza, and these belong to what he defined as the "pedagogy of the concept." Therefore, it is important to underline in our brief introduction to these volumes that the form of the vocabulary is meant neither to be exhaustive nor to encapsulate the totality of the concepts belonging to the Deleuzian corpus. But then, how could it? That is to say, if one of the recognized characteristics of Deleuze's style of "doing philosophy" is the frenetic, almost schizophrenic, creation of concepts, then the idea of a total glossary could be comparable only to the Borgesian fiction of the total encyclopedia. Zourabichvili himself calls attention to absence of certain concepts from his vocabulary (the cinema concepts, in particular, with the notable exception of the "crystal of time"), and to other concepts that deserve more attention (such as "plane of immanence"), but whose full exposition was aborted to function only as a relay or connective link to other concepts; and, finally, the fact that the arbitrary character of the alphabetical order is the most sure means of not superimposing upon the relations of multiple imbrication between concepts an artificial order of reasons that would divert attention away from the true status of necessity in philosophy. However, to avoid becoming completely partial or arbitrary (or merely subjective) in its assemblage, Zourabichvili defends his method of selection as "sampling" [*échantillonnage*], employing a term that is derived from the philosophy of Leibniz and from Deleuze's short commentary on Whitman. The modern and technical sense of the term "sampling" belongs neither to the seventeenth-century philosopher, nor the nineteenth-century American poet—unless only figuratively applied—so we might ask what is the literal sense of this term from both sources?

In the *Monadology*, "sampling" can be employed to describe the process by which the monad reads all the totality it includes; nevertheless, this process is described both as method of reading and as an art, and in this case the specific problematic is how to unfold all of the predicates that belong to each monad as its own singular point of view, defined as "a clear zone of expression." However, for Deleuze, the problem is determined by a movement that does not go from part to whole, "because the totality can be as imperceptible as the parts," but rather from what is *ordinary* to what is *notable* or *remarkable*" (L 87–8). In this sense, the process of "sampling" can actually indicate the precise manner in which conscious perception occurs in the monad, by a means of a selection that begins "as if through a first filter that would be followed by many other filters," and almost in the same manner that in the act of exposition a concept is extracted to serve as a sieve of sorts that is first applied to ordinary perceptions (i.e., the previous conditions of intelligibility), "in order to extract from them whatever is remarkable (i.e., clear and distinguished)" (L 91). Likewise, in the brief commentary on Whitman we find that Deleuze employs the *échantillon* ("sample") as a translation of the term "specimen" (from Whitman's *Specimen Days*) in reference to what he describes as "the law of the fragment," and where we find the following maxim: "To select the singular cases and the minor scenes is more important than any consideration of the whole" (CC 57). Here, we have the most succinct and clear expression of the logic that Zourabichvili employs in his own exposition of the concepts he regards as the singular cases and minor points of view. Moreover, as Deleuze writes, "the fragments—as remarkable parts, cases, or views—*must still be extracted by means of a special act, an act that consists, precisely, in writing*" (CC 57; emphasis added). Again we return to the earlier observation that in the art of exposition, by means of the special act that is writing, the concept must first be extracted from a prior assemblage that previously determined the conditions of intelligibility, much in the same manner that using citation words are extracted from their original sentences in order to be placed into new sentences and new possible arrangements—not only, as we have seen, with other concepts in a philosophical understanding, but primarily in relation to a movement that tends toward an outside that is composed by new percepts and affects. Accordingly, we must neither presuppose that concepts already belong to an organic totality that would determine their relations, nor presuppose that in their raw state the concepts have no preliminary artificial order of reasons that would divert our attention away from the act of assembling them according to an order that becomes necessary, and not in the least bit arbitrary, because it expresses a unique point of view. Therefore, following the preliminary entry in the original French edition, the concept of "assemblage" [*agencement*] is the first concept Zourabichvili selects in the *Vocabulary*, where we find the following description: "In reality, the disparity of the cases of the assemblage can be ordered only from the point of view of immanence—hence existence reveals itself to be inseparable from the variable and modifiable assemblages that ceaselessly produce it."[17]

We would like to thank Kieran Aarons, not only for his superb translation, but for his tireless efforts to see this book through to its publication. Paul Patton's assistance was crucial in first communicating with the French publishers concerning our proposal to combine the original works into one combined volume. Carol MacDonald at Edinburgh University Press has been a model editor, full of patience and critical acumen. Finally, we would like to thank Anne Nancy for her support and friendship throughout this project. This book is dedicated to Anne and her sons, Félix and Timotheé.

Notes

1. See below p. 135.
2. From the back cover of the French edition of the *Vocabulary*.
3. See below p. 37.
4. François Zourabichvili, *La littéralité et autres essais sur l'art* (Paris: PUF, 2011). The book includes three essays in particular that are devoted to the theme of literality: "Event and Literality," "The Question of Literality," and "Are Philosophical Concepts Metaphors? Deleuze and his Problematic of Literality."
5. François was the son of the composer Nicolas Zourabichvili, the cousin of the writer Emmanuel Carrère (author, most notably of *Un roman russe*, Paris: POL, 2007) and the nephew of Hélène Carrère d'Encausse, a French historian who specialized in Russia and was elected to the Academie francaise in 1990. His father's cousin was Salomé Zourabichvili, a French diplomat who served, among other positions, as the French ambassador to Georgia in 2003. His great-great grandfather, Ivane Zourabichvili, had been a minister in the Georgian government from 1920–21.
6. See below p. 37.
7. See below p. 26.
8. As Deleuze and Guattari argue, "a concept is not a set of associated ideas like an opinion [since] ideas can only be associated as images and only ordered as abstractions; to arrive at a concept we must go beyond both of these and arrive as quickly as possible at mental objects determinable as real beings" (WP 207).
9. See below p. 141.
10. See below p. 140.
11. See below p. 35.
12. See below p. 56.
13. See below p. 49.
14. See below p. 141.
15. Of course, Deleuze himself recognized this temptation with respect to one other philosopher, Spinoza, who constitutes perhaps a precedent for understanding the same problem in the reception of his own

philosophy. It is true, Deleuze observes, that often writers and artists "understand" Spinoza in the sense of incorporating his plan(e) of immanence into their own creative composition without necessarily understanding his philosophical concepts; whereas, most philosophers have left his system in a state of abstraction. In other words, Spinoza unites philosophy and non-philosophy in one and the same sense, which is why Deleuze and Guattari later on refer to him as the "Christ of philosophers."

16. See below p. 141.
17. See below p. 145.

DELEUZE: A PHILOSOPHY OF THE EVENT

François Zourabichvili

Contents

New Introduction: The Ontological and the Transcendental (2004)

This book, first published ten years ago, attests to a period in which it was not obvious that Deleuze ought to be considered a full-fledged thinker, a major figure in the philosophical twentieth century. I set out from the paradox of his contentious reputation: he's not an original philosopher because he writes commentaries, nor is he an historian since he always writes pure "Deleuze." Moreover, I refused to distinguish between Deleuze, Deleuze-and-Guattari, and Deleuze once more (just as there is a Beckett before Pim, during Pim, and after Pim—a quite muddled affair, as it should be).

It is uncertain, given the fatigue of the times, whether this double misunderstanding has dissipated. Ingenuous or not, there is a call today for philosophers who know once again how to attend to an *object*: as if "experience" or "life," that sole affair of the philosopher, that "thing itself" with multiple irreducibly imbricated dimensions among which philosophy figures, had been partitioned in advance into *terrains* for academic busywork, *major themes* for the idle talk of honest men. Experts or rhetors, there is no lack of claimants to this new and diversely cognitive philosophy. As for the history of philosophy, current academic trends tend to present Deleuze as a mild-mannered species of eclectic perhaps worthy of memory, as is any species from the point of view of the scholar, but which has fortunately run its course.

As regards the other misunderstanding (Deleuze from the point of view of Pim), the last decade has witnessed the proliferation of exegetes: either experts in Deleuzological purity or, conversely, Deleuzo-Guattarologists indifferent to the pre-Guattarian era (and even the lesser Guattarian age, when *A Thousand Plateaus* radiates in their eyes like a unique and absolute source). If my bias was resolutely ahistorical, it is because I sought to bring forth a systematic Deleuzian thought while avoiding such vulgar chronological traps (in many ways, for example, the turn of *Anti-Oedipus* is a *trompe-l'oeil*, as the true renewal of concepts—Becoming-animal, the refrain, the war machine, etc.—occurs only later).

However, the fact is that new stakes have arisen. I will address only two of these here, since they concern this book. On the one hand, in its worst moments as well as its best, Deleuzology has made extensive use of the "pompous name of ontology," as Kant put it, installing an equivocation all the more difficult to extirpate given that this word recovers from Heidegger something of the latter's aura. On the other hand, in some of its tendencies, phenomenology today lays claim with all the ardor of the newly converted to a monopoly over the notion of the event, even if this occasionally means revising history or simply ignoring it.

There is no "ontology of Deleuze." Neither in the vulgar sense of a metaphysical discourse which could inform us, in the last instance, what there is of reality (which would be fluxes rather than substances, or lines rather than persons) . . . Nor in the deeper sense of a primacy of being over knowledge (as is the case with Heidegger or Merleau-Ponty, where the subject appears to itself already preceded by an instance that opens the possibility of such an appearing).

Let us remind those who hold the first view of the resolutely "critical" (in the Kantian sense) anchor of Deleuze's thought: that of a philosopher who, from start to finish, questioned the conditions of experience, unsatisfied with Kant as well as phenomenology (the well-known usage he made of Nietzsche and of Bergson figure in this context).

To the more subtle partisans of the second version, we attest by means of the same oeuvre of Deleuze that the overflowing of the subject in experience does not necessarily inscribe itself in ontological terms, that another diagnosis has emerged according to which being is a category that itself cannot withstand this overflowing. It is true that the prestige enjoyed by the term "being" tends to remove it (as if by distraction) from the critical work of those who are most vigilant: it would be the obvious correlate of thought, so obvious that any suspicion regarding it would be almost bad faith. The counterpart of a privilege no less exorbitant is the acceptance without reserve of any possible content or, better still, of no content—this is to say, inconsistency itself: Being, withdrawn from all possible predication, and as its very source. It is certainly possible to construct a concept of the contentless (whether one obtains this by resorption or by suspension) and name it, for example, the nothing, the neuter, or otherwise still; but there is no reason to baptize this being—except to force language to the point where all becomes equal, where one no longer speaks.

If there is an orientation of the philosophy of Deleuze, this is it: *the extinction of the term "being" and therefore of ontology.* Those for whom to comment on an author consists in inscribing him in the grid of *philosophia perennis* do not return from it [*n'en reviennent pas*] (but after all, as Deleuze said, if the eternal return has a meaning, it is that of a selection). However, time and again Deleuze spoke clearly—and literally—of his program: substitution of IS by means of AND or, what amounts to the same thing, substitution of becoming for being. The introduction of *A Thousand Plateaus* ends with these words: "establish a logic of the AND, overthrow ontology."[1] Contemporary philosophy—Foucault, Derrida, to say nothing of the Anglo-Saxons—has abandoned or overcome ontology; what fun, naive or perfidious, to want by all means to rediscover one in Deleuze!

Nevertheless, one might object, didn't Deleuze himself explicitly write that "philosophy merges with ontology" (LS 179)? Let us assume this—the apologist for the term "being" must then explain how, in the same work, a concept of the transcendental field can be produced (LS 14th–16th Series). We may begin by restoring the second half of the statement, intentionally ignored or poorly weighed: ". . . but ontology merges with the univocity of being."[2] A formidable example of the style or of the method of Deleuze—there is enough in it to pervert the entire ontological discourse.

Hence the two authors to whom Deleuze attributes the affirmation of univocity, after its initiator, Duns Scotus: Spinoza, and Nietzsche (DR 39–42). Is it not from his incessant meditation on Spinoza that he draws the expression "plane of immanence," destined to supplant that of the "transcendental field," itself become inadequate?[3] And is it not of Nietzsche that he says: he fulfilled, beyond Kant, the hope of a true critique (NP 87 ff.)? The question that every reader of Deleuze must confront if he wants to avoid the bias (without, for all that, abstaining from taking a position, i.e. from assigning to Deleuze a new place in philosophy, one which shatters its landscape) is how this thinker could coordinate two modes of approach which at first blush seem incompatible: transcendental and ontological.[4]

Is it enough to recall that Husserl had already reintroduced ontology by subordinating it to phenomenological interrogation? Is it enough to add that the difficulties phenomenology found itself confronted with (the limits of a "constitution" on the basis of the transcendental subject) conversely led a Fink or a Heidegger to re-inscribe phenomenology—in order to accomplish it rather than betray it—in an ontological perspective? Certainly not. The ontological inspiration surfaces in Deleuze *alongside* his critical approach, and as its double.

Deleuze returns to the heart of the genuine ontological tradition: that which, developing in the Middle Ages well before the learned formation of the word, is first and foremost a meditation on language, contrary to the classical "metaphysics" with which ontology is often confounded (as a result of being historically annexed to it). Heidegger is certainly the first to have restored this linguistic dimension—inasmuch as he pursued the Scotist adventure. However, the thesis of univocity is not a source of inspiration for him, whereas Deleuze sees in it the most glorious act of ontology—one that also leads to its auto-abolition as a doctrine of *being*.[5] It is not ontology in itself that interests Deleuze; as he indicates in the latter half of the statement cited above, it is the moment of its history where the thesis of univocity arises, and the secret posterity of this statement, well beyond the Middle Ages.

The *coup de force* therefore consists in identifying ontology with one of its theses: Deleuze believes himself authorized to do so by the fact that the affirmation of univocity is sustained by the quest for a pure logic of sense (even if—in accordance with the Deleuzian definition of humor as an art of consequences—this logic leads to a special sort of political anarchism, one of perversion rather than destruction: founding, on the idea of the irreducibility of the small to the large, an original and not at all pious concept of resistance which pretty well sums up the "joyful pessimism" of our philosophy). At the same time, it is at the point of its highest accomplishment that ontology finds itself condemned, not to cross out the notion from whence it takes its name (to cross out is not Deleuze's way), but to erase it through a force of *sobriety*. And if one wishes to mark the Deleuzian style with a symbol, without insisting on it here any more than did a thinker who always maintained his distance from linguistic cleverness, emphasis will once again be placed on that silent amputation of a letter that the French language permits: E(S)T.[6]

From a logic of being and knowledge, philosophy shifts toward a logic of relation and belief. That the "naive" Hume reemerges *after* Heidegger, not under the form of a return-to, but under the deterritorializing injunction of the most contemporary questioning, is certainly one of the surprises that delivers us over to this sobriety without which, for Deleuze, there is no philosophy in becoming.[7]

As for the question of where Deleuze believes he can tie together the two threads of his discourse, transcendental and ontological, we will of course invoke the category of "immanence" and the strange treatment he causes it to undergo.[8] But if one asks, "at which precise moment of this category's emergence?," we must reply: when the affirmation of the univocity of being, deployed in all its consequences, leads to the concept of *affect* and is converted into a thought of experience. The schema of demonstration is as follows: *if* the univocity of being implies that beings are distinguished only by their degree of power [*puissance*], and *if* this degree of power, before being compared to others, is first subject to an intrinsic test where it is measured only against itself (to go to the limit of what one can do—where oppression consists less in suffering the yoke of the more powerful than in being "separated from what one can do," henceforth unfit for any sort of resistance), *then* a being allows itself to be defined only through the singular declination of its affects (rather than by a generic and specific difference), and this evanescent ontology, which knows only becomings, transversal couplings or mutual diversions, coincides with the description of a field of experience freed from the supervision of a subject (since no one can know "what a body can do" in advance). Here we pass from a regime of literal meaning and controlled [*reglée*] metaphor to a regime of anarchic "literality," where everything communicates in principle with everything else.[9]

Immanence is not the moment where ordinary experience re-ascends to its ownmost conditions in order to have some sort of transcendental experience, even if this going-back recognizes that its ultimate condition is not the *ego* but Being or the Event (the phenomenologico-Heideggerian style); it is rather the moment where this transcendental re-ascension proves to be dependent on the coming-into-consistency[10] of a "real" experience—in other words, on the alteration of the conditions under which something is recognized as possible (the Deleuzian style). This event attests to itself through the production of singular categories and by the emergence of a new *belief*. For if knowledge, regardless of what one says of it, remains the fundamental disposition of a thought that addresses itself to being, only belief answers to the event, given the irreducible exteriority that the latter envelops, and the challenge it issues to reason.

"Belief" no longer has here the traditional sense of an attitude whose relative validity is measured by the yardstick of a truth (already) present or to come, possessed here below [*ici-bas*] by another, the scholar, or beyond in some infinite understanding. Only the sense of a non-reasoned conviction is preserved, but whose negative value is reversed as soon as the *necessity* to which the philosopher aspires reveals itself to be unthinkable within the limits of "reason" (which is to say, of a thinking that masters itself). "Belief" refers to the tireless return, in the mind, of a new and problematic relation, of a conjunction of terms as unforeseeable as they are unjustifiable, the difficult affirmation of which presupposes the breaking-open by effraction of a new field of experience, able to tame a share of the chaotic occurrences of life and to transmute their shocks into signs (the well-known examples: the unconscious is/and [*e(s)t*] a factory and not a theatre [AO *passim*]; the brain, grass rather than a tree— statements, Deleuze tells us, which are to be taken literally and not as simple metaphors, since no division of meaning allowing us to assign a literal usage and a figurative usage precedes this shifting ground of transitory relations). To think, in this sense, is to "contract a habit," restoring to this notion all its value of innovation or of creation.

Thus there is no event except in the plural, the event is always at least two. In other words, the event is less the absolute occurrence of a birth on the background of negativity (nothingness or *doxa*) than a becoming in which the before and the after spring forth at the same time, on either side of a caesura that thought cannot reduce (the before is not nothing, which is to say not before me or before thought, but me-before-otherwise [*moi-avant-autrement*] or what thought was—"I is an Other"). In addition, the event, always plural and preceded by other events, does not, as in phenomenological thought, have the character of an advent.

With Deleuze, thought ceases to take the neutrality of the event for a neutral event, everywhere reiterable (even though, for Merleau-Ponty or Heidegger, its ante-predicative status protects the event *in principle* from the test of the same and the other, the test itself being neutralized).[11] Henceforth, thought attempts to fulfill Nietzsche's wish: to articulate names which would not be avatars naming a poorly killed God. Which is why the function of belief does not disappear, but rather changes its meaning; and we would be mistaken in thinking that the variable has only taken another value, while the function remained intact. It is for this reason as well that the Deleuzian assemblage cannot ever completely fit with philosophy in becoming, and still less does it suffice for it eternally. But philosophy in becoming suits the Deleuzian assemblage, in the active and strong sense, or, even better: *they fit with one another*, as long as philosophy in becoming finds here a space to displace itself, to surprise itself, and to test itself without recognizing itself. Consequently, to write on Deleuze is not to commemorate a philosophical revolution already made. Nobody knows nor claims to say what "the" philosophy of Deleuze is; we feel affected by Deleuze, we who are its explorers, inasmuch as we try to do philosophy today; we assume that philosophy will not emerge from the Deleuzian adventure unscathed, but we know that it is up to us to demonstrate this and to pursue it.

Notes

1. ATP 25. On the substitution of the AND for the IS, cf. D 56–9; ATP 25, 98; C2 180. On the substitution of becoming for being, cf. ATP 237–8 (from which the emphasis on lines emerges).
2. "The univocity of being" means: being is said in a single and same sense of everything of which it is said.
3. Referring to Spinoza, *A Thousand Plateaus* speaks of a "plane of immanence or univocity" (ATP 254 and 266).
4. To take but one example, the same concept of "pre-individual singularities" is introduced twice in *The Logic of Sense*: first, as composing the new concept of the transcendental field (15th Series), then as an ontological category in a text on Klossowski (Appendix III).
5. Deleuze, however, is very close to annexing Heidegger in his lineage of univocal thinkers; he does not exclude him except *in extremis* (cf. DR 35, 66).
6. This untranslatable symbol is formed from the French words *est* ("is") and *et* ("and")—Trans.
7. The appeal to sobriety is one of the leitmotifs of *A Thousand Plateaus* (cf. ATP 99, 279, 344). It is addressed to everyone, thus equally to Deleuzians.
8. Husserl restored life to the notion of immanence by inscribing it in the framework of a philosophy of experience beyond Kant. Deleuze reactivates the old—metaphysical—usage of the notion to give consistency to his anti-phenomenological project of radicalizing critical thought (cf. EPS, Ch. XI; ATP 253 ff.; SPP Ch. VI).
9. Cf. DR 37, as well as the illuminating course of January 14, 1974, available at www.webdeleuze.com
10. This formulation, *prise de consistance*, functions here as a perversion of the expression *prise de conscience* (becoming conscious of something, becoming aware) —Trans.
11. On the neutrality of the event, cf. LS 9th and 21st Series.

Preface (1994)

Gilles Deleuze constantly comments on other authors, while at the same time putting forward his own original thought. The same logical motifs, and often the same concepts, reappear from one book to the next, though each time varied and displaced. The work, which is still in progress, is like a play of echoes and resonances. We have tried to bring to light this recurrent logical configuration, which presents enough unity, coherency, and problematizing force to be taken on its own as a philosophy—a philosophy of the event: "In all my books, I have tried to discover the nature of the event," "I spent a lot of time writing about this notion of the event" (N 141, 160, translation modified).

The nature of this strange philosophy—constantly innovating and meticulously stubborn, stationary and mutating in accordance with the paradoxical definition of *nomadism* that it proposes—seems both to legitimate and to compromise my intention. Moreover, it may seem derisory to present the prototype of a thought that is always engaged in a variable element, and inseparably ethical, aesthetic, and political. As a result, this book makes sense only as an auxiliary to reading, or as an adjacent logical exercise: it is written for people who read Deleuze or would like to read Deleuze. Like any guide, it proposes an itinerary, one that has been followed by the author, but the guide cannot take the place of the reader (the latter is naturally free to amend it or to depart from this itinerary, provided that they in turn follow their own).

However, the difficulty involves another aspect. It is erroneous to divide Deleuze's work into two parts—commentaries on one side, and works written in his own name on the other. Starting with *Nietzsche and Philosophy*, whose title announces a confrontation rather than a simple commentary, the tone Deleuze employs alerts the reader to the underlying and autonomous presence, not of a commentator, but of a cause that is common to both the author doing the commenting and the author being commented upon. There appears here for the first time the nonconventional use of *free indi-*

rect discourse that will characterize many of Deleuze's subsequent texts, before becoming itself an explicit theme: a way of giving one's voice to the words of another that ends up merging with the other—speaking in one's own name by borrowing the voice of another. Commentary and co-authorship [*écriture à deux*] are cases of free indirect discourse. One could apply to Deleuze what he says, in the first person, of the filmmaker Pierre Perrault: "I gave myself mediators, and this is how I can say what I have to say" (N 125, translation modified). Reciprocally, the presence or insistence of admired authors is no less ubiquitous in the so-called independent works than that of the commentator in his monographs; consequently, we thus cannot consider a book such as *Proust and Signs* to be less important from the point of view of Deleuze's "own" thought than *Difference and Repetition* or *The Logic of Sense*, since the concepts elaborated in these works often emerged through a reworking and telescoping of motifs that came from elsewhere.

In most cases, then, the statements presented here have been attributed to Deleuze alone. Is he a Spinozist, a Nietzschean, a Bergsonian? (Is he good? Is he bad?) What belongs to Deleuze and what belongs to others is hardly *discernible*, and cannot be evaluated in terms of authenticity or influence. By contrast, the new and anonymous configuration that is affirmed in this free indirect oeuvre is *distinct*, and it can bear no name other than that of Deleuze. And it is that which interests us here.

1

Thought and Its Outside (Critique of the Dogmatic Image)

The most general problem of thought is perhaps that of its *necessity*: not the necessity of thinking, but how to arrive at a necessary thought. The first experience of thought is that we have no choice, that we do not want to have a choice, that we will not state what we want. The thinker is happy when he no longer has a choice.

Philosophy has always understood and admitted this correlation of thought and necessity. Moreover, it has even recognized the relation of necessity with *exteriority*. Thought does not itself choose what is necessary—what it thinks absolutely must not depend on itself alone. Philosophy has called this necessity truth. It has seen in truth not merely the object of a revelation, but the precise content corresponding to what must be said or thought—which led it to double truth with a correlate outside the mind, independent of it and identical to itself (reality and its essence). In philosophy, thinking first of all meant knowing.

Philosophy thus readily admits that the fate of thought depends on its relation to exteriority. The problem is knowing whether it can indeed succeed in thinking this exteriority, whether it can affirm an authentically exterior relation between thought and truth [*le vrai*]. Deleuze offers the following diagnosis: however much philosophy recognizes in truth an element independent of thought, it ends up *interiorizing* the relation and postulating that thought and truth have an intimate or natural relation. The philosopher does not choose the true, he wants to submit himself to the law of the outside [*dehors*]; but at the same time he constantly claims to be the friend or intimate companion [*l'intime*] of this outside; it is he who seeks after it spontaneously, who finds himself naturally on its path. The truth has not yet been conquered or possessed, but the thinker gives himself its form in advance; thought "possesses the true formally," even if it still has to be conquered materially (DR 131). Thought does not yet know what is true, but it at least knows itself to be well-endowed

44

for the search, *a priori* capable of finding it. Whence the idea, for example, of a truth forgotten rather than unknown (Plato), or the theme of the innate idea rather than the forged or adventitious idea, even if this means interiorizing the relation to God as an absolute outside or a transcendence (Descartes).

Deleuze thus undertakes a critique of the concept of truth, or the determination of the necessary as true. The problem he poses is the capacity of thought to affirm the outside, and the conditions of this affirmation. Is it sufficient to think the outside as an external reality that is identical to itself? Despite appearances, does this not remain a relative exteriority? And is the necessity to which the thinker aspires in fact on the order of a truth, at least in the way we have defined it? Does it refer to a discourse that could express what things are, a statement that could establish a correspondence between sense and essence? Is the outside of thought something that can be known, or made the object of a content of thought? It is certainly hard to renounce the idea of an external reality . . .

Deleuze notes that a certain *image of thought* has been affirmed throughout the history of philosophy, an image that he terms *dogmatic* because it assigns, *a priori*, a form to the outside (NP 103–10; PS 94–105; DR Ch. III). This image impregnates all philosophy—at least formally—up until the great Nietzschean crisis, even if it has occasionally been contested within a given system (for instance, in Spinoza's system, where the idea of composition, which is developed through the concept of the common notion and the affective theory of the body, tends to invert the entire system into an empiricism, requiring a reading "from the middle" (EPS 149 and Ch. XVII; SPP Chapters V–VI).

The dogmatic image derives from the internalization of the relation between philosophy and the outside, or between philosophy and necessity. It is expressed: (1) in the belief in a natural thought; (2) in the general model of recognition; and (3) in the claim to grounding.

Willing

It is presumed in philosophy that we think naturally—the *good will* of the thinking subject is already presupposed: "The philosopher readily presupposes that the mind as mind, the thinker as thinker, wants the truth, loves or desires the truth, naturally seeks the truth. He assumes in advance the good will of thinking . . ." (PS 94; cf. equally NP 73, 94–5, 103; DR 130 ff.). The desire for truth belongs by right to thought as a faculty; seeking the truth is a constitutive and originary orientation of thought. Thought finds in itself the desire for and the motivation toward a search: it wants the truth. And this will is not simply a wish, since it is enough to put us on the path of truth. From the start, there is a relation of affinity between the thinker and what he is seeking: to discover (or rediscover) the direction of the truth, it is enough for him to will. Good will does not only mean the intention to do good, but an intention that by itself already puts us on the path of the good, a guide that orients thought. That the will is good means that to will is to will the truth (and persevering in error, in accordance with a well-known moral motif, is to be attributed to a lack of will). Commit an act of will, decide that you want the true, and you will already be on its path; all that is missing then is a method by which to avoid mishaps. "From a certain viewpoint, the search for truth would be the most natural and the easiest; the decision to undertake it and the possession of a method capable of overcoming the external influences that distract thought from its vocation and cause it to take the false for the true would suffice" (PS 94, translation modified). Thinking is perhaps difficult in fact, but it is easy in principle: it suffices to will it (decision) and to apply oneself (method) (DR 133).

But if thought is supposed to find the necessary orientation within itself, this is because it always already possessed it. The good will of the thinker is guaranteed by the *upright nature of thought* (DR 131; NP 103). Since thought is naturally well oriented [*bien orientée*], if we are not only in search of the true but in search of the path that leads to the true (the orientation), it must be the case that thought has been led astray [*détournée*] or diverted [*divertie*] by harmful forces that are foreign to it. The concept of error, where philosophy locates all that constitutes the negative of thought, is constructed on the schema of an external intervention that leads thought astray from itself and accidentally (therefore provisionally) conceals its natural relation to truth. Thought always retains the resources to reconnect with its own force through an act of will. Exteriority, in philosophy, is thus divided: truth no less than error finds its source outside of thought—yet we have an essential and intimate relation with the former, and only an accidental relation with the latter. The good outside lies in the depth of our hearts, like an "inside deeper than any internal world"[1] (and we shall see that Deleuze retains this schema, while shattering its signification); the bad outside is exterior, it perverts thought.

Thought is naturally *well* oriented, or oriented toward the *good* [*bien orienté*]. How can we not suspect, following Nietzsche, a moral motivation behind this dogmatic image? A good-thinking [*bien-penser*] at the origin of this presupposition? "Morality alone is capable of persuading us that thought has a good nature and the thinker a good will, and that only the good can ground the supposed affinity between thought and the True. Who else, in effect, but Morality, and this Good which gives thought to the true, and the true to thought . . ." (DR 132). What assures us of this in-principle relation between thought and truth? Why would thought have to have an affinity with the truth? Nothing guarantees that thought is always already in search of the truth, or that it wants it naturally. There is no *a priori* relation except through the moral idea of the Good.

Recognizing

The second consequence of the internalization of the relation between thought and truth is the model of *recognition* (PS 27; DR 131 ff.). The object of thought is less the object of a discovery than of a recognition, since thought—since it is not in a relation of absolute strangeness with what it thinks or endeavors to think—in a certain way precedes itself by prejudging the form of its object. We do not seek the truth without postulating it in advance—in other words, without presuming, before even having thought at all, the existence of a reality: not the reality of a world (Deleuze does not challenge this), but that of a "truthful world" [*monde veridique*], identical to itself, a docile world faithful to our expectations whenever we try to know it. As soon as thought interprets its object as reality, it assigns it *a priori* the form of identity: homogeneity and permanence. The object is subjected to the principle of identity in order that it may be known, and as a result all cognition [*connaissance*] is already re-cognition [*reconnaissance*]. Thought recognizes what it has first identified—it does not give itself anything to think that it has not first passed through the screen of the Same.

It is thus easy to see that a "truthful" world is inevitably surrounded by a *transcendence* that guarantees it an identity, precisely because this identity can only be a presumed identity, thought giving an *a priori* form to what it does not yet know (whence begins the confusion of immanence with closure). Belief in an external reality refers in the last instance to the position of a God as the absolute outside. In sum, the dogmatic image of thought is recognizable by the way it links the outside to a transcendence, necessarily referring to a beyond as the necessary guarantor of the *a priori* that it postulates and imposes here below.

Yet how can thought know in advance *what* it has to think? How can it be that thought applies itself to an object that has already been recognized, and is assumed to be preexistent? Are we to believe that it attains necessity in this way, that it manages to seize upon something that does not depend on it? A philosophy of immanence must go so far as to call into question the attributive logical schema which privileges questions of essence while prejudging the identity of the interrogated object, and which always asks: what is it? We will see that thought, insofar as it thinks, does not intend a self-identical object, and does not function in an objective-explicit field. It attains the necessary—which is to say it truly thinks—only in a "distinct-obscure" zone.

The model of recognition involves at least two other postulates: error, as the negative state *par excellence* of thought, and knowledge, as the element of the true (DR 148 ff. and 164 ff.). Philosophy measures its ambition by the nature of its intended object, which is identical and permanent. Thus, thought is but a provisional process, destined to fill the distance separating us from the object; it lasts exactly as long as it takes to recognize. Its *raison d'être* is negative: to put an end to the frustrations of ignorance. Unless it is the inverse, and thinking amounts to the happy contemplation of the known object, or the mechanical exercise of a sovereign power of recognition. By making knowledge its goal, thought is trapped in the alternative of the ephemeral and the immobile. In both cases, it is a matter of appropriating contents we do not yet have at our disposal (and the "pedagogical" critique of knowledge remains powerless; worse yet, it has a sophistical inspiration, when it contents itself with devaluing knowledge in favor of empty or formal capacities, which are nothing but its correlates: one does not critique the content except by abandoning the dualism it forms with the container). Thus, the philosopher imagines himself to have arrived, he dreams himself to be in possession; the dogmatic image of thought is indeed a thought of enrichment. Under these conditions, how can the element of knowledge dispel the specter that haunts it: stupidity [*la bêtise*]? Deleuze emphasizes the degree to which the postulate of recognition, with its two avatars—knowledge and error—encourages a servile image of thought grounded in *interrogation*: to give the right answer, to find the right result, as if one was in grade school or on a televised game-show. The act of thinking is modeled on puerile and scholarly situations. "We are led to believe that the activity of thinking, along with truth and falsehood in relation to that activity, begins only with the search for solutions, that both of these concern only solutions" (DR 158). "From earliest times philosophy has encountered the danger of evaluating thought by reference to such uninteresting cases as saying 'Hello, Theodorus' when Theatetus is passing by" (WP 139; cf. also NP 105 and DR 150).

Whence emerges the pious and humanistic idea that the problems are and have always been the same, that they constitute a common cultural patrimony beyond time, and that thought navigates between entirely divergent solutions, themselves equally incomplete and unsatisfying. Philosophy is presented with the dilemma of either seeking out new solutions that would condemn its entire past, or else tending to the cult of the eternal enigmas posed to man (and philosophers would at least have the social merit of accepting this role on behalf of others), often by deploying a disinterested ardor in the conservation of past solutions (fortunately, the history of philosophy has not always remained at this level).

Grounding

Finally, the *a priori* relation of thought and truth is expressed in the equivocation of the *beginning* [*commencement*] (DR 129 ff.). Philosophy has always been preoccupied with beginnings, constantly seeking out the right principle: Ideas, causes, the Cogito, the principle of sufficient reason, etc. It is not only a question of introducing an order within concepts; the demand for an order implies a division, a difference in status between those concepts that ground and those that are grounded—the former, absolutely necessary, are supposed to guarantee the necessity of the latter. "Once and for all": this applies not only to the end (knowledge), but also to the beginning. Philosophy demands *a* point of departure as a definitive rupture with that which it is not. Philosophy requires a grounding [*fondement*] as a mark indicating that it has finally begun to think, that it has left behind for good the horizon of a thought that would be merely possible (opinion, *doxa*). Here again, as with the theme of exteriority, it is a question of knowing whether or not philosophy, by posing the problem in terms of grounding, can claim to effectively go beyond the simple possibility of thinking.

Deleuze emphasizes the inability of philosophers to truly begin

(DR 129–32). A genuine beginning requires the expulsion of every presupposition. Try as one might to begin by selecting a concept that does not effectively presuppose any other concept (such as the Cogito, which is opposed to the definition of man as rational animal), one does not for all that escape presuppositions of another order, implicit or pre-conceptual, which can only rely on common sense. Thus is it "presumed that everyone knows, independently of concepts, what is meant by self, thinking, and being" (DR 129). At the very moment philosophy believes itself to be beginning, it falls back into the pre-philosophical, so that it can never possess itself or autonomize its ground. In order to begin or to ground itself, philosophy cannot cling to a difference in status among concepts, since the latter in turn rests on a difference of status between itself and *doxa* or opinion. Philosophy can arrive at a grounding only by selecting universal opinions (empirical, sensible, and concrete being in Hegel, the pre-ontological understanding of being in Heidegger) or else an originary Opinion (the *Urdoxa* of phenomenology). Heidegger decisively contests the dogmatic image when he says that thought remains in a position in which it is not yet thinking, but he links this to the theme of a *philia*, and thus maintains "a homology between thought and that which is to be thought" (DR 321 fn.). As long as the beginning is conceived as grounding, it is subject to an initial recognition that borrows its form from common sense, and thus philosophy never manages to break free of a preliminary affinity with what it is to be thought. The inability to break free of presuppositions is obviously related to the model of recognition: the thinking that grounds circles around opinion, which it claims both to surpass and to conserve; as a result, it winds up merely rediscovering or recognizing the *doxa* (we will see in Chapter 3 how much the Hegelian dialectic is implicated here as well).

To put this supposed affinity into question is to provoke a complete disruption of the way in which philosophy understands its own necessity. To break with the thought that grounds . . . but for the sake of what? By renouncing the ground, are we not led back to doubt, but now with the assurance of never escaping from it? Is not the only certainty the minimal and paradoxical certainty of skepticism? Yet the problem is knowing whether the very enterprise of grounding is not quite simply in contradiction with the concept of necessity. By grounding, we claim to possess the beginning, to master necessity. Thought is supposed to return to itself, and to conquer its necessity from within (recall, for example, the impressive opening of

Malebranche's *Dialogues on Metaphysics*). Once again, philosophy seems caught in an equivocation between an outside that is sometimes threatening (the external sensible world) and sometimes salutary (God, the intelligible), the necessary relation to the outside being inscribed inexplicably in the very nature of thought. The failure of grounding is not extraneous to the fragility of this postulate. It is not surprising that necessity escapes us when we try to close thought in on itself. The ground itself rests upon a breach that is, for better or worse, more or less covered over by opinions.

As a result, it is not clear that thought renounces the beginning simply by noting its own incapacity to dominate or comprehend it. On the contrary, perhaps thought truly begins only at such a price, by giving up its possession of the beginning, by admitting that it takes place "behind its back". What philosophy believes itself to have lost when it affirms a radical exteriority is perhaps won in this way for the better. There is no contradiction between the "true beginning" invoked in *Difference and Repetition* and the affirmation in *Dialogues* according to which thinking happens only "in the middle," without beginning or end. We do not begin by grounding, but in a "universal ungrounding"; there is no beginning "once and for all." To understand that there is nothing skeptical about this statement, and that it is perfectly compatible with the idea of a radical or effective beginning, we need to link it with the rejection of the model of recognition, which was the result of challenging the postulate of an intimacy with the outside ("the dubitable will not allow us to escape from the point of view of recognition"—DR 139). The concept of a beginning implies unicity only when the identity of what is to be thought is presupposed. We will see that the beginning must be repeated, and even affirmed on "all occasions,"[2] because the world does not have the reality or reliability that we think: it is heterogeneous. It is at one and the same time that thought affirms an absolute relation to exteriority, that it challenges the postulate of recognition, and that it affirms the outside *in this world*: heterogeneity, divergence. When philosophy gives up grounding, the outside abjures its transcendence and becomes *immanent*.

For Deleuze it is thus a question of affirming the relation of exteriority that links thought to what it thinks. If thinking necessarily fails to grasp its beginning, perhaps it is because the beginning does not depend upon thought. As a result, Deleuze is able to think the conditions of a radical absolute beginning while at the same time declaring that "we are always in the middle," and that a philosophy does not begin, does not think on the basis of a principle it takes to be first (cf. D 62 and SPP 122 for Spinozism). The true beginning is necessarily outside the concept [*hors-concept*], or at the limit of the concept, and depends on the capacity of the latter not to close in on itself [*se refermer sur soi*], to implicate on the contrary the relation to the outside [*dehors*] from which it draws its necessity. We can already see that this relation will put in play something very different from an "exterior reality" (an event, a becoming).

Deleuze ceaselessly challenges the false alternative that forces us to choose between transcendence and chaos, between necessity understood as preexisting truth and the absence of necessity pure and simple. The idea of truth is not absent from his work, but he rejects the traditional concept that would associate it with an external objective reality. He maintains the idea of revelation (PS 46), but it is less a matter of revealing a hidden object than a becoming-active of thought and of the paradoxical distinct-obscure "objecticities" [*objectités*] thought apprehends when it sets out to think. "Truth [is] solely the creation of thought ... thought is creation, not will-to-truth" (WP 54). Yet creation does not mean an arbitrary decision or a decree. To make truth depend on an act of creation is not to confine it to a subjectivism, to submit it to the caprice of an individual will (a relativism which, as we know, annuls the idea of truth). Deleuze shows on the contrary that the act of thinking necessarily puts subjectivity into crisis, and that necessity, far from fulfilling the wishes of an already constituted thinking subject, can only be conquered in the state of a thought outside of itself, a thought that is absolutely powerful only at the extreme point of its powerlessness.

Note on the Event, the End, and History

Deleuze does not see a logical link between the event and the idea of an *end*. For him, the modern problem is not expressed in terms of an end, since these are the terms of a thinking that is precisely incapable of finishing anything, or being finished with finishing. We will not achieve the end through interrogation: "Getting out never happens like that. Movement always happens behind the thinker's back, or in the moment when he blinks. Getting out is already achieved, or else it never will be" (D 1).

The problem of modernity—whose thinking of the end is in a certain way the derived reading, the negative reflection—is that we are already seized by something else, by other signs. An end is not enough to constitute an event, to throw us into the event; an epoch comes to an end only because another has already begun. The end is the reactive shadow of an emergence, the misinterpretation *par excellence* of the event. Something has happened, but philosophy is not simply closed, since the closure that is thereby announced does not imply that we abandon thinking with concepts, even if they must change their nature: philosophy enters into a new epoch, or, more precisely, is replayed again anew. This is to say, for Deleuze philosophy is not tied to an identity—marked by the concepts of truth, essence, grounding, reason, etc.—that would allow us to declare its end: of philosophy we must say "we don't know what it can do," because we have before our eyes only its past, eminently contingent, a past that cannot be taken for a center or an absolute reference.

The event puts the idea of history into crisis. That which happens, insofar as it happens and breaks with the past, does not belong to history and cannot be explained by it (N 31, 152–3, 170–1; WP 111–13). Or else nothing happens, or history is only the homogeneous representation of a succession of irreducible events (which are so often subjected to a transcendent judgment from the future, rather than to an immanent evaluation that would in each case draw out the intrinsic consistency or the weight of existence of a becoming). If it is still possible to relate these becomings to a "same" subject that is deduced from them— much more than it conditions them—it is always as a function of one or more *faculties*, in this case the faculty of creating concepts, which is linked to the very nature of language (cf. below Ch. 5). Yet this faculty has no sense in and of in itself—as we will see, it depends on the forces that seize it and that impose on it a "plan(e)" [*plan*] of thought, an "image of thought."

Or else there is something new, and it is this novelty that allows us to see what we are ceasing to be when we murmur "it is finished," because we no longer recognize ourselves in it; or else history is a development, and the end, already existing in germinal form at the beginning, appears as the truth of what is now ending—but then the truth is internal to the process it brings to a close, unable to break away from it, and it usurps the name of the end:

> Hegel and Heidegger remain historicists inasmuch as they posit history as a form of interiority in which the concept necessarily develops or unveils its destiny. The necessity rests on the abstraction of the historical element rendered circular. The unforeseeable creation of concepts is thus poorly understood. (WP 95)

53

It may be that we are experiencing a great weariness, a fatigue that is perhaps sufficient to define our modernity: but the sensitivity to the *intolerable*—the affect that paradoxically leaves us without affect, disaffected, disarmed in the face of elementary situations, power-less in the face of the universal rise of *clichés*—constitutes a positive emergence in the least moral sense of the word, the emergence of something that did not exist before, and which introduces a new image of thought (C2 18). Certainly contemporary thought testifies to a rupture that needs to be evaluated. But what we precisely need to ask is, "What happened?" (ATP 8th Plateau), which is the same as asking: what is philosophy *becoming*?

It is true that along with many philosophers before him or con-temporary with him, Deleuze seems to interpret his epoch as being the happy moment when the essence of philosophy is revealed, where the issue that distinguishes it absolutely from both the techniques of communication and religion appear as clear as day: *immanence*. The modern image of thought is thereby related to the new necessity of affirming immanence (WP 54). Yet, on the one hand, this revelation does not emerge at the end. On the contrary, it is the beginning of an epoch, and philosophy's past was perhaps only a first age, one in which philosophy still extricated itself poorly from what preexisted it:

> We know that things and people are always forced to conceal themselves, have to conceal themselves when they begin. What else could they do? They come into being within a set which no longer includes them and, in order not to be rejected, have to project the characteristics which they retain in common with the rest. The essence of a thing never appears at the outset, but in the middle, in the course of its development, when its strength is assured. (C1 2–3)

On the other hand, it remains no less the case that philosophy was already present in this first age: philosophers create their concepts only by immanence, even when they have transcendence for an object; and here and there, philosophers were already subverting the dominant image—Chryssipus and the event, Lucretius and the simulacrum, Spinoza and encounters, Hume and circumstance. And perhaps this subversion was already inscribed in Plato himself, the great ambivalent (cf. DR 67–8; LS 1st, 2nd and 23rd Series; CC 136–7).

The theme of the event lies at the center of today's philosophical preoccupations, nourishing the boldest and most original endeavors.

But the spirit of the time does not itself constitute a philosophy, and it should not mask irreconcilable differences: for Deleuze, a philosophy of the event is incompatible with negativity.

Notes

1. Cf. F 96; WP 59—Trans.
2. Cf. DR 283—Trans.

2

Encounter, Sign, Affect

Philosophy fails in its search for a first concept because beginning does not depend on it. If there is no natural link between thought and truth, if thought is not originally related to the truth, then it does not depend on philosophy to commence the search for truth, and it would not even originally have the taste for it. The love of truth is not spontaneous.

> There is always the violence of a sign that forces us into the search, that robs us of peace ... Truth is never the product of a predisposed good will but the result of a violence in thought ... Truth depends on an encounter with something that forces us to think and to seek the truth ... It is the accident of the encounter that guarantees the necessity of what is thought ... What is it that the man who says "I want the truth" wants? He wants the truth only when it is constrained and forced. He wants it only under the rule of an encounter, in relation to such and such a sign. (PS 15–16)

Something must *force* thought, shocking it and drawing it into a search; instead of a natural disposition, there is a fortuitous and contingent incitation derived from an *encounter*. The thinker is first of all a patient (DR 118–19), he undergoes the effraction of a sign that imperils the coherency or relative horizon of thought in which he had moved until now. The emergence of an idea is certainly not amicable—it implies a discomfort quite different than the dissatisfaction associated with the so-called desire to know, and which cannot fail to accompany the thinker so long as he thinks, even if it is only the reverse or the counterpart of a joy, a desire, or a love that emerges simultaneously:

> A philosophy that saddens no one, that annoys no one, is not a philosophy. (NP 106)

> What is a thought which harms no one, neither thinkers nor anyone else? Thought is primarily trespass and violence, the enemy, and nothing presupposes philosophy: everything begins with *misosophy*. (DR 135–6, 139)

The question is no longer "how do we attain the truth?," but "under what conditions is thought led to seek the truth?" An "encounter" is the name of an absolutely exterior relation, in which thought enters into relation with that which does not depend upon it. The *exteriority of relations* is a constant theme in Deleuze's thought, beginning with his first book (ES 98–9). Whether it is a question of thinking or of living, it is always a matter of the encounter, the event, and therefore of the relation as exterior to its terms.

Defined in this way, the relation is contingent and hazardous [*hazardeuse*], since it cannot itself deduce the nature of the terms that it is relating: an encounter is always inexplicable. Yet just as necessity depends precisely on the exteriority of the relationship, *chance* [*hazard*] loses here its traditionally negative value. The arbitrary is no longer determinable as chance, and the opposition is no longer between chance and necessity. On the contrary, the arbitrary refers to a thinking that claims to begin in itself, by itself, that proceeds in a deductive manner or by reflecting on an object given in advance. On the other hand, when thinking assumes the conditions of an effective encounter, of an authentic relation with the outside, it affirms the unforeseeable or the unexpected, it stands on a movable ground that it does not control, and thereby wins its necessity. Thought is born of chance. To think is always circumstantial, relative to an event that happens unexpectedly to thought. The idea that philosophy finds its point of departure in something it does not control comes as somewhat of a shock to reason: how is it supposed to find a foundation [*assise*] in that which defeats it, in the inexplicable or the aleatory? But who still speaks of a foundation, when the logic of grounding or the principle of reason leads precisely to its own "ungrounding," comical and disappointing (DR 200 and 272–7)? We cannot give the reason for an event. Insistent on the difference between irrationalism and illogicism, Deleuze draws the consequences of his critique of the dogmatic image: thought refers to a *logic of the outside*, necessarily irrational, that challenges us to affirm chance (for example, CC 81–2). Irrational does not mean that everything is permitted, but that thought only thinks out of a positive relationship to what is not yet thinking. Deleuze notes that the discipline that is institutionally called "logic" was responsible for this confusion of illogicism and irrationalism, when it fixed its limits by insisting that the outside could only be "shown" (following Wittgenstein's term): "Then logic is silent, and it is only interesting when it is silent" (WP 140).

57

Stupidity, Sense, Problem

Conversely, if thought thinks only under the condition of an encounter, it is "naturally" in a state of torpor. *Stupidity* is this condition of thought taken as a simple faculty, "precisely the fact that it does not think so long as nothing forces it to do so" (DR 275). Here Deleuze is at once closest to and most removed from Heidegger. The closest because he takes up the idea that the faculty of thought concerns a simple possibility and not yet a capacity, appropriating the famous motif according to which "we are not yet thinking."[1] The most removed because, as we have seen, he reproaches Heidegger for not breaking with the dogmatic theme of friendship—"whence the metaphors of gift which are substituted for those of violence" (DR 312 fn.). Heidegger's statement is thus related to a problematic of stupidity. The latter concerns not simply facts but principles: it belongs to the very concept of thought, since nothing guarantees the existence of a natural affinity between thought and truth. Stupidity constitutes a much more formidable menace than error, which is always extrinsic.

> Mature, considered thought has other enemies; negative states which are profound in entirely different ways. Stupidity is a structure of thought as such: it is not a means of self-deception, it expresses the non-sense in thought by right. Stupidity is not error or a tissue of errors. There are imbecile thoughts, imbecile discourses, that are made up entirely of truths; but these truths are base, they are those of a base, heavy and laden soul. (NP 105)

> Teachers already know that errors or falsehoods are rarely found in homework (except in those exercises where a fixed result must be produced, or propositions must be translated one by one). Rather, what is more frequently found—and worse—are nonsensical sentences, remarks without interest or importance, banalities mistaken for profundities, ordinary "points" confused with singular points, badly posed or distorted problems, all heavy with dangers, yet the fate of us all. (DR 153)

As a result, thought is pitted against an enemy much more formidable than the false: non-sense [*non-sens*]. The game of the true and the false is no longer enough to define the lived test of thought: "Can we still claim to be seeking the truth, we who debate amongst ourselves in non-sense?" (N 148, translation modified). "It is pointless to rely on such a relationship to define philosophy" (WP 54)—It would be much better to seek that which would make it possible to think, on the one hand, the state, graver than error, in which thought is both materially *and* formally separated from truth; and on the other hand, the circumstances in which it enters into a relationship with the element of truth, and in which the distinction between the true and the false itself takes on a sense. This relationship is that of sense and non-sense. "A new image of thought means first of all that truth is not the element of thought. The element of thought is sense and value" (NP 104, translation modified). It is not a question of invoking a value higher than truth, but rather of introducing difference into truth itself, of evaluating truths or the subjacent conceptions of truth. This is to say that Deleuze is not suppressing the true-false relation but modifying its sense, raising it to the level of problems, independent of every act of recognition. "Apply the test of true and false to problems themselves" (B 3; DR 157): the relationship between sense and non-sense is not opposed to the true-false relationship but rather is its higher determination, which no longer appeals to a postulated reality (by non-sense we mean a false problem).

"There are imbecile thoughts, imbecile discourses, that are made up entirely of truths" (NP 105). The brutal true-false opposition is surpassed through the introduction of a difference within truth itself, between "base" truths (correct recognitions) and "noble" truths (positions of problems). The element of truth is subjected to the differential criteria of sense and non-sense. Difference is introduced into the false as well: error or incorrect recognition / false problem. Truth is not relegated to a second plane, which would be contradictory, but conceived of as a multiplicity. To submit the true and the false to the criteria of sense is to introduce into the element of truth—or the true-false opposition—a difference of level, a plurality of degrees; not degrees of probability going from the true to the false, from 1 to 0, as in plurivalent logics, or variable distances between the true and the false, but different hierarchizable planes of truth and falsity. In other words, the model of recognition does not belong in principle to the concept of truth; it is but one determination among others, from which is derived the notion of adequation, which presupposes the preexistence of an object to which thought then becomes equal. At a higher level, the "true" describes the act of posing a problem, while the "false" no longer designates an incorrect recognition or a false proposition, but a non-sense or a false problem, which corresponds to a state that is no longer error but stupidity (DR 157). Yet according to what criteria can a problem be deemed true or false? Is Deleuze not going to reintroduce the postulate of recognition at this level?

Deleuze elaborates a theory of the problem capable of accounting for this pluralization of the concept of truth. At first sight, this seems paradoxical, since it is grounded in a devaluation of the role of interrogation in philosophy. In the name of the same illusion, the same incomprehension of what a problem really is, Deleuze will denounce both the interrogative process as a false procedure of apprenticeship, since it organizes the becoming of the student as a function of the result acquired in advance by the teacher, as well as the idea that philosophy would be the art *par excellence* of the question, rather than the art of the response. "As the creation of thought, a problem has nothing to do with a question [*interrogation*], which is only a suspended proposition, the bloodless double of an affirmative proposition that is supposed to serve as its answer" (WP 139). When we pose a question and presuppose a response as if it preexisted in principle in some theoretico-ontological sky—as if philosophy suddenly attended to a heretofore neglected region, as if this region awaited its glance not in order to exist but in order to have the right to reside among men—we are seeing only the question-response ensemble already belonging to a problematic context that conditions the one just as much as the other. That truth is not an ensemble of scattered responses, that it is irreducible to a collection of particular truths, was a constant philosophical theme until Hegel. Sublation, however, even in Hegel, is sought at the level of the proposition, rather than ascending to a more profound genetic element from which even contradiction and the negative are derived. Hence we fail to reach the veritable motor of thought. It is by virtue of a certain problematic that a question becomes possible, and above all, a proposition derives its *sense*. Sense is nothing other than the relation of the proposition, not to the question to which it is the response (its sterile double), but to the problem outside of which it has no meaning [*sens*]. Which problem is it necessary to pose, or how must the problem be posed for such and such a proposition to be possible?—such is the principle of a logic of sense that Deleuze's first book, *Empiricism and Subjectivity,* had already outlined in a vocabulary that will later be corrected:

> What a philosopher *says* is offered as if it were what he *does* or as what he *wants*. We are presented with a fictitious psychology of the intentions of the theorist, as if it were a sufficient criticism of the theory. Atomism and associationism are therefore treated as shifty projects which disqualify, *ab initio*, those who form them. "Hume has pulverized the given." But what does one think has been explained by this? Does one believe something important has been said? We must understand what a philosophi-

cal theory is, the basis of its concept, for it is not born from itself or for the fun of it. It is not even enough to say that it is a response to a set of problems. Undoubtedly, this explanation has the advantage, at least, of locating the necessity for a theory in a relation to something that can serve as its foundation; but this relation would be scientific rather than philosophical. In fact, a philosophical theory is an elaborately developed question, and nothing else; by itself and in itself, it is not the resolution to a problem, but the elaboration, *to the very end*, of the necessary implications of a formulated question. (ES 105–6)

Deleuze thus turns to a pluralism of problems inseparable from a new conception of the object of philosophy. "To think means to experiment and to problematize" (F 116): at once to pose and to critique problems. At the root of thought there is no relation of fidelity or adequation, or even of identification with what thought thinks, but an act, a *creation*, whose necessity implies criteria distinct from that of a supposedly external object, independent and preexistent (and this act and this creation are paradoxical since they do not properly speaking emanate from the thinking subject: DR 199). What depends on such an act of problematization, on such a problematizing creation, is not truth in its simple opposition to error, but the *content of truth*, in other words the sense of what we are thinking. Questions are not given to the philosopher any more than they emerge from a lacuna or a state of ignorance: they are created. As we will see later, the feeling of ignorance is the shadow or the negative image of a positive act. To not know, it is necessary to capture precisely those signs that launch us on an apprenticeship (the old Socratic motif). And yet why is philosophical creation "problematic," why is affirmation in philosophy concerned with problems rather than propositions, the latter being dependent on the former? To pose a problem amounts to objectivizing, in a paradoxical way, a pure relation to the outside. Thought, insofar as it thinks, does not state truths, or rather its acts of truth are the problems themselves, which are not born ready-made.

The determination of sense as a relation between a thesis and a higher instance that conditions it returns in Deleuze's second book, *Nietzsche and Philosophy*. This book outlines the concept of *force* in relation to a problematic of sense and of evaluation. A preliminary remark is in order here. To establish a relation between forces and sense is a very new idea in philosophy, given that force is habitually considered as the mute instance *par excellence*, brutal and stupid: force says nothing, it strikes and imposes itself, nothing more. And a single preoccupation cuts across the entire history of philosophy, to which the fate of philosophy itself seems tied: to radically oppose the *logos* to violence, without any possible compromise. Yet is force reducible to violence? Perhaps the concept of violence should instead be differenciated. There is a theme of violence in Deleuze: however the violence described is that which thought undergoes, and under the impact of which it begins to think. It is this critical aggressivity that is too often missing in philosophy. It is therefore entirely contrary to a spontaneous violence characterized by a will-to-dominate, by a thought that is aggressive from the outset and which would seek its motor in negation (separated from the conditions of necessity that would compel it to think, such a thought only converts its stupidity into spite). As we shall see, a differential concept of violence implies a critique of the negative. For now, it is enough to simply note the following: insofar as he thinks, the thinker is no more able to will the violence that befalls him from the outside than he can be said to naturally desire the truth. Such a violence is taken up—as critical aggressivity—only in a second moment, and on the condition that it be directed against his former ego or his own stupidity. As long as we are content to oppose the logos to violence in a highly general way we remain deaf to the essential—the conditions of a true act of thought, and the specificity of the will-to-dominate.

From what point of view can a logic of forces renew the theory of sense? A "thing" –phenomena of every order, physical, biological, human—has no meaning in itself, but only in accordance with a force that seizes it. It has no interiority or essence: its status is that of being a *sign*, of referring to something other than itself, namely, to the force that it manifests or expresses. Interpretations relating to the explicit contents of the thing teach us nothing of its sense, and, believing themselves to be speaking of its nature, in fact restrict themselves to describing a phenomenon. Sense appears only in the relation of a thing to the force of which it is the phenomenon (NP 3). Sense refers to an affirmation. Manners of living and thinking are affirmed through things/phenomena (man testifies to his modes of existence through the phenomena described as cultural—religion, science, art or philosophy, but also social and political life—therefore through concepts, feelings, and beliefs).

A conception of the philosophical object emerges here. Thought does not bring the explicit contents of a thing into relief, but treats it as a sign—the sign of a force that affirms itself, makes choices, marks preferences; in other words, that exhibits a will. To affirm is always to draw a difference, to establish a hierarchy, *to evaluate*: to institute a criterion that permits the attribution of values. Above all, what interests thought is the heterogeneity of manners of living and thinking; not in themselves, so that it may describe and classify them, but in order to decipher their sense, which is to say the evaluation they imply. Sense concerns a will rather than a thing, an affirmation rather than a being, a cleavage rather than a content, a manner of evaluating rather than a signification. Thing, being, content, signification: this is what the phenomenon is reduced to when it is separated from its genesis, from the conditions of its apparition, when it is not longer seized as a sign.

The formulation in *Empiricism and Subjectivity* was that a statement had a sense only by virtue of the problem that rendered it possible. The book on Nietzsche begins to define what a problem is. Every act of problematization consists in an evaluation, in a hierarchical selection of the *important* or the *interesting*. A problem is not a question posed to the philosopher; on the contrary, every question already implies the position of a problem, even implicitly, a manner of posing "the" problem, which is to say, of redistributing the singular and the regular, the remarkable and the ordinary:

> The problem of thought is tied not to essences but to the evaluation of what is important and what is not, to the distribution of the singular and the regular, distinctive and ordinary points . . . To have an idea means no more than this, and erroneousness or stupidity is defined above all by its perpetual confusion with regard to the important and the unimportant, the ordinary and the singular. (DR 189–90)

> Philosophy does not consist in knowing, and is not inspired by truth. Rather it is categories like Interesting, Remarkable, or Important that determine success or failure. (WP 82)

What does it mean to apply the test of true and false to problems themselves? What criteria will decide between rival problematics? The criteria must logically follow from the way in which necessity was defined: a problem is true or necessary, or rather a problem truly emerges, when the thought that poses it is forced, when it undergoes the effect of an exterior violence, when it comes into contact with the outside. The criteria lies not in an adequation to what is given or to an exterior state of things, but in the efficacy of an act of thought that introduces a hierarchy within the given. A problem, as a creation of thought, carries its necessity or its "power of decision" within it (DR 199), which has no other criteria than the displacement it implies, and which precisely makes of it a problem: it makes us think, it forces thought. The criteria is thus simultaneously violence and *novelty* (WP 111). Violence and novelty signal the contingency and exteriority of an encounter that gives rise to an authentic act of problematization, a creation of thought. Truth, raised to the level of problems and released from every relation of adequation to a presupposed exterior reality, coincides with the emergence of the new. To the good wills that attempt to give sense to the present, the thinker opposes an exigency that appears to be both more modest and more formal: to think *otherwise* (F 117–20; WP 51). Which does not mean that thought has no relation to the times, to their miseries and their urgencies; but this relation is not what we take it to be. To think is to think otherwise. We think only otherwise.

However, the criteria of novelty has a conciliatory air, and seems to compromise the very possibility of the false problem. At this point will not every problem, solely by virtue of its being new, be said to be necessary? Yet the expression "false problem" precisely designates that which is not a problem, that which does not testify to any genuine act of problematization: the absence of any encounter or relation with the outside. What makes a problem false is not a matter of a confrontation between the diverse forms of problematization and a supposedly neutral, impassible and indifferent reality (and Deleuze shows that science thinks no less than philosophy or art, insofar as it too has a "plane of reference" that must be drawn, which completely removes its experimental activity from the ambit of recognition: WP 214–15, and above all Ch. V, notably 123, 125, 129–30, 133). It remains for us to understand what false problems consist in, those evaluations which, so to speak, are not evaluations, and which signal the death of all evaluation. A philosophy that refuses the recognitional postulate must ground the criteria of the true and the false, or of the necessary and the arbitrary, on something other than an external pseudo-reality: on a critique of the *negative*.

Heterogeneity

However, the difficulty would appear to have less to do with the possibility of a new critique than with what seems to result from it: the loss of the exterior world, a thought that, if it is not enclosed within itself, is at least confined to a closed sphere of almost pure intellectuality. Is this not the opposite of what was hoped for? By seeking to affirm the outside do we not fall into an even worse confinement? In fact, the outside invoked here has nothing to do with an exterior world: "an outside more distant than any exterior world" (C2 206–8; F 86, 118; N 97; WP 59–60), a "non-external outside" (WP 60).[2] Moreover, when Deleuze describes himself as an empiricist because he "treats the concept as object of an encounter" (DR xx), this refers to an empiricism that is *superior* or *transcendental*, which apprehends an exteriority far more radical than the always relative exteriority of sensory givens.

It should be understood that the existence or nonexistence of a world exterior to the thinking subject is not at stake here, and that such a question has no meaning within the Deleuzian problematic. The existence of plants, rocks, animals and other men is not being disputed. It is a question of knowing under what conditions the thinking subject enters into relation with an unknown element, and whether to do so it suffices for him to take a trip to the zoo, to inspect an ashtray sitting on the table, to speak with his fellow man or to travel the world. It is a question of knowing what determines a mutation of thought, and whether it is really by such means that thought has an encounter. Certainly, the *body* is not the same as thought, and to be sure, "obstinate and stubborn, it forces us to think, and forces us to think what is concealed from thought, life" (C2 189). When the body—whether it is mine or not—stubbornly persists, resisting thought, does it do so as an exterior object endowed with its own identity? Is it not rather through the *heterogeneity* of its postures and aptitudes (sleep, fatigue, effort, resistances)? (Cf. C2 189, and the reference to the cinema of Antonioni.) Deleuze is not amazed that there are bodies—only the body "exists," and it is rather thought that must be explained—but, following Spinoza, he is amazed by what a body can do (NP 39; EPS Ch. 14; D 59–60; ATP 256; SPP 17). What we call the external world refers to an order of contiguity or separation that belongs to representation, and which subordinates the diverse to the homogenizing condition of a unique point of view. The position of an external reality given by the criteria of the Same which condemns thought to the sterile exercise of recognition must be related to the norms of representation. The diversity of the panorama is nothing, or remains relative, so long as one does not cause the point of view to vary, or, more rigorously, so long as one does not bring into play the difference of points of view.

Thinking displaces the subjective position: not the projection of the subject's identity into things, but the individuation of a new object that is inseparable from a new individuation of the subject. The latter goes from point of view to point of view, but rather than being a point of view *on* supposedly neutral and external things, these points of view are those *of* the objects themselves. For Deleuze, the problem of exteriority leads to a perspectivism. However, the point of view is not to be identified with a subject who is opposed to an object ("relativity of the truth"): on the contrary, it presides over their double-individuation ("truth of relativity"). The Deleuzian rehabilitation of the medieval problem of individuation can be understood only in light of this conjoint and variable genesis of the subject and the object. Consequently, the relative exteriority of the represented world—not only of things exterior in relation to a subject, but the respective exteriority of things amongst themselves—is overcome in the direction of a more profound, absolute exteriority: a pure heterogeneity of planes [*plans*] or of perspectives.

> Each point of view must itself be the object, or the object must itself belong to the point of view. The object must therefore be in no way identical, but torn asunder in a difference in which the identity of the object as seen by a seeing subject vanishes. (DR 56)

What the point of view is, as well as the heterogeneity that belongs to it, can be revealed only little by little: in a sense, Deleuze's entire philosophy is in play here, and the sole ambition of our study could be seen as an attempt to understand the concept of the "thing" sketched therein. For the moment, what is essential is to pose this distinction between the relative outside of representation (*extensio, partes extra partes*) that only presents thought with a homogeneous diversity, and an absolute outside in the world or of the world, which escapes the design of an exterior world. The fact that heterogeneity does not "exist" outside of thought—which is to say that it can be seized only by an act of thought—does not prevent it from being said *of* the world, or from concerning the "things themselves." The difficulty does not therefore have to do with losing the world or not, but rather with the logic that will enable a thought of the outside, the relation thought has with the outside, the exteriority of relations. Can we conceive of a positive mode of relation between thought and the unknown or the un-thought that accounts for the act of thought? It is no longer only a matter of asserting the exteriority of the relation, but of producing its concept.

Signs 1: Points of View and Forces

What is the status of this object that is encountered without being recognized? What escapes representation is the *sign*. The exterior world becomes interesting the moment it produces signs, thereby losing its reassuring unity, its homogeneity, its truthful appearance. And in a certain respect, the world never ceases to produce signs, is composed of nothing but signs, on condition that we be sensitive to them. Why is there an encounter only with signs? What must a sign be if it is to constitute the object of the encounter as such? That which is encountered is not simply different from thought (as, for example, an image or fact is, etc.), but is exterior to it as thought: it is what thought does not think, does not know to think, and does not yet think. It is not in affinity with thought, and it refuses itself to thought no less than thought refuses itself to it, since it is still not thinkable, since thought still doesn't desire its attainment. And yet it is there, both unthought or unthinkable and that which must be thought: pure *cogitandum* (DR 141, 147, 153). Consequently, thought cannot fail to experience its own stupidity the very moment it sets out to think. The encounter presents all the traits of a non-relation, and yet it must be the case that "the non-relation is still a relation" (F 63; N 97). To encounter is not to recognize: the encounter is the very experience [*épreuve*] of the non-recognizable, the failing of the mechanism of recognition (and not a simple misfire, as in the case of an error).

The sign is this positive instance that does not merely refer thought to its own ignorance, but orients it, sweeps it along, engages it. Thought does indeed have a guide, but a strange guide, elusive and fleeting, always emerging from the outside. Neither an object deployed within representation, a clear or explicit signification, nor a nothing: such is the sign, or that which forces thought. For we would fall back into the trap of recognition were we to suppose a content prior to the sign, one still hidden but nonetheless indicated, as if thought preceded itself and imagined the content to have come in principle from another thought (the infinite understanding of the divine in classical thought, the understanding of the master in the traditional scholarly schema).

What characterizes the sign is *implication*. Deleuze also uses the terms envelopment, rolling-up [*enrouler*]. The sign implicates its sense, presents it as implicated. Better still: sense, as the very movement of thought, and distinct from explicit significations, surfaces only in the sign and merges with its explication. The sign does not implicate sense without simultaneously explicating or expressing it, so that the structure of the sign or of expression is defined by the two movements of implication and explication, which are not contrary but complimentary: one does not explicate without implicating, and vice versa (PS 89–90; EPS 16; L 6, 7). Sense is like the other side [*l'envers*] of the sign: the explication of what it implicates. Yet what is it that is both implicated and explicated by this sign-sense? What accounts for the unity or the identity of the sign and sense? If there is a sign, if a depth hollows itself out in the relative and unmysterious exteriority of representation, it is because a heterogeneous element surfaces: another point of view. "Signs involve heterogeneity" (DR 22). The sign is always that of the *Other* [*d'Autrui*], always an expression of an enveloped "possible world," virtual and incompossible with mine, but which would become mine if I were to become other by occupying the new point of view (DR 260–1, 281–2). We shall see below why all fields of representation necessarily involve signs, which is to say they communicate virtually with other fields, other points of view. For now, three remarks are in order.

The sign surfaces in a field of representation—which is to say a field of explicit significations or recognized objects—by implicating the heterogeneous or that which escapes representation in principle. Firstly, then, this is why the heterogeneous or the other point of view is implicated (it cannot be the object of an act of recognition). Secondly, this is also why sense, as expression or explication, can be said to consist in the putting-into-communication of two points of view, two planes or heterogeneous dimensions. There is sense only in the interstices of representation, in the gap between points of view. Sense is divergence, dissonance, disjunction. Sense is problematic: "discordant harmony," unresolved dissonance (DR 146; L 81–2; and the "irrational cuts" of cinema, C2 179–82, 185). Thirdly and finally, sign-sense affects only a mutating subject, a subject in becoming, split between two individuations. Which is why Deleuze calls this subject "larval":

> In this sense it is not even clear that thought, insofar as it constitutes the dynamism peculiar to philosophical systems, may be related to a substantial, completed and well-constituted subject, such as the Cartesian Cogito: thought is, rather, one of those terrible movements that can be sustained only under the conditions of a larval subject. (DR 118)

In addition to points of view, we have seen that Deleuze invokes forces in the definition of the sign. The explicit content of a phenomenon does not in itself furnish its sense; this content must be related to the evaluative point of view it affirms (its way of thinking and existing). The Nietzschean account assimilates force and point of view, or at least sees in force the affirmation of a point of view. But why resort to a concept of force? Because force is always related to an emergence, that is, to a process of actualization (C1 98). The "thing" is not only a point of view, nor is it merely split apart within the difference between points of view: it is a relation of forces, because the sign is a sensation or *affect*, the emergence of a new point of view exercised upon an undefined subject. The very notion of the affect refers to a logic of forces.

The concept is set forth in two steps:

> 1. "Every force is thus essentially related to another force. The being of force is plural, it would be absolutely absurd to think about force in the singular. A force is domination, but it is also the object on which domination is exercised" (NP 6). "Force is never singular but essentially exists in relation with other forces, such that any force is already a relation, that is to say power: force has no other object or subject than force" (F 70).

> 2. "The relationship between forces is in each case determined to the extent that each force is *affected* by other, inferior or superior, forces. It follows that will to power is manifested as a capacity for being affected" (NP 62). "Force defines itself by its very power to affect other forces (to which it is related) and to be affected by other forces" (F 71).

Force exists only in relation, which is to say as exercised. In addition, it is in relation with another force, since its superior effects are of domination and not of simple destruction. Whence its irreducibility to violence, which consists in a destruction of form, the decomposition of a relation. The concept of violence considers force in as much as it is exercised on a determined being, that is, upon an object (F 70). To reduce force to violence is to grasp as original what is in fact the derivative or the shadow of a real relation. Not only do we overlook the fact that a force is from the outset exercised on another force, but we prevent any understanding of the phenomenon of affect, which is to say a force that exercises itself upon another not so much in order to destroy it as to induce a movement. Certainly, it is a question of a "forced movement," which marks an obedience or a submission: what would be contradictory would be a voluntary affect. The affect is nonetheless a positive effect, and cannot be explained by destruction. To be sure, in annulling others, this movement imposes a new form incompatible with what preceded it. But this is precisely the sign that violence is "a concomitance or consequent of force, but not a constituent element" (F 70). Thus Deleuze is not saying that force has nothing to do with violence, but rather that force, which is essentially the installation of a relation, cannot be defined exclusively by the negative relation of violence.

In fact, Deleuze goes even further than this—with Nietzsche, he undertakes a genesis of the exclusively negative use of force. What must be understood is that in certain cases force can have no other finality than violence or domination: a force that negates before it affirms, in order that it may affirm; a force that finds no other means to affirm than negation. We will not say of such a force that it acts but that it re-acts, unable to command absolutely, to exert itself without conditions, to *create*. A force never demonstrates its weakness and its proclivity to obey as clearly as when its will is reduced to a will-to-dominate:

> It is characteristic of established values to be brought into play in a struggle, but it is characteristic of the struggle to be always referred to established values: whether it is struggle for power, struggle for recognition, or struggle for life—the schema is always the same. One cannot overemphasize *the extent to which the notions of struggle, war, rivalry, or even comparison are foreign to Nietzsche and to his conception of the will to power*. It is not that he denies the existence of struggle: but he does not see it as in any way creative of values. (NP 82)

> When nihilism triumphs, then and only then does the will to power stop meaning "to create" and start to signify instead "to want power," "to want to dominate" (thus to attribute to oneself or to have others attribute to one established values: money, honors, power, and so on). (PI 76–7)

Hence the profound affinity between the misinterpretation of the concept of force, which reduces force to violence, and the uniquely negative use of force. There is consequently no need to be surprised if the mistakes of the "anti-Nietzschean" humanist reading of Nietzsche resemble those of his Nazi readers.

From the relational nature of force arises its principal attribute: a *power [pouvoir] to affect and to be affected*. On this point Deleuze sees Nietzsche and Spinoza as having a common intuition (EPS Ch. 14; SPP *passim*). The concepts of force and of affect are logically related in as much as force is the very thing that affects and is affected. Every affect implies a relation of forces, the exercise of one force upon another, and the passion that results from it. Force is not only the affecting power [*puissance affectant*] but affected power [*puissance affectée*], sensible matter or material on which a force is exerted. Power [*puissance*] is divided, sometimes active, sometimes passive. Consequently Power [*pouvoir*] no longer has the typical meaning of possession or of action, since it is related first and foremost to sensibility: "Force is in direct relation with sensation" (FB 34; NP 62–4). "Force, however, is not what acts but, as Leibniz and Nietzsche knew, what perceives and experiences" (WP 130). Which is why from the moment we consider a matter as something affected, we no longer speak in terms of an object: we are already in the element of forces. Apropos of Bacon, Deleuze shows that once painting assumes the task of "rendering" sensation, it confronts a new problem: that of "painting forces" (FB, title of Ch. 8). It abandons the formed, figurative body, and attempts by means of deformations to attain something else: the figure, which is to say a body no longer defined by its functional parts (organs) but by zones of intensity that are just as much thresholds or levels, and which compose a body that is "intense" or "without organs" (FB Chapters 6–7).

Why does the theory of sense and of thought need a logic of forces? Because thought is in a fundamental relation with affect. We do not think without being sensitive to something, to signs, to this rather than that—and contrary to the opinion so prevalent in philosophy according to which there is no more compromise possible between thought and the passions (the compromise of reason) than there is between violence and discourse. Thought begins with difference: "something distinguishes itself" (DR 28), produces a sign, and distinguishes itself as enveloped, implicated—*distinct-obscure* (DR 28, 146, 243). If there is a problem, if there is sense, it is in accordance with a sign encountered by thought, fracturing the unity of the given, and introducing a new point of view. Which means that thought does not evaluate so long as it remains enclosed within a point of view, and so long as it represents things from this point of view. Certainly, such a representation implicates a cleavage, a repartitioning of the values carried over from a past act of evaluation; but the latter, being completely explicated, developed, objectivized, has ceased to be sensible. Certainly, to every point of view there corresponds a problem, but this refers to the originary difference between points of view: one does not problematize—one does not think—except by arriving at a point of view, by changing points of view (we have yet to understand why each point of view refers virtually to other points of view). Thought will never be engendered within thinking if the latter is not first affected. The three concepts of force, the outside, and affect are interdependent: to encounter the outside is always to be forced, to be involuntarily affected; or rather, an affect is involuntary by nature since it comes from the outside, since it is the index of a force exerting itself on thought from without.

Transcendental Field, Plane of Immanence

An encounter is an affect. Put differently, it is a sign that causes points of view to communicate, rendering them sensible as points of view. The sign forces thought, putting it into relation with new forces. In so far as it thinks, thought is affected: "Thinking depends on forces which take hold of thought" (NP 108). Are we to understand that thought itself, as a faculty, is a force? When considered independently of signs or of the encounter, thought appears as a simple *faculty*; however this is an abstract view, or the state of a thinking "separated from what it can do" and which consequently thinks abstractly, restricting itself to reflection on the givens of representation. For Deleuze, the state of a simple faculty, a mere possibility without any effective capacity, is neither natural nor originary. The rejection of the dogmatic image of thought entails not only that thought does not think all by itself, but moreover that it is not even *a priori* a faculty (we have yet to see precisely in what the emergence of thought consists, and under what conditions it falls back into the state of a faculty).[3]

As long as it remains in the state of a simple faculty, thought operates abstractly, reflexively, and within the closed horizon of representation: it is not affected by or confronted with forces. What are the forces that seize it? Taking his cue from Foucault's "historical" cuts (the three events or major becomings affecting thought since the seventeenth century), Deleuze proposes the following examples: forces capable of being raised to the infinite in the classical century, under the influence of which thought elaborated a "God-compound"; forces of finitude in the nineteenth century, that inspired a "Man-compound"; and perhaps today forces of an "unlimited finity" [*fini-illimité*] . . . (F 131). These examples call for two remarks.

First of all, these forces are all "forces of the outside," which do violence to the forces of the inside, that is, the "forces within man" or faculties. Yet this apparent dualism finds its *raison d'être* in a genesis of the negative or the reactive. Thus the former must be understood as *active forces*, the latter as *reactive forces*, following the schema extracted from Nietzsche (NP Chapters 2 and 4). We will see later that what characterizes reactive forces is the denial of heterogeneity or the exteriority of relations, the re-enclosure of a point of view upon itself and the blocking of the affect (thought thus valorizes interiority: the dogmatic image). In other words, they are not called "forces of the outside" because they come from outside, but because they put thought in a state of exteriority, hurling it into a field in which points of view enter into relation, where homogeneous combinations and significations give way to relations of forces within sense itself.

Secondly, the forces that seize thought are those of sense itself. We can now understand why Deleuze can say that sense insists within thought as its own outside, or that it is the outside of thought even though it does not exist outside [*hors*] of it. Forces are not exterior to thought; they are its outside. Thinking consists in the emergence of sense as force: classical thought is affected by the infinite, "it continually loses itself in infinity" (F 125). Infinity ceases to be a simple signification in order to become the very event of thought, that which haunts it and inspires it, that which it encounters and with which it continually clashes. The field of forces is nothing other than the field in which sense is produced—a *transcendental* field.[4]

The encounter with a sign therefore presents itself as follows: 1. A violence is exerted upon existing or composed significations, upon the homogenous milieu in which thought exercises itself facultatively. 2. Thought becomes active because it experiences a relation of forces between points of view. The encounter therefore avails itself of a double reading according to which we take account of the violence exerted upon a form, or the new relation of forces that subtends it and of which it is the concomitant:

> The transformation occurs not to the historical, stratified and archeological composition but to the composing forces, when the latter enter into relation with other forces which have come from the outside (strategies). Becoming, change and mutation concern composing forces, and not composed forces. (F 87, translation modified)

The encounter can be located as much at the limit of the thought-faculty as within a field of radical exteriority, and this ambiguity points to the problematic relation between the subject and thought. When the transcendental field has become a field of forces or heterogeneous points of view, it is no longer governed by the ego; sub-representative, it no longer bears the form of consciousness (LS 98–9, 102). Inversely, Deleuze can take Kant at his word and reproach him for having produced only the conditions of possible experience rather than real experience, for having described the transcendental field of a thought that reflects but does not think, that recognizes objects but does not distinguish signs—in short, which encounters nothing (and does not experiment). Kant conceives the field as a form of interiority, he "traces" the transcendental field from the empirical form of representation (the identity of an unspecified object and the unity of the "I think" correlated with it). On this point, Husserl can hardly be said to break with him (LS 14th and 15th Series).

The transcendental field is impersonal, asubjective, unconscious. The act of thinking is certainly not unconscious, but is engendered unconsciously, beyond representation. The disjunctive encounter of forces or points of view enters consciousness only in an implicated state (sign, affect, intensity). "Thought thinks only on the basis of an unconscious" (DR 199). It is in this sense that philosophical activity—concept formation—always takes place in the middle, and does not master its own beginning. In a paradoxical way, thought becomes active when the subject is made a "patient"; the act of thought is engendered in a *passive synthesis*. For Deleuze, the unconscious is nothing other than this informal field where forces enter into relation; it comprises neither forms nor representations, and "resembles" a factory more than a theatrical scene. Oedipus does not structure the affective field in an *a priori* way, but is only the form under which this field is submitted to a process of closure or interiorization, "the familial relation becoming 'metaphorical for all the others'" (AO 24 and 307 ff.).

When Deleuze speaks of the Outside, this word has two complimentary senses: 1. the unrepresentable, or the outside of representation; 2. the very consistency of the unrepresentable, which is to say the exteriority of relations, the informal field of relations. The *plane of immanence* is Deleuze's name for this transcendental field where nothing is presupposed in advance except the exteriority that precisely challenges all presuppositions:

> We will say that THE plane of immanence is, at the same time, that which must be thought and that which cannot be thought. It is the nonthought within thought. It is the base of all planes, immanent to every thinkable plane that does not succeed in thinking it. (WP 59)

Notes

1. This formula is almost as frequent in Deleuze's work as the one drawn from Spinoza according to which "we don't know what a body can

do." See NP 108; DR 144, 153, 275; C2 167; WP 56. Moreover, the two formulas enter into relation at the beginning of Chapter 8 of the *Time-Image*.

2. Cf. equally L 111: an outside of the monad that is nonetheless not exterior to it. And F 84: the relation of forces "does not lie outside the strata but forms the outside of the strata." An analogous formulation is found in *Critical and Clinical*: sights and sounds that "are not outside language, but the outside of language" (CC 5).

3. In *Difference and Repetition*, Deleuze appears to assume the existence of a faculty of pure thought, but he specifies that "[his] concern here is not to establish such a doctrine of the faculties" (DR 144). It will be noted that thought is absent from the enumeration of the "forces within man" in *Foucault* (F 124 and 130): this is because thought is polymorphous and is not related to any one faculty in particular, but rather merges with the becoming-active of faculties; for Deleuze, the arts and the sciences think no less than philosophy. The concern of *Difference and Repetition* was rather to show how thought is engendered in the disjunction that occurs when faculties are raised to their superior exercise: the same theme is taken up once more in *Foucault* (the disjunction of seeing and speaking).

4. Keep in mind that the word "transcendental," which must not be confused with "transcendent," has since Kant been related to a questioning of the *conditions* under which thought experiments, which is to say enters into relation with something that does not depend upon it.

3

Immanence

Let us return to the question we left in suspense earlier, that of the false problem. To affirm an authentically exterior relation between thought and what it thinks (even in not thinking it), is to apply the test of truth to problems themselves: the sense of a thesis, or the content of its truth, appears when we relate it to the problematic act to which it responds. Necessity—or truth—depends on an act of thinking, on the effective capacity of thought to confront an outside and consequently to pose a new problem from which flows a new set of statements. But if every act of thinking is a problem, a true problem, and if the becoming of philosophy testifies to innovations rather than to a progress, how is a critique still possible? And if critique consists in the denunciation of false problems, how can their possibility be accounted for? In other words, what is nonsense?

Critique of the Negative: The False Problem

"Erroneousness or stupidity is defined above all by its perpetual confusion with regard to the important and the unimportant, the ordinary and the singular" (DR 190). Deleuze speaks of an inverted or reversed image of the problem, but how do we distinguish the important from the unimportant if critique is the very act of evaluation? Problems are not given and there is no neutral or objective standard by which to distinguish the upside down from the right side up . . . Yet this is not the question, for stupidity consists less in a permutation of the important and the unimportant than in its indifference regarding the two, in its incapacity to distinguish between them and consequently to distinguish anything whatsoever. The false problem refers to a powerlessness to evaluate, it is a way of reflecting and interrogating without actually beginning to think. Deleuze finds in Nietzsche a logical schema capable of furnishing a criteria conforming to the very conditions he had himself posed: a false problem is a shadow, a secondary enunciation that affirms only by negating. The false problem is not an act of thinking, it does not create—it refers back to a creative act that it inverts and reverses, and thereby denatures. Inversion consists in taking as originary what is in fact a derived affirmation, in taking *negation* to be the motor of thought (NP 180): stupidity, nonsense, and false problems all testify to a promotion of the negative. The false problem is not poorly posed, it poses nothing at all—it believes it brings about movement, but moves only shadows.

Certainly, Deleuze has in mind first and foremost those who live off of the work of others and who count on critique to afford them the status of thinkers: amateurs trifling with *discussions* and *objections*, who have ample time to busy themselves with the problems of others, to direct their progress, who demand that they explain and account for themselves. In place of a truly problematic creation capable of making us sensitive to a difference in points of view or problems, and thereby freeing up a new power of evaluation, they do nothing but judge, elevating established values drawn from old problematics to a transcendent status by converting them into references (the famous "return to. . ."). The alternative *judge/evaluate* defines the practical problem, and we must choose between a moral attitude that relates existence to an opposition between transcendent values (Good/Evil), and an ethical attitude that experiments with the qualitative and intensive difference between modes of existence, ordering the typology on the basis of the immanently differenciated scale of the good and the bad (EPS Ch. 15; SPP 23, 37–8; CC Chapters 6 and 15). Judgment testifies to the link between the postulate of transcendence and the primacy accorded to the negative; from this point of view, critique must come first, for it is what ensures progress within thought. The point of departure of evaluation lies, on the contrary, in the feeling-out of differences between modes of evaluation (points of view, or problems), so that critique arises first of all from out of a positive act.

The question is not therefore whether critique is well-founded in general or not; rather it is a matter of determining the precise place or role of critique within intellectual activity: is it a cause or merely a consequence of the becoming of thought? The violence of that which forces us to think is converted into a critical aggression toward a problematic that, although still present, has already been compromised. The interest of critique will be addressed later, when we consider the notion of "disappointment"; for now, let us say that critique has a meaning only in accordance with an act of rupture already initiated: we must have already passed over to another plane, we criticize only from another point of view. The critical component of a philosophy, no less than its conceptual component, depends on an act of thought that situates the philosopher *elsewhere* from the start. It measures the distance that separates this philosophy from those that preceded it, showing how a problem or a concept comes to lose its sense from the point of view of the new act (cf. already ES 105–12). Moreover, this is why, when seen from the point of view of that which has been criticized, a critique will always appear inoffensive. Spinozism does not emerge from a critique of Cartesianism but can critique the latter because it has already separated itself, and thus can measure the incompatibility of the two points of view; inversely, the Spinozist critique presents no real threat from Descartes' point of view. The relation of exteriority separating the two philosophies prevents them from being positioned as two "moments" within a single history, which in fact would account only for their critical component, thereby according to critique the role of a motor that it does not possess—as if Philosophy [*LA philosophie*] changed and advanced through development and rectification. Is this an irenic conception of philosophy? Obviously not, since the incompatibility of points of view distances itself equally from eclecticism and skepticism, and is accompanied by an immanent evaluative criteria: exteriority and its affirmation.

Deleuze reproaches discussion both for its absurdity as well as its uselessness, since it rests on misunderstandings and on intolerance, ill will, or an implicit reactive violence (concealed by its partisans beneath what is in principle a pacifistic demand for a democratic consensus). According to his diagnosis, discussion is possible only insofar as one remains solely at the level of propositions (opinions, theses) without referring them back to a problematic that could give them their sense, that is, only if one separates them from the problematic that gives them a sense (the reduction of philosophical statements to opinions). This is why the objections made to philosophers more often than not seem to fall under the logic of a kind of table talk: true opinions are selected on the basis of recognition, and oscillate between two criteria, that of adhesion and judgment: concurrence with "common" (i.e. majority) opinion and participation in a transcendent Idea (WP 144–50; CC 136–7). As we will see, against the abstract, scholarly, and vaguely Socratic image of philosophical work founded on the dialogue as a discussion, Deleuze will present another conception of exchange defined as an "act of fabulation" or "free indirect discourse" (see, of course, *Dialogues*). Since this criticism of discussion has still not been understood, I will supply some long quotations:

> Every philosopher runs away when he or she hears someone say, "Let's discuss this." Discussions are fine for roundtable talks, but philosophy throws its numbered dice on another table. The best one can say about discussions is that they take things no farther, since the participants never talk about the same thing. Of what concern is it to philosophy that someone has such a view, and thinks this or that, if the problems at stake are not stated? And when they are stated, it is no longer a matter of discussing but rather one of creating concepts for the undiscussible problem posed. Communication always comes too early or too late, and when it comes to creating, conversation is always superfluous. Sometimes philosophy is turned into the idea of a perpetual discussion, as "communicative rationality," or as "universal democratic conversation." Nothing is less exact, and when philosophers criticize each other it is on the basis of problems and on a plane that is different from theirs and that melt down the old concepts in the way a cannon can be melted down to make new weapons. It never takes place on the same plane. To criticize is only to establish that a concept vanishes when it is thrust into a new milieu, losing some of its components, or acquiring others that transform it. But those who criticize without creating, those who are content to defend the vanished concept without being able to give it the forces it needs to return to life, are the plague of philosophy. (WP 28)

> Philosophy has absolutely nothing to do with discussing things, it's difficult enough just understanding the problem someone's framing and how they're framing it, all you should ever do is explore it, play around with the terms, add something, relate it to something else, never discuss it. (N 139)

> It is already hard enough to understand what someone is trying to say. Discussion is just an exercise in narcissism where everyone takes turns showing off. Very quickly, you have no idea what is being discussed. But it is much more difficult to determine the problem to which a particular proposition responds. Now, if you understand the problem which someone has posed, you have no desire to discuss it: either you pose the same problem, or you decide to pose another problem and continue in that direction. How can you have a discussion without a common source of problems, but what is there to say when you share a common source of problems? You always get the solutions you deserve depending on the problems that have been posed. For indeterminate problems, discussion is just a waste of time. Conversation is something else entirely. We need conversation. But the lightest conversation is a great schizophrenic experiment happening between two individuals with common resources and a

taste for ellipses and short-hand expressions. Conversation is full of long silences; it can give you ideas. But discussion has no place in the work of philosophy. The phrase "let's discuss it" is an act of terror. (TR 380)

The morality of discussion consists in granting to critique a role that it does not have, mistaking its function, and inverting the real hierarchy by attributing to the negative that which actually belongs to affirmation. The false problem *par excellence* therefore consists in attributing the motor of thought to negativity—which is why Hegelianism is the current of thought Deleuze despised the most, and with which no compromise is possible (cf. notably NP 8, 156 ff., 195; DR ix).

Deleuze's conviction is that the reprisal of the theme of the master and the slave in Nietzsche remains unintelligible so long as it has not been situated in its polemical or critical context: the refusal of a dialectical conception of the relation between forces. Hegel "dialecticized relations": according to him, terms enter into relation with one another only via the negative, each negating the other; there is consequently no relation between forces except in the mode of contradiction. Such a concept of relation is incompatible with the idea of a radical encounter, for the conception of negation as a motor implies that the other is already comprehended in each term as "all that it is not"—and therefore that the identity of a Whole first be given. In a dialectical relation, difference is only thinkable in accordance with the implicit presupposition of the Whole. Thus alterity envelops within itself unhappiness and abstraction: instead of alogical, aconceptual hazardous encounters in a field of pure exteriority, it presupposes a scission and is only the shadow of the Same. The relations are interior to the Whole: in pushing difference all the way to contradiction, Hegel subordinates it to the identical. For Deleuze, the implicit presupposition of the Whole is sufficient reason enough to not believe in the movement promised by the dialectic, since it compromises in advance the temporalization of truth. This presupposition enables a permanent suspicion of circularity to linger over Hegelianism, a circle by means of which we rediscover at the end what we gave ourselves at the beginning; under these conditions the passage from the abstract to the concrete risks being only a "false-movement," making the negative only a pseudo-motor.

The negative presupposes the identical and therefore participates in the dogmatic image of thought. But Deleuze goes even further than this. The dialectic is not a simple avatar of the dogmatic image, but its culmination, its greatest consequence and its highest achievement (DR 164). Not only does the negative not move thought, it is the symptom *par excellence* of a thought that does not move, habituated to the primordial concern for conservation. Hegelianism is only a failure at first view, that is, from the point of view of a project that had the aim of creating movement, of introducing becoming into thought. At bottom, it fulfills perfectly the wish of the forces animating it: to conserve (understood here perhaps above all in a moral and political sense, as Deleuze specifies).

It is here that the analysis of Nietzsche takes on its full meaning. It is not a question of brutally contradicting Hegel by affirming that the master-slave relation is not dialectical, but rather of showing that it is only dialectical on one side, from the point of view of the slave. Hegel is partly right: he states the point of view of the slave. Yet he poses the problem poorly, since the relation above all concerns *points of view*. By invoking a relation between points of view, one does not change merely the nature of the terms, one also makes the point of view on the relation internal to the relation itself, which then finds itself doubled. It is therefore no longer a matter of asserting that the relation between forces is or is not dialectical in itself. The latter is the point of view of the slave, who affirms only in accordance with the master (obedience); the concept of the slave includes the relation to the master because his mode of affirmation is essentially relative. But the relation is not at all dialectical from the point of view of the master who affirms absolutely (creation), this affirmation having a relation to the slave only secondarily (we have seen that the phenomenon of domination cannot always be explained by a will to dominate, which implies an inversion of roles, where violence becomes the cause or agent rather than the consequent or concomitant). Hence the misinterpretation of force emerging from the slave, which can be understood only from a point of view of conservation and obedience.

By invoking a misinterpretation, does this not in the last resort send us back to the problem of the nature of relations? The Deleuzian challenge is the following: to think hierarchy within a relativistic framework, or, what amounts to the same thing, to conceive of a non-relativistic perspectivism. Deleuze insists on the necessity of not confusing the banal and contradictory idea of a truth that varies according to one's point of view with the idea—attributed to Leibniz and Nietzsche—of a truth relative to the point of view, where all points of view are not of equal value (L 19–20, 21).[1] In a first moment sense is pluralized according to diverse points of view; from there, one of these may be selected as a superior truth.

In such a case, we are confronted with the problem of the relation between forces, and it is a matter of showing why the negative can only be derived from affirmation. The response or the argument lies in the very difference between points of view. The disequilibrium favoring the master, the exteriority of relations, and the primacy of affirmation stems from the fact that the difference between the points of view only appears from one point of view, namely that of the master. Perspectivism cannot lead to a relativity of the true because it presents us with points of view that deny it: one cannot affirm the difference of points of view without at the same time posing their inequality. Perspectivism therefore dispenses with the obviousness of a criteria. Can one therefore reproach it for remaining without [hors] criteria?

In short, it is a question of knowing whether master and slave do in fact correspond to different points of view. This is where the logic of force intervenes. For a relation of forces is unequal by nature, implying a phenomenon of domination, a force that affects (active) and a force that is affected (passive or reactive). This in itself is still not enough to produce a difference in points of view, since the vanquished, dominated force limits itself to obedience or to being affected; in other words, to affirming only the point of view of the master. What we must try to explain is what Hegel presupposes from the beginning: a will to knowledge, a will that affirms itself in taking an other into account. Seeing the recognition of an other, conceiving of domination as the attainment of recognition, testifies to a force that is absolutely powerless to command, powerless to begin. The Hegelian master resembles a "successful slave" (NP 10). Hegel does not think the origin of this subjection [l'asujettissement], presenting us instead with forces already subjugated, and which from then on enter into dialectical relations wherein one never really knows who dominates whom, or where the negative truly governs, or by reason of what each force comes to lack the other and to be nothing without it. It is therefore imperative to return to the original relation between forces, to the precise threshold where commanding and obeying, action and reaction, differentiate themselves. Now, a relation between forces entails an action and a reaction, a force that affirms itself and exerts itself upon another, becoming master of this force and its will precisely by imposing its own upon it. Such a rela-tion does not yet presuppose a negation (self-affirmation through negation of the other): domination, as we have already emphasized, is a positive relation as such, productive of a new effect. Negation enters the concept of the relationship between forces as a consequence rather than an origin, and this relationship is in principle exterior to its terms (even if, inversely, the terms are interior to it owing to the fact that they are defined only in relation to one another):

> Not all relations between "same" and "other" are sufficient to form a dialectic, even essential ones: everything depends on the role of the negative in this relation. Nietzsche emphasizes the fact that force has another force for its object. But it is important to see that forces enter into relations with *other* forces. (NP 8)

At this point, we are still not dealing with points of view but only with terms that are originally exterior to each another. Perspectival difference requires an interiorization of the relation: the negative must no longer be a simple consequence, but the very motive of force as such. How does it come about that a force first and foremost negates, and finds in the negation of an other the very principle of its affirmation? It can only be explained by a force that includes the other within its own will, or who obeys this other. To create movement through negation, whether in thought or in life, is always the hope of a subjected force. Here we have the appearance of a point of view distinct from that of the master, a point of view affirming a force of negation (instead of negating by affirmation). The struggle may now be taken up at another level: for despite his efforts, the slave does not become active or capable of a pure affirmation, but struggles by diffusing his point of view, by inspiring reactivity in the active force itself, by *separating it from what it can do* (NP 57). In fact, from the point of view of the slave the division of active and reactive is not inverted; it is both forces together—master and slave—who are becoming reactive and who have no relation other than that of the negative. We can see in this way how perspectivism not only hierarchizes points of view, but also how it manages to avoid falling prey to a circularity: the very terrain on which Hegel installs himself, that of the relation of forces, seems to favor a difference of point of view.

What consequences does this have for a theory of thought? The negative appears as the *false problem par excellence*: the point of view taken by reactive forces—forces of consciousness or representation—on the encounter. "The negative is an illusion, no more than a shadow of problems" (DR 202). The shadow of problems, which means at the same time their necessarily denatured insistence within the world of representation. A thought that confronts a problem with the aim of determining its conditions can only represent it negatively, because the positivity of signs is not representable. There remains only a shadow of signs within representation, which is that of the negative: whence the formula according to which we *are not yet* thinking that which nevertheless forces us to think (and this applies just as much to the representation of desire as lack). Which is why Hegelianism is not an error but a phenomenon simultaneously worse and more interesting, the development of a necessary transcendental illusion. It was fatal that Hegel attributed the motor of thought to the negative, he who sought to introduce movement into thought, but who thus remained at the level of representation (DR 10). Certainly, the negative is the best way to represent movement, but precisely to represent it and not to bring it about. And more generally, how is thought represented if not as paradoxically confronting that which it does not think? How is desire represented, if not as a lack? Under these conditions, how can we avoid sacrificing the efficacy of both thought and desire—i.e. the always mutating jubilation of their vagrancy at the whim of signs and forces of the outside—by reducing them to their monotonous shadow? (Cursed or neurotic, the man of representation perceives in the diversity of signs only the forbidding underside that always returns to the same—*the* negative, lack *as such*.)

The apprehension of a problem thus runs up against a paradox that Plato liked to state even as he overcame it: how can you seek something you do not already know, if by definition you do not know what it is you are seeking? Or at least we stumble over it so long as we are seeking the resolution of a problem in a reflection on given and representable contents. Deleuze occasionally represents the effort of a thinker as follows:

> How else can one write but of those things that one doesn't know, or knows badly? It is precisely there that we imagine having something to say. We write only at the frontiers of our knowledge, at the border that separates our knowledge from our ignorance and *transforms the one into the other*. Only in this manner are we resolved to write. To satisfy ignorance is to put off writing until tomorrow—or rather, to make it impossible. (DR xxi)

> You give courses on what you are investigating, and not on what you know. (N 139)

To be content with knowledge and ignorance is to stupidly remain before a negative frontier that retains nothing of the real dynamic of thought (the harnessing of signs and the positivity of the problem unfolding itself out of them). To think is neither to know nor to not know but to seek [*chercher*], and one seeks only if one has already found the minimum enveloped—a sign—that draws thought into a movement of searching [*recherche*]. Thus it is necessary to "transform the one into the other." Can we really believe that the dialectic reaches this point, endeavoring as it does to take up the concrete movement by mixing or combining what one has and what one does not, Being and Nothing, with the hope that the negative can ground the opposition in a movement (Becoming)? The dialectic believes itself to be capable of obtaining the non-representable through a work of representation,

> but of what use is a dialectic that believes itself to be reunited with the real when it compensates for the inadequacy of a concept that is too broad or too general by invoking the opposite concept, which is no less broad or general? The concrete will never be attained by combining the inadequacy of one concept with the inadequacy of its opposite. The singular will never be attained by correcting a generality with another generality. (B 44)

"To transform one into the other" requires a non-dialectical theory of *becoming*, where it is no longer a matter of combination (contradiction) but of rendering indiscernible (what Deleuze will call "vice-diction"). There are two ways of "rendering representation infinite": push difference all the way up to contradiction (Hegel), or follow it all the way down to the infinitesimal (Leibniz). Deleuze chose the latter path, which, once extricated from any reference to the infinitely small, leads us to consider a pure *differential relation* (DR 42–50, and all of Ch. 4).

Disappointment and Fatigue

The pressure of reactive forces has two poles: disappointment and dogmatism. Sometimes they struggle and take over before an encounter could even take place, or could crystallize; sometimes they take over after the fact, testifying rather to the fatigue of the thinker.

To say that thought encounters its outside means that it is newly affected, and that a problem that it had lived up to this point has ceased to occupy its center, even if it continues to act upon it negatively. When it is in contact with the outside, thought is in becoming: it becomes-other and struggles against that which it is ceasing to be.

By an overlapping that is characteristic of the event, it is still what it is ceasing to be, and not yet what it is becoming. Thus the philosopher must respond to the pressure of the *involuntary* (the sign) with an active *ill will* (critique) that challenges the dogmatic image of a naturally good thought. The thinker is a double character—"jealous" insofar as he captures signs that do violence to him and which he must decipher (PS 15), an "idiot" inasmuch as he must turn away from the dogmatic image of thought, "not managing to know what everybody knows" (DR 130). These two postures are not moments, as if the thinker first had to pass from one to the next. He is both at once, creator and critic, even though critique draws its inspiration from the beginning of a creation. The idiot is first jealous, but we will see that in a sense the inverse is also true, since there is a sensitivity to signs only on the basis of a rupture of the sensory-motor schema by means of which representations are produced (C2 44). An involuntary will and an ill will: both are necessary in order to think, and we must not see in the latter a lack of will or a broken will, for on the contrary it is precisely the obstinacy or *stubbornness* capable of destroying the sterile and paralyzing good will of the thinker that prevents him from thinking, that constantly diverts him from that which has seized hold of him.[2] Stubbornness is the erratic and necessarily delirious pursuit of the sign, the mad and disorderly gesture, the opposite of good sense in every way; it is the means by which thought affirms its own *hauntedness* or the superior urgency seizing it.

And yet, it is no easy thing to renounce the dogmatic image of thought, and Deleuze invokes a necessary *disappointment*: thought is not what we believe it to be. Lending his voice to Proust, or vice versa, he says:

> To be sensitive to signs, to consider the world as an object to be deciphered, is doubtless a gift. But this gift risks remaining buried in us if we do not make the necessary encounters, and these encounters would remain ineffective if we failed to overcome certain stock notions. (PS 26–7)

Where does the resistance to encounters come from? Thought is first of all a passion, and it is only by assuming the role of a patient that the thinker becomes active and conquers his power of thought. Thinking must be conquered, engendered in thought. This paradox inherent to becoming-active is developed in relation to Artaud:

> Henceforth, thought is also forced to think its central collapse, its fracture, its own natural "powerlessness" [*impouvoir*], which is indistin-

guishable from the greatest power [*puissance*]—in other words, from those unformulated forces, the *cogitanda*, as though from so many thefts or trespasses in thought. Artaud pursues in all this the terrible revelation of a thought without image, and the conquest of a new principle which does not allow itself to be represented. He knows that *difficulty* as such, along with its cortège of problems and questions, is not a *de facto* state of affairs but a *de jure* structure of thought; that there is an acephalism in thought just as there is an amnesia in memory, an aphasia in language and an agnosia in sensibility. He knows that thinking is not innate, but must be engendered in thought. He knows that the problem is not to direct or methodically apply a thought which pre-exists in principle and in nature, but to bring into being that which does not yet exist (there is no other work, all the rest is arbitrary, mere decoration). To think is to create—there is no other creation—but to create is first of all to engender "thinking" in thought. (DR 147)

Disappointment is related first of all to this powerlessness: to not manage to work, or to undertake the announced project (PS 21). It then concerns the transcendental discovery that explicates this powerlessness, that of the paradox of creation. Thought is engendered at the extreme point of powerlessness; in other words, there is no pure power, no sovereign self-mastery acquired for all time and there from the start. Thought advances only from one act to another, not from principle to consequence or from ground to sky, and replays itself completely each time. Such is the revelation of the "ungrounding" echoing Artaud's "central collapse."

Is this not already the etymological meaning of disappointment (deprivation [*dessaisissement*], a loss of control or a forced renunciation of mastery)? "What violence must be exerted on thought for us to become capable of thinking; what violence of an infinite movement that, at the same time, *deprives us* of our power to say 'I'" (WP 55, translation modified); "Far from presupposing a subject, desire cannot be attained except at the point where someone is *deprived* of the power of saying 'I'" (D 89, emphasis added [FZ]).[3] It is disappointing to discover that thought begins in an encounter, that it does so as a result of the renunciations that such a revelation implies and the absolute precarity it promises: the philosophy of the event begins by saddening (cf. DR 200: "How disappointing this answer seems to be. . .").

Thought confronts a double deception that it must surmount. On the one hand, the acknowledgement of powerlessness as its condition (idiocy); on the other, the illusory nostalgia for a thought that would be easy in principle and agreeable (jealousy). It has at its disposal a paradoxical will, drawn from the involuntary as such (the sign that haunts it), a "will that the event *creates* in [the thinker]" (LS 101), a stubbornness or obstinacy. But it also confronts something else, undermining its resolution to take this will up, for the second disappointment is amplified by a suspicion that threatens to cloud everything: what if the renunciation were after all only the elegant dissimulation of powerlessness ... The philosopher gives up trying to interpret the world, to give a meaning to life and to his time—in short, he stops treating reality as an object of recognition—for he senses a certain servility in all of this, a presumptuousness foreign to the act of thinking. But he must still escape the voices that call him to return to Opinion, and first and foremost from within himself. Such is the case for Proust's narrator, when he confronts the conception of art which had long been his own:

> But then, why does he suffer so intense a disappointment each time he realizes its inanity? Because art, at least, found in this conception a specific fulfillment: it espoused life in order to exalt it, in order to disengage its value and truth. And when we protest against an art of observation and description, how do we know that it is not our incapacity to observe, to describe, that inspires this protest, and our incapacity to understand life? (PS 33)

Let us now consider things from the other side. It is no longer a disappointment that the thinker confronts, but a *fatigue*, one which equally calls him back to Opinion and freezes his problematic into a dogmatism. What is the limit of a thinker's capacity to endure the "ungrounding" of his own thought? Is he not bound to rely on an enunciation that is itself only possible in the ungrounding, and to utilize it from then on as an orienting sign or a reference point for merely relative movements (WP 49)? How long can active forces hold sway in thought? Is there not an eventual "becoming-reactive of all forces" (the recurrent question of *Nietzsche and Philosophy*: 64 ff., 166 ff.)?

Critique's oscillation between the theme of a "thought without image" (DR 132, 167, 276; ATP 376; CC 82) and that of a "new image of thought" (NP 103 ff.; PS 100; N 148 ff.) perhaps signals the moment where Deleuze confronts the question for himself. In fact, this oscillation reflects the paradox of a transcendental philosophy that, wanting to be immanent, seeks conditions "which are no larger than the conditioned" and which constitute a transcendental field that is in a certain way "plastic" (NP 50; DR 68). Yet, what good can a theory be that claims to do without an image, while at the same time describing the conditions of an act of thought? If Deleuze were to claim to escape all images, to evade all presuppositions regarding what it means to think, this would be the time to apply to him his own dictum, "we make ourselves prisoners of the relative horizon" (WP 49). But this oscillation is not to be attributed to a hesitation. In reality, the paradox is that the new image—the "rhizome" (ATP, 1st Plateau)—is *the image of a thought without image*, an immanent thought that does not know in advance what thinking means.

Deleuze explains this in a recent text (WP Ch. 2): every philosophy admittedly has presuppositions—an image of thought—but which do not as such constitute an opinion or a postulate of transcendence. Presuppositions are not always there, like a region of belief remaining intact: they emerge at the same time concepts do, implicated in them as their condition (so that the very problem of *belief* changes its sense, no longer being related to prejudice or stupidity). The image of thought merges with the plane or the field drawn up by philosophy, and THE plane of immanence must be conceived of as the field of virtual coexistence of all the planes, of all philosophies (cf. above, end of Ch. 2). In this sense thought creates without a preconceived image, by tracing a new image of thought.

On the other hand, it is a fatigued thought that confuses the two lines of creation, taking concepts to be the plane itself, and aspiring to first concepts as transcendent principles. It therefore ends up a "prisoner of the relative horizon": the problem is no longer distinguished as such in the distinct-obscure gleam characteristic of the sign or the encounter, but subsists in a disfigured, denatured way, in the caricatured form of a dogmatic tree stump (WP 49, 212–13; and on the confusion of planes with concepts, 39–40, 50).

"Our" Problem

Beyond the misdirection of the false problem and the many dangers that thought confronts, two questions remain: if each plane has its own necessity, what compulsion leads us to change planes? And what renders a plane null and void? Falsity and obsolescence: critique exerts itself from these two points of view. Certain problems usurp their name, but all problems pass away [*vient à passer*]. Deleuze is not at all saying that truth itself passes away; he even insists on the fact that a problem to which we have ceased to be sensitive conserves in itself its force of novelty in a sort of virtual eternity where it waits to eventually be reactivated and transformed. A problem passes away because another appears, ceding place to a still more urgent novelty. A problem is *ours* not because it corresponds to present reality (recognition), but because it is new and because the renewal of historical conditions emits new signs (WP 27–8 and 110–13).

By maintaining that problems pass away—and this contrary to the scholarly prejudice that would seek to make them into eternals (and this is how they appear when they are treated as vague and general statements)—Deleuze is not making a vague and negative remark, but is indicating a positive relation between truth and time. To justify such a passing by seeking its reason in the nature of problems themselves is an absurd endeavor. Problems pass away because thought is exposed to time, and the latter can here be determined only as chance, or a field of encounters. When Deleuze relates truth and time, it is the entire field of exterior relations that is temporalized. And we will see that the force-sense relation is surpassed toward a sense-time relation, that an authentic relation is always a relation to time (could forces not be in the last instance *forces of time*? cf. FB-LS Ch. 8; C2 42; WP 182).

Deleuze always presents our contemporary situation according to an event: something has happened, "the problem changed." We can celebrate it or deplore it, we can cling to the old problematic, but it imposes itself nevertheless as *our* problem, since it elicits creation. We don't choose what makes us think, the philosopher does not choose his themes and problems; the only criteria—the appreciation of the new or of what forces thought—certainly appears fragile since it puts sensibility into play, but it is a matter of a non-recognitional sensibility[4] no longer relative to a constituted subject. There is certainly a *cruelty* here—for example in the statement that "God" today no longer provokes thought. We rediscover here the general problem of the active and the reactive, of creation and conservation: is not what emerges interesting by nature? The real question is that of a good diagnostic. It is not a matter of asking whether the problem presented to us is better than the previous one, but of whether or not we can say that a new problem has emerged. The thinker's task is to isolate the authentic event among the "great resounding events" (NP 156). The philosopher must become a *clinician*, and Deleuze's work is first of all the description of a modern mutation in the field of thought. A new problem has surfaced, which no longer has anything to do with believing or not believing in God:

The problem would change if it were another plane of immanence. It is not that the person who does not believe God exists would gain the upper hand, since he would still belong to the old plane as negative movement. But, on the new plane, it is possible that the problem now concerns the one who believes in the world, and not even in the existence of the world but in its possibilities of movements and intensities, so as once again to give birth to new modes of existence, closer to animals and rocks. It may be that believing in this world, in this life, becomes our most difficult task, or the task of a mode of existence still to be discovered on our plane of immanence today. This is the empiricist conversion (we have so many reasons not to believe in the human world; we have lost the world, worse than a fiancée or a god). The problem has indeed changed. (WP 74–5)

Deleuze draws up a clinical picture of modern thought by creating the necessary concepts, he develops the signs that haunt current thought, captures the forces exerted upon it. Of course, not all the representatives of this world of thought are affected by these forces and signs, concerned as so many are with conserving or discrediting, being unfit for encounters as a result of their distrust. Yet there are others still who would perhaps draw up the picture differently, and it is between Deleuze and them that the decision is to be made.

To believe in this world is to affirm immanence. The new forces are those of the intolerable and of shame:

For it is not in the name of a better or truer world that thought captures the intolerable in this world, but, on the contrary, it is because this world is intolerable that it can no longer think a world or think itself. The intolerable is no longer a serious injustice, but the permanent state of a daily banality. Man *is not himself* a world other than the one in which he experiences the intolerable and feels himself trapped. The spiritual automaton is in the psychic situation of the seer, who sees better and further than he can react, that is, think. Which, then, is the "subtle way out"? To believe, not in a different world, but in a link between man and the world, in love or life, to believe in this as in the impossible, the unthinkable, which nonetheless cannot but be thought: "something possible, otherwise I will suffocate." It is this belief that makes the unthought the specific power of thought, through the absurd, by virtue of the absurd. Artaud never understood powerlessness to think as a simple inferiority which would strike us in relation to thought. It is part of thought, so that we should make our way of thinking from it, without claiming to be restoring an all-powerful thought. We should rather make use of this powerlessness to believe in life, and to discover the identity of thought and life . . . The modern fact is that we no longer believe in this world. We do not even believe in the events that happen to us, love, death, as if they only half-concerned us.

It is not we who make cinema; it is the world which looks to us like a bad film . . . The link between man and the world is broken. Henceforth, this link must become an object of belief: it is the impossible which can only be restored within a faith. Belief is no longer addressed to a different or a transformed world. Man is in the world as if in a pure optical and sound situation. The reaction of which man has been dispossessed can be replaced only by belief. Only belief in the world can reconnect man to what he sees and hears. (C2 169–72)

Why is it still a problem of belief? Contrary to knowledge, belief implies a relation to the outside, it is the affirmation of such a relation: to affirm what we neither perceive nor think, what we are not yet thinking (immanence: "we do not know what a *body* can do"), or else what we will never think (transcendence: God, the unknowable or the concealed, whose perfections surpass and humiliate our understanding). Deleuze insists on the difference in nature between the two types of belief, for the modern fact is that of the inclusion of the outside *within* the world, and not outside it or beyond it. Today the outside is becoming an immanent category, and this conceptual mutation is at the same time the condition of a radical thought of immanence.

To affirm the outside or divergence not as a beyond but as the condition of immanence: such is the response of thought to its own exhaustion, to its own lassitude (no longer believing in love, in philosophy . . .), which substitutes a paradoxical belief for the faith in achieved forms, in totalities, or interiorities. This lassitude is opposed to the fatigue which, no longer capable of sustaining the event, replaces it with an *a priori*. Depriving thought of its power to signify or speak essences, it makes it capable of seizing new forces, of sensing new signs. This new belief in immanence and no longer in an essence of "reality" is expressed thus:

The play of the world has changed in a unique way, because now it has become the world that diverges. Beings are pushed apart [*écartelés*], kept open through divergent series and incompossible totalities that pull them outside, instead of being closed upon the compossible and convergent world that they express from within . . . It is a world of captures instead of closures. (L 81)

Notes

1. It is a commonplace to treat as proponents of nihilism the very thinkers who diagnosed it, by drawing up the clinical picture and endeavoring to

92

surpass it without being willing to evacuate the problem of relativism. This stubborn misinterpretation testifies to the difficulty of renouncing the dogmatic alternative of transcendence or chaos.

2. On the stubbornness of the idiot and its relation to the theme of a "thought without image," cf. DR 131, 132; CC 82.

3. The expression comes from one of Blanchot's phrases, cited in ATP 541, fn. 43; and CC 185, fn. 7.

4. The French term *la sensibilité* can mean both sensitivity (which we have employed up until this point) and sensibility, as for example in Deleuze's formulation in *Difference and Repetition*, "*la sensibilité des sens*," or "the sensibility of the senses" (DR 73)—Trans.

4

Time and Implication

Forces and affects refer to a field of exteriority or pure heterogeneity, a field of absolute difference. Deleuze arrives at the conception of this field through a meditation on time. He shows that when difference is raised to the absolute it becomes an authentic relation, so that the motif of the exteriority of relations is achieved in the articulation of difference and repetition. The logic of forces thus turns into a meditation on time that devalues the relation of succession. Time works on bodies, and the heterogeneity operative within bodies (affect) and at the limit of bodies (sense) is in the last instance temporal.

"Chronos wants to die," writes Deleuze (LS 164). Time is heterogeneous before being successive; the passage of time (chronology) is only an empirical form of time, the way in which it is represented. Succession is not an appearance, but it cannot account for itself and refers back to a more profound genetic instance, to relations of another nature, no less real and no less temporal.

Habit, Becoming, Chance

Difference and Repetition (Ch. 2) describes three temporal modes that are at the same time ways of living time, or simply of living. Each of these "times"—present, past, future—will in turn become dominant in its own way (Deleuze provides a reason for this triad: an originary distribution of three times that "eludes" one of them—the present). The first of these temporal modes is an alternating, periodic time corresponding to organic cycles. This mode corresponds in particular to the image of a circular movement, always passing through the same points: cardinal time, docile and regular, "rhythmic" in the vulgar sense of the term. First of all, there is a contraction of instants or punctual excitations giving birth to a present that lasts, to a duration. This present, which Deleuze names *habit* with reference to the Anglo-Saxon empiricists, is less something we are in than something we *are* (our activities are what take place in it). It is the very consistency of our existence, differenciated and qualified. This present is necessarily finite, limited, bounded by a certain capacity for contraction. At the organic level, each organ has its present or its own duration, so that the differences here are not only from one species to another: several presents, durations, or relative *speeds* coexist in the same organism. The relaxation of contraction (fatigue) corresponds to the eruption of need, an openness enabling further contractions by preventing its perilous closure. Contraction continues, giving rise to need, because the contractive repetition of instants (habit) engenders a "claim" or an anticipation, "our expectation that '*it*' will continue" (DR 74). There are indeed lacunae between contractions, however we cannot say that the present passes, since it continually produces itself anew, its claim being to continue or to preserve itself. In its principle or its logic, periodicity is a perpetual present, punctuated [*scandé*] only by the intermittences of fatigue and need. We contract anew, but it is always the same cycle that begins again—the present lasts, is perforated, but does not pass.

This contraction or variable present is also what Deleuze calls—to be content with a provisional approximation—a *milieu*, which serves as a frame, at both an organic and an existential level, for our acts, for our "effectuations" (our buildings, streets, friends, professions, conjugal life, the army, the country, the region, etc.). The milieu is defined by a habituation, a periodic and qualified space-time, a "relative speed" corresponding to the scale of its cycle (ATP 312; C1 Chapters 8–9).

The concept of the milieu may seem imprecise: sometimes we act in it, sometimes we are it. This is because it implies a theory of subjectivity, according to which being or identity is deduced from a *having* or a claim (DR 78; L 109–10). "We are all contemplations, and therefore habits. *I* is a habit" (WP 105). Who am I? A contemplative habit, drawn through a contraction of the material and sensorial elements composing a milieu in which I live and act. Or else the multiplicity of habits related to the diverse milieus I contract, some of whose formation did not await my arrival: social milieus, linguistic milieus, etc. I have exactly the consistency of my habits; my actions and reactions presuppose the prior contraction of a milieu which I henceforth *am*. This is the literal meaning of habit, and the Deleuzian cogito is an "I inhabit" ["*j'habite*"] or an "I claim" (that which I contract).

However, we all know this temporal mode does not exhaust the entirety of our experience. On the one hand, even within a single person the milieus that serve as a frame for existence are diverse,

95

which already poses problems of accordance or composition, and requires that we think lateral, non-successive temporal relations from one dimension of time to another. On the other hand, it happens that we pass from one milieu to another, from one periodicity to another: to grow up, to leave, to fall in love, or out of love, is a becoming, an event, a rupture or an encounter (but there is a rupture in every encounter). Succession itself becomes discernible and thinkable here, once we take account of the fact that—to repeat once again—our present is plural, and that each of us simultaneously lives on several lines of time (PS 25–6). Moreover, some lines become blurred or brutally interrupted, while others continue, etc. Contrary to periodicity, there is no longer only the present that persists, but the present that passes, and that passes to the benefit of *another* present (whether it be one line relaying another, or a change in the composition of presents). Every existence straddles several milieus, but it happens that sometimes they are no longer the same ones, or the multiple present becomes augmented by a new dimension.

The present does not account for its own *passing*; thus there must be a more profound aspect of time, a mechanism explaining this passage of time. To say that we live in the present is not enough. Certainly, action requires that we have a present, but once the present that constitutes us passes, depriving us thereby of our power of acting, we are left with only an obstinate contemplative question: "what happened?" (LS 154–5; ATP 8th Plateau). The situation has changed, and it would be enough to contract a new habit in order to react anew; but in the interval something surfaces that is more profound than any situation: a pure insistent caesura, a difference between two irreconcilable dimensions of time that makes us *idiots*. This is the event.

It is necessary at once to account for the possibility of the passage of time, and to describe the temporality proper to the event as such: not the new situation or the new milieu, but the between-two-milieus. We can equally imagine a kinship between the heterogeneity of variable presents and the succession of presents. In both cases, the idea of a cardinal time, related to periodicity, testifies to a local, partial, and abstract viewpoint, and is surpassed toward an *ordinal* conception of a multi-dimensional and multi-linear time; whether past or present, as relations in time dimensions are of the same nature, so that it is a matter of ascending or descending amongst them, or even of exploring horizontally the different actual lands. As Bergson already knew, time is not a fourth dimension added to those of space, it itself contains "more dimensions than space" (PS 26).

Before analyzing this question of passage or of the past, and the consequences it has for the theory of relations, it must be noted that Deleuze is not satisfied with these two temporal modes, the present dominating in one case, the past in the other. He seeks a third mode, sensing its necessity: a temporality in which the future would have primacy. Why? The third temporal mode not only affirms the present and the fact that it succeeds another (past), but in a certain way it requires this substitution itself, and in this substitution it sees the fate of all presents. Becoming is not simply acknowledged but affirmed: all that exists is in becoming, nothing is given "once and for all." The question has become: "what is going to happen?" This temporal mode, eminently precarious, can be experienced only at the extreme point of the livable; it threatens the present, and therefore also the identity of the subject who affirms it. "I is an other," I will be an other, or even more radically still: the other who will surface in my place excludes me. It is impossible to *represent* myself in this affirmation of the future which consequently differs from every anticipation, the latter referring to a future of action that remains included within my present periodicity. If we attempt to give the future an independent meaning, and to view it as the reference of a really distinct temporal mode, we are led to the paradoxical affirmation of a new coherence, a *"chaoerrance"* that excludes the subject that affirms it (DR 57–8, 89–90, 93–6, 112–13). The affirmation of becoming is thus tainted with death, and Deleuze occasionally links it to the psychoanalytic death drive (DR 111 ff.; M 115 ff.). Nonetheless, it remains foreign to any dialectic, for death is not at all conceived as a moment of life, a moment that would nourish life and which constitutes its surpassing [*dépassement*].

"Time must be understood and lived as out of joint, and seen as a straight line which mercilessly eliminates those who embark upon it, who come upon the scene but repeat only once and for all" (DR 298). But who could live in the future tense? In a philosophy of immanence that announces the perpetual "ungrounding" of the present, is not the ethical problem precisely this? "To believe in this world," the very formula of immanence, is inseparable from a "belief of the future, a belief in the future" (DR 90), which obviously has nothing to do with some indeterminate hope, or with a confidence in progress (sentiments that refer in fact to an anticipated future and which keep us in the present of action, of which this future is only a modality). As an original temporal mode, the future is related to the conditions of emergence of an act of thought. To think—but also to love, to desire (we will see why later)—depends on the possibility of affirming the future as such, and in a certain manner living the unlivable.

We can therefore understand the necessity of seeking a third temporal mode. What is at stake is the "last form of the problematic" (DR 112). It is a question of knowing whether thought and desire can meet and affirm their own conditions—in short, whether they can affirm immanence and the conditions of the emergence of a problem. What is at stake is our highest mastery, even if it is conquered in precarity and powerlessness. Are we capable of such an affirmation? At least we can define the conditions: they would be those of a game of *absolute chance*, where all of chance is affirmed in each throw, where each throw consequently creates its own rules, as in a game of roulette where we would constantly rethrow the ball again and again. To the rule of a unique throw in which an initial and relative chance is tolerated "once and for all" [*une foise pour toutes*] is opposed an indefinite succession of throws reaffirming all of chance each time, and appearing thus as fragments of the same unique Throw "for all times" [*pour toutes les fois*]. This infinitely subdivided unique Throw, "numerically one but formally multiple," is the affirmation of absolute chance, or becoming: an affirmation of the future and a selective repetition which ensures that what has only been affirmed once and for all does not return. The affirmation of becoming implies that all of chance is restored each time: it thus excludes finality, but also causality and probability, to the benefit of a *non-causal correspondence* between events (EPS 326; LS 170). Such is the substance—if one can say this—of the Deleuzian interpretation of the Eternal Return in Nietzsche. And this is perhaps a game to the death for every well-constituted subject; *one* does not leave it without always winning by definition (DR 116, LS 10th Series, "Of the Ideal Game," and the first analysis of the dice throw in NP 25–7).

The Heterogeneity of Time

Let us return to the question of the dimensions of time. Deleuze shows with reference to Bergson that it is impossible to account for the passing of the present by sticking to the relation of succession, and that it is necessary to explore a more profound domain of "non-chronological" temporal relations (C2 111). But how can one maintain that time is not essentially successive? Is not time defined by succession (an order of before and after)? Time is indeed a caesura, but the latter is static, a pure Instant, and does not account for succession.

It is therefore necessary to explain the passing of time. The reason for the change is not in the present, which aspires only to continue. We never get to the past, still less to the future, so long as we make the present continue: what we call past and future (retention and anticipation) is only incorporated within a larger present that excludes any difference in kind. And nevertheless we live this continuation as a passage, as the incessant discharge [*rejet*] of the present into the past. It is correct to say that we pass from one present to *another*, rather than it being a simple change of content. But this statement is obscure for two reasons. First, the present does not lead to another present of its own accord; second, it is not clear why the former present can now appear as *past*. A juxtaposition of segments does not explain the passage of the present.

What makes the present pass, thereby causing time to move, and making it appear in itself as change, rather than the latter being merely that which effectuates itself in the present? The new present always implies an "extra dimension" in relation to the one it replaces (DR 80), and the succession of presents has as its condition a "constant augmentation of dimensions" (DR 81). Between the before and the after there is a potentialization: time is ordinal (DR 88). In place of the traditional image of time as a line on which presents come to be juxtaposed is substituted the idea of a time that progresses intensively by an augmentation of its dimensions. The concept of duration that appears here has a Bergsonian origin, and differs radically from the present defined above, for here duration is defined as that which is "divided only by changing in nature" (B 40). Thus between variable presents there must be a difference in nature that operates in another dimension than that of the present. Or rather, difference passes between an unlimited number of dimensions, whereas the present is defined as an homogeneous unidimensional continuity.

Deleuze shows how Bergson is obliged to have another field intervene that doubles the present. The present is conceivable only if it is simultaneously present and past, for otherwise we can't explain how a present can become past when it is supplanted by another. The passing of the present is thinkable only in light of this paradoxical coexistence of the past with the present. The field invoked here is not that of a past relative to a present: in it coexists every dimension capable of being actualized, and not merely those which were formerly present. It is not a receptacle in which all the old presents could accumulate; on the contrary, it conditions the difference and substitution of presents, it is the very field of difference in kind. It is an absolute past, and must be called a *pure* or *virtual past* if we are to distinguish it from empirical memories belonging to representation ("a past that never was present, since it was not formed 'after'"—DR 82).

Succession therefore refers to the *actualization* of a new dimension (hence the force-time relation). Certainly, the same flow of duration being given, the successive dimensions are accumulated in a memory whose contents are always expanding; but this accumulation presupposes in principle something else entirely: the relations between the dimensions themselves, the field of the virtual past in which these coexist. A new present is certainly an "extra dimension," but it is first of all an *other* dimension. The parts of the virtual past—pure dimensions of time—are not memories or images of a past experience, and the different presents do not refer to contents of experience: each present actualizes a temporal dimension the consistency of which is purely *intensive* (level, degree . . . or else plane, point of view). And as we shall see, there is no reason here to suspect some sort of substantializaton of time, since intensity is said only of bodies. Time is the intensity *of* bodies.

If we ask why Deleuze invokes a difference of intensity, the answer is that the difference of the past and the present is intelligible only at this price. To neglect the intensive temporal difference (pure difference, stripped of all resemblance, and consequently not subjected to an identity that subsumes it) would reduce each of our lives to an alignment of facts within an homogeneous and continuous present, from birth to death. In this way we miss the ruptures that are not only material and spatial, but profoundly temporal, and which are factually signaled when one no longer recognizes oneself in who he or she used to be. The concept of the event requires this intensive conception of time. Inversely, an encounter draws the one whom it catches by surprise into a new temporal dimension that breaks with the previous one.

Time is pure change, since its dimensions do not resemble each other whatsoever; and succession is not illusory, it is simply its least profound aspect. Between two dimensions there is a disjunction, a relation of incompossibility (according to Leibniz's term): the presence of the one makes the other plunge into the past. Two dimensions cannot be actualized at the same time "in" the same subject. Actualization transports the subject from one to the other, causing him to change or become, passing irreversibly from one period to another or—in the same period and by virtue of the plurality of lines— from one *hour* [*heure*]¹ of existence to another. Each dimension is individuating, which is why time is *actually* [*actuellement*] successive: the coexistence of dimensions is incompatible with the conditions of actualization or of existence, which are those of individuation (which as we shall see does not prevent a persistence of the virtual in the actual: individuality is always already a transindividuality).

What results from this? Time, pure change, is the passage from one dimension to another (becoming). It merges with its dimensions, which it reunites virtually; better still, each dimension exists only in its difference from all the others. What, therefore, is time? Absolute difference, the immediate placing-into-relation of heterogeneities, without a subjacent or subsuming conceptual identity. Time is nothing properly speaking, it consists only of differences, and in the referral of one difference to another. It has neither center nor pole of identity (Deleuze credits Resnais with having discovered this in cinema, while Welles still saw in death an ultimate center: C2 116–19). A pluridimensional or intensive conception of time such as this is vertiginous. There is no reason why the present dimension should have any privilege over the others, or constitute a center or an anchoring; the ego bursts into distinct periods that each take turns occupying the center, without an identity ever being able to become fixed (and death does not order anything, nor decide anything). The same applies horizontally, if we consider that a life is unfolded on many planes at once: in depth, the dimensions of time, successive or simultaneous, are related to one another in a "non-chronological" and non-successive manner.

These relations are non-causal correspondences, in the sense we invoked above regarding formally or qualitatively distinct "cuts," which renders every causal explanation trivial and stupid. "What happened?"—the false problem is to invoke causes, to seek an explanation, which is certainly possible at the level of the material effectuation of the event, but powerless before the irreducible hiatus of heterogeneities. Incidentally, even for purely physical phenomena it is banal to say that causality explains nothing, and that this is not its role (which doesn't necessarily imply that we have to seek a superior mode of explication). It must be understood that Deleuze is not opposing this correspondence of events to causality. He is highlighting the fact that causality does not account for the heterogeneity of what takes place. Time puts causality in crisis at a more profound level: beneath causality there reigns an irreducible chance that does not contradict it, but renders it ontologically secondary (even the regularity of a relation does not prevent it from being fundamentally irrational, since heterogeneous terms have only an exterior relation, through their difference).

Multiplicity: Difference and Repetition

Time is the relation between heterogeneous dimensions. These dimensions are concurrent, by virtue of their individuating power: each actualizes itself by excluding the others (from a given individual), but all are time, differences of time, or even differences as such, insofar as time is only pure difference. They all return to the Same thing, "at different levels" (DR 83). We cannot speak of them as numerically distinct things, but only as differenciations of a single paradoxical thing, never given in itself and never identical to itself. Time is the difference of differences, or what relates differences to one another. It is *internal difference*, difference "in itself": something that exists only by differenciating itself and which has no other identity than to differ from itself, no other nature than to divide itself by changing nature—a thing having no "self" except in and by this division [*écartèlement*]. Internal difference? Only the form of pure change can correspond to this concept, which has the great merit of defining time without bestowing on it an essence or an identity. Time is at once the Anonymous and the Individuating: impersonal and unqualifiable, yet the source of all identity and all quality.

Of internal difference, one can say that "there is *other* without there being several" (B 42). Certainly, it is hard to see how we can maintain the unity of that which ceaselessly changes in nature—if not verbally—since nothing is conserved of its identity. One may object that no object is actually intended here, insofar as that which changes has no identity. Yet this is the very nature of difference, and is precisely what is sought since, according to Hamlet's expression, time *out of joint*[2] has no cardinal points (*cardo* = joint) capable of marking it out and imposing on it a regular curve, the form of a circle. Time floats in the void, itself void (DR 88-9; CC 27-8).

"There is *other* without there being several" also means "numerically one, formally multiple" (EPS 65-6; DR 40, 300-4; LS 59). Internal difference is neither one nor multiple: it is a *multiplicity*. Under this concept Deleuze puts forward a mode of immanent unity, the immediate identity of the one and the multiple. There is multiplicity when the unity of the diverse does not require the mediation of a genre or a subsuming conceptual identity (B Ch. 2; DR 182; ATP 32–3, 482–8; F 13–14). Difference must be the only relation that unites these terms, and it must be a real relation: a relative resemblance would fall back on a superior identity. It is possible to speak of Difference [*LA différence*], where this means differences mutually differenciating themselves, and renewing themselves in each other; but can difference appear as a link or a relation, as a positive connection? Can we think a strictly relational or differential interiority, an inside *of* the outside? Such a relation would be entirely *virtual*, since the differences could not actually coexist in the same individual. It is therefore a question of the consistency proper to the virtual, between nothingness and the actual.

What remains to be understood is how difference can be united [*reunir*], and how the multiple can be called *a* multiplicity. It is because difference thus defined has a correlate: *repetition*. Difference [*LA différence*] ceaselessly returns in each of its differenciations, in each of its differences. The paradox is immediately visible: difference repeats itself by differenciating itself, and yet never repeats identity (such an idea would obviously be absurd within the field of representation, where repetition is confused with the reproduction of the same; this makes it all the more delicate to think). The differenciation of difference has as its correlate a repetition that diverges or that rings hollow, and *Difference and Repetition* is the logic of intensive multiplicity as a concept of time. The difference-dimension returns each time, but it returns as differing, thus at another level, on another plane, in another dimension. The Deleuzian interpretation of Nietzsche's eternal return rests on this correlation of difference and repetition (hence a very peculiar relation between the past and the future, between memory and belief).

Difference consequently no longer appears only as an intensive dimension but as a point of view (on other dimensions): it is reciprocal *implication*. Difference returns in each of the differences; each difference is therefore all the others, notwithstanding their difference [*à la différence près*], and constitutes a certain point of view on all the others which in themselves are also points of view. The passage from "being" to "being a point of view" is made possible here by the displacement [*décalage*] associated with this paradoxical repetition: each difference is repeated, but at a distance, in another mode, at another level than its own. Each difference virtually envelops its distance from all the others, and itself consists of an ensemble of distances (point of view). For a difference to repeat is for it to reprise at a distance, and thus to open a perspective on . . .

From the idea of difference in itself we passed to its divergent repetition from difference to difference, and finally to the repetition of each of these differences by one another (differences that are mutually enveloped according to their distances). These two repetitions are one and the same, for Difference [*LA différence*] exists only in the differences that differenciate it, and repetition proceeds only from one of these differences to another. The divergent, irregular, alternating character of repetition leads to the idea of a reciprocal implication. For Deleuze there is no confrontation between things, but rather a mutual envelopment, and an unequal one at that, since the terms in play are heterogeneous points of view. Contradiction, the negative, is only the effect of the difference between points of view—the shadow projected by the sign, through which a heterogeneous point of view announces itself ("Other").

This logic of multiplicity destroys the traditional alternative between the same and the other. What happens when we suppress the identical? The Same—or the One—is rediscovered *after the fact*, as the positive effect of difference rather than the presupposed common term between merely relative differences. It stems from a play of positive differences, where differences are always included within one another. Its consistency is no longer that of the identical but of distance, reciprocal implication. It now designates the *univocal*, or the possibility of treating the manifold of what exists as universal self-modification (Nature), where each being implicates all the others by responding in its manner to difference as pure question. And this question is certainly not "what is being?" but "*who*—or how—is being?" For Deleuze, difference is not even being, since it merges with *becoming*, and since becoming does not go from one being to another, but takes place in the *in-between* (cf. below, Ch. 5). Deleuze shows how immanence is affirmed in the history of philosophy through the theme of univocity: formal difference occurs in being and no longer between numerically distinct beings (DR 39 ff.). According to the formulation cited earlier, being is formally diverse and numerically one. Henceforth difference of quality or of nature refers to intensity: not that everything refers back to the Same, where there are only differences of degree; rather every difference [*les différents*] (qualities, species, modes of existence) resonates at a distance in all its heterogeneity, and is mutually repeated as "degrees of Difference" itself (B 93).

What authorizes us to speak of Difference [*LA différence*], of Multiplicity [*LA multiplicité*]? Divergent and therefore enveloping repetition, as the immediate unity of the multiple or consistency of the univocal (the manifold no longer has to be unified, subsumed in advance under an identical and common concept assuring a minimum of resemblance for the differences, or a minimum convergence of points of view). As the product of repetition rather than an original identity, the Same is the self of difference. Consequently, it may be called "internal": difference that differenciates "itself," interiority without identity, inside of the outside.

Implication is the fundamental logical movement of Deleuze's philosophy. In nearly every one of his books, it is only ever a question of "things" that are rolled up and unrolled, enveloped and are developed, folded and unfolded, implicated and explicated, as well as complicated. But implication is the fundamental theme because it appears twice in the system of the fold: *complication* is an implication in oneself, *explication* an implication in something else. Together they form a logic of expression. It must be specified that expression here has nothing to do with a process of externalization beginning from an inside. The contrary would even be the case. The Deleuzian conception of subjectivity rests on the idea of an inside of the outside, an interiorization *of* the exterior, in the double sense of the genitive (there is no presupposed interiority: we must not lose sight of the repetition at a distance in which envelopment consists).

For now it will suffice to indicate the *raison d'être* of the implicative theme: the problem of relations is posed at the level of intensities, and the relationship between one intensity and another, between one dimension and another, cannot be one of contiguity or of juxtaposition, but must be one of implication. Two temperatures or two speeds are not added together; one temperature is not composed of other temperatures, but envelops others that envelop it as well, and the same goes for speeds (DR 237; ATP 31). A period in someone's life is not composed of anterior periods, even if it reprises them in its own way (it "does not divide itself" into them "without changing in nature"). One can certainly say that a life continues, but its way of continuing is to replay itself entirely on another plane, so that beyond the recollections [*les souvenirs*] that neurotically fix us to what has happened, memory [*la memoire*] on the contrary registers irreducible distances that no longer spare the present, but put the latter in perspective. The idea of destiny thus takes on an immanent meaning: for Deleuze, "a life" is a condensation or complication of periods in a single and same Event, a system of non-causal echoes or correspondences (DR 83; LS 170; ATP 262–3; C2 100). Destiny is like the dice throw: ontologically one, formally multiple.

Thus "differences are not composed of differences of the same order but imply series of heterogeneous terms . . . An intensive quantity may be divided, but not without changing its nature" (DR 237). Pure difference is intensive, for intensive differences do not participate in any common identical genre capable of guaranteeing them a minimal resemblance. Between two intensive quantities there is only heterogeneity or difference in kind. Implication therefore appears as exterior relation in itself, as the proper logical movement to describe relations in a field of exteriority. A philosophy of the Outside is a philosophy of Implication.

The system still seems to be static and to exclude encounters, since all relations are already saturated by reciprocal virtual implication. How can Deleuze see a philosophy of "mobility" here (DR 254, 257, 302)? It could be considered a hesitation: sometimes differences are "all communicating," other times they must "enter into communication" in order to have an encounter (for example DR 222 and 257; ATP 238 and 239, or even 233). But this objection could only make sense if Deleuze had moved from virtual to the actual, from time to the body, as from a transcendental principle to its consequence, by proposing the metaphysical task of deducing existence. Yet he does not ask why there are bodies—he asks if it is possible to account for their effectuations and their relations without invoking the virtual, which is to say the process of actualization. The question is the following: in the name of the concrete, of existence and of becoming, is it not necessary to have recourse to a perspectivism of intensive dimensions, and to the concept of a necessarily virtual heterogeneity? Is this not the only means of introducing and of thinking *difference in existence*, as the divergence in the world?

> In fact, a lot has happened, outside as well as inside: the war, the financial crash, a certain growing older, the depression, illness, the flight of talent. But all these noisy accidents already have their outright effects; and they would not be sufficient in themselves had they not dug their way down to something of a wholly other nature which, on the contrary, they reveal only at a distance and when it is too late—the silent crack. "Why have we lost peace, love and health one after the other?" There was a silent, imperceptible crack, at the surface, a unique surface Event. It is as if it were suspended or hovering over itself, flying over its own field. The real difference is not between the inside and the outside, for the crack is

neither internal nor external, but is rather at the frontier. It is imperceptible, incorporeal, and ideational. (LS 154–5, in reference to Fitzgerald)

The Deleuzian decision is as follows: there is no shortcut that can
enable us to do without the "abstract line" (the incorporeal or the
mind, beyond all representations) that doubles the effectuations or
the mixtures of bodies and passes between dimensions; no shortcut
can avoid the virtual, even and above all in a philosophy of immanence. This is how Deleuze poses the problem of immanence: the
unity of the one and the multiple, "pluralism = monism," univocity—
the proposed solution being the concept of virtual or intensive multiplicity (DR 300–4; EPS 178; ATP 20). The virtual is not a second
world, it *does not exist outside of bodies* even though it does not
resemble their actuality. It is not the ensemble of possibilities, but
that which bodies implicate, that of which bodies are the actualization. The abstraction begins once bodies are separated from the
virtual they implicate, retaining only the disincarnated appearance of
a pure actuality (representation).

    Henceforth, the "communication" of differences is no longer the
object of a dilemma. For Deleuze, 1. bodies implicate the time that
they explicate, or that is actualized in the spaces-times they deploy
(milieus); 2. the time implicated in bodies is implicated in itself, and
complicates the points of view in which it is divided ("all communicating" differences); 3. mixtures of bodies effectuate certain relations
of time, certain coexistences of points of view, which insist at the
limit of bodies as mind (the "putting-into-communication" of differences, which is to say of relations). Bodies implicate what they explicate, or explicate what they implicate: they are signs, and lose their
semiotic potential only in representation. The latter "separates them
from what they can do" and retains from them only a pure actuality
in which intensity is cancelled out, a presence without the presence
of the objective-explicit (PS 92–3; LS 280 ff.: "this objective power of
hesitation in the body"). Time communicates with itself, but does not
become sensible, or does not "enter" into communication with itself,
except by encountering the different fluxes of duration that incarnate
it (mixtures of bodies).

Aion and Chronos

Let us return to the three temporal modes. We may notice that the
second (the virtual past) is less the complement than the concurrent

of the first (the present of action), insofar as becoming ceaselessly eludes the present: "Chronos wants to die." Two distinct conceptions of duration collide: first, that of the present of action, which is periodic and seemingly immobile in its circular perpetuity; second, that which "does not divide without changing in nature" (B 40, 42), a perpetual becoming that undoes the circle, stretching it out along a line without contour, an "abstract line." The complementarity is thus rather between the second mode (the virtual past of dimensions) and the third (the affirmation of the future of eternal return). The repetition of each difference-dimension in all the others causes us to pass imperceptibly from one to another, and the Deleuzian eternal return is nothing other than the affirmation of the intensive virtual multiplicity of time, of the reciprocal implication of differences. No dimension functions as the center of time, but each returns in all the others, and itself causes them to return. Each is therefore still a kind of circle, but one that is de-centered in relation to the others, and which doesn't coincide with itself in its return (since it returns in the others). We are far from the "insipid monocentricity of circles" (DR 263) characterizing the Hegelian dialectic. The circle repeats itself in becoming other circles, and thus repeats only the difference of the circles: from one circle to another, or to still others, runs the abstract line or *line of flight*, which does not create an outline but is rolled up by being unrolled from one circle to another. To affirm the present in its absolute chance—like a dimension plucked as a number is from a hat, where we ourselves are drawn in the same way, and certainly not "once and for all"—is to affirm chance "each time" "for all times."

There is a rupture between the first temporal mode (the periodic present) and the two others. Deleuze constantly highlights this alternative: one cannot simultaneously act and seize the event as such. When the samurai defending a village asks himself what he is doing there, "what is a samurai today, in this moment in History?," or when a fugitive or mortally wounded soldier sees himself fleeing or dying, he experiences an urgency higher than that of the situation, he asks useless questions that paralyze action but which are nevertheless of great importance to it. He ceases to act in order to see, but recognizes nothing in what he sees. The world has ceased to be recognizable. They become "seers," perfect "idiots" (LS 101; C1 189–92; C2 5–6, 128, 176—we shall see in the final chapter that if "becoming-active" means anything, it is precisely in a similar crisis of action).

Everything happens as if the event is played out in two temporal modes at once: the present of its *effectuation* in a state of affairs, or its incarnation in a "mixture of bodies"; but also a paradoxical eternity where something is *ineffectuable*, something *incorporeal* overflows and survives the effectuation. Deleuze's constant thesis is this: the event is not reducible to its effectuation. Doubtless, the event could never be effectuated were there not the continuity of a homogeneous present; yet when the effectuation has come to an end we find ourselves in another present succeeding the former. The event has been conjured away. This is because in itself it has no present, and strangely makes the future (not yet here and nevertheless already here) coincide with the past (still present and nevertheless already past). Such is the paradox of becoming:

> When I say "Alice becomes larger," I mean that she becomes larger than she was. By the same token, however, she becomes smaller than she is now. Certainly, she is not bigger and smaller at the same time. She is larger now; she was smaller before. But it is at the same moment that one becomes larger than one was and smaller than one becomes. This is the simultaneity of a becoming whose characteristic is to elude the present. (LS 1)

The event is located in a time without duration, paradoxically empty, in which nothing is happening. Despite its being pure change, the event is static, and is only perceptible after the fact—or else during its effectuation if the latter is long—in an interminable waiting, in which the not-yet and the already remain stuck to one another. The event as such is always happening, it is impossible for it to finish. Happening (*evenire*) is what never ceases, despite its instantaneity. In the event, the different moments of time are not successive but simultaneous.

Thus the ternary schema becomes more complicated. It is not only the present, but Chronos as a whole (the succession of presents) that vacillates. The event is deployed under two temporal modes at once, Chronos and *Aion*. The present could not account for itself, since in its claim to continue it does not in itself pass. Logically, it could pass only by virtue of a pure past (the virtual and its actualization). But the course of the explanation has led to the subversion of what was supposed to be explained, and has opened onto something entirely other than a present that passes: the interminable instantaneity of the event (hence the word *Aion*, borrowed from the Stoics). The instant does not pass, for the future and the past coincide within it. This is no longer the relative speed of variable presents or of milieus, but is now an absolute speed, instantaneous, a pure spatio-temporal differential which is thus no longer dependent upon a space to be traversed or a time to be determined. The distinction between Chronos and Aion can also be stated differently: time no longer measures movement, it is no longer the "number of movement." The relation of subordination is reversed, and it is now movement that is subordinated to time, to its heterogeneity, to the infinity of its dimensions (DR 89; C2 271; CC 27–8). The event is no longer what takes place *in* time, as a simple effectuation or movement; it is the transcendental synthesis of the irreversible, which gathers and distributes the before and the after on either side of a static caesura, the Instant. It is from this that succession is derived, as the "empirical course of time" (C2 271, 272–3).

Finally, the distinction between Aion and Chronos, between the event and its effectuation, escapes any pure and simple dualism of mind and body, for the physical effectuations already implicate that which differs from them in nature (the event). Mind is really distinct from body, but does not constitute an originally separate or independent order of reality: it is sensibility itself (or the affect), or rather its incorporeal and ineffectuable dimension, the momentary virtual coexistence that it implies. The mind emerges at the surface of bodies, it is the event within what happens. The apparent dualism of mind and body is only derived from the fact that language—itself made possible (as distinct from the body) by this status of the event— is reduced by its everyday employment to an exchange of information or opinions that installs thought in what appear to be separate milieus (we will return to this). We should therefore not say that the mind exists, but that it *insists* at the limit of bodies (and of the brain), that it *haunts* a pure surface, eminently fragile.

"The depth of the mind" is first of all "delirium . . . change and indifference" (ES 23): an intensive chaos comprised of evanescent sketches, fleeting sensations, non-related vibrations. For the mind to *become subject*, requires that these sketches then be contracted, be conserved as "habits," and that the difference thereby produced not be equalized in the active representation of a milieu. The distinct-obscure glimmers of thought are produced in this precarious interval.

Notes

1. The peculiar use François Zourabichvili makes of this term, particularly in the following chapter, is somewhat difficult to translate into English. Another option would have been to translate *heure* as "moment in

time." However, as this would lose the stubborn insistence he confers on the term, which sounds strange even in the original French, I have opted instead for the slightly more awkward (but authentic) construction throughout—Trans.

2. In English in the original—Trans.

5

Becoming

Put into reflection?

✳ First, thought proved to be dependent upon an encounter, on the emergence of an exteriority: sense, implicated and explicated in the sign, put heterogeneous dimensions into contact. This was the transcendental hypothesis of a field of forces. But this field now merges with Time as internal difference or multiplicity, the complication of differences or irreducible intensive points of view. Not only must sense and time be related, but sense must be thought as time, or rather as a temporal relation. We have said that truth is inseparable from an *hour*, since it does not preexist the act of thinking, its revelation here and now. Now we must understand that it is itself an hour: what is revealed is nothing other than a relation of time. "Truth has

✳ an essential relation to time" (PS 15). "Every truth is a truth of time" (PS 94). The misinterpretation would be to think that Deleuze assigns a content to truth. The truth *of* time certainly does not mean "about time"; revelation is a presentation of time itself, in its multiplicity. Time is what is true, insofar as it presents itself. Truth is here thought as *becoming*, independently of all content.

A living person experiences successive presents that mark out the periods of his or her life, and which are not arranged end to end but constitute different planes, with leaps or ruptures from one to another: a life does not unfold from beginning to end in the present. Is it a question solely of events, of contents of time, rather than time itself? Certainly not, since the event implies a potentialization, an ordination of existence that fractures the apparently continuous duration into heterogeneous levels, and without which there would be no past. The facts that fill out our life take place in heterogeneous dimensions, and what is called an event is the passage from one dimension to another: an effectuation in bodies sufficiently singular to implicate an intensive mutation on the scale of a life (encounter, separation, etc.). To fall in love, or out of love, does not belong to any present. Beyond acts and feelings, these are temporal crises, subversions of the present from which the subject does not emerge unscathed or identical to who he was.

112

Deleuze underlines how much Bergson's conception of levels of the pure past differs in kind from recollections [*souvenirs*], which only represent effectuations. A dimension, a pure point of view or difference of intensity, should not be confused with the milieu derived from it, the "block of space-time" composing a periodic present. Each space-time envelops a temporal difference, each milieu is the actuality [*actualité*] or the accomplished development of a virtual dimension. The milieu *does not resemble* the pure intensity of which it is the actualization.

Signs 2: Habit, Disparity, Singularity

Let us return to the analysis of the concepts of habit and milieu. It was said that on one side habit faces an intensive dimension that belongs to it, and on the other the milieu that envelops this dimension. Through repetition, contraction produces a difference called habit, and this is nothing other than the *sign* (DR 73, 78). Contrary to the current sense of the word, habit here refers less to the faculty of reproducing the identical ("cadence-repetition," or melody) than to the harnessing or the "preservation" of a difference ("rhythm-repetition," or a *refrain*). Doubtless, in some ways it amounts to the same thing, as in the case of a song we have listened to so many times we no longer hear it or follow it: the second repetition is "only" the empirical representation of the first, the manner in which it appears to representation (DR 21). But it is precisely from the point of view of the second repetition, or of representation, that they return to the same, since this means only that they are related to the same object of representation (the piece of music).

Beneath the periodic and measurable present, we must consider the return of an intensity constituting the sign. In fact, the intensity does not last; a simple sketch or evanescent present, it tends toward 0, whatever its level may be. Such emergences would trap us in a pure chaos if the passive syntheses were not effectuated in us, contracting the vibrations and the recurrent instant of intensity. It is from out of these syntheses that the "actively represented repetition" emerges (DR 76), the living present or the milieu that converts the sensed sign into the urgency of a situation to which we must react (DR 78). To react is to interpret the sign, to develop it (DR 73). Every milieu or situation is therefore conditioned by a passive synthesis without which no reaction would be possible, for the body would undergo only a punctual excitation, a simple shock, an unrelated pulsation

113

("jolts that beat like arteries"—WP 201). The body clings to the milieu just as the mind clings to the *opinions* that constitute the milieu of thought, less in order to think than in order to act intellectual, i.e. to reflect (voluntary thought). Opinion submits ideas to a regulated sequence "following an order of space and time" (ibid),[1] and the false dualism of mind and body depends upon the installation of such milieus of thought. The eye has its milieus as well, optical milieus or *clichés*, where it is no longer a question of seeing but of recognizing and "rediscovering itself" (on clichés, see C1 208–end, and C2 20; see also FB 60). A milieu is precisely an order of conformity that we rely on in order to act: given identical conditions of experience, we expect that the same sensation will be reproduced. Consequently, habit induces an expectation, a presumption or a claim that converts the return of a difference into a reproduction of the same, and deploys the sensation within an active field of representation. An organ is nothing other than a recognized and therefore useful habit, so that the organism refers to a *body without organs* where the organs are sensed before being acted, where beneath their periodic and reproductive work the functions are so many constituent and individuating sensations. This "intense body" is not opposed to the organs but to the organism as the coordination of constituted forms. It consists in an incessant birth of emergent-evanescent organs (AO 323–31; ATP 6th Plateau; FB Ch. 7—the notion appeared in *The Logic of Sense*: 88, 351 fn., 198–9, 203, 224).

A milieu is the representation of a difference, of a temporal dimension that actualizes itself in a contraction. Let us take two examples from Proust. Combray was a milieu, and reappears much later as an originary world: "Combray reappears, not as it was or as it could be, but in a splendor which was never lived, like a pure past" (DR 85 and PS 12, 56, 60–1). The "in-itself of Combray" is an intensity, a sign that envelops a virtual world. Inversely, Albertine is not—or not yet—a milieu; she would become one if between her and the narrator an ordered conjugal relation subordinated to cardinal points were to be established. Which is why Albertine is so interesting: as long as the explicative fervor of the narrator (action) does not triumph over his capacity to be derailed by her (passive synthesis), she is pure rhythm in his life, the insistent return of difference rather than the reproduction of identical traits submitted to the routine of recognition. Contemplative habit is not routine, even if the latter can conceal it and eventually defeat it, as rhythmic inequality is defeated by melody.

What is this inequality enveloped in sensation? This question is linked to that of the plurality of lines and times within one "same" subject. To the question "who (or what) am I?," Deleuze speaks of habits, contractions that engender expectations and claims: I am what I have, being is a having. I am what I have—in other words, I am inseparable from something else whose prehension constitutes me: I am so long as I prehend. From this stems the retrieval of a Plotinian conceptual movement: turning back toward what one "proceeds" from in order to "contemplate" it (such that, at the limit, we are ourselves contemplations):

> We do not contemplate ourselves, but we exist only in contemplating— that is to say, in contracting that from which we come . . . and we are all Narcissus in virtue of the pleasure (auto-satisfaction) we experience in contemplating, even though we contemplate things quite apart from ourselves . . . We must always first contemplate something else . . . in order to be filled with an image of ourselves. (DR 74–5)

The mechanistic objection would be that in order to contemplate we must first be, and not the reverse—and that consequently this means we must be a subject. But Deleuze goes back prior to receptivity (or the capacity to perceive), toward to an originary sensation that constitutes it (DR 78–9). Moreover, it will be noted that *Cinema 1: The Movement-Image* establishes a difference in nature between affect and perception, where the latter is associated with action. The perception of a milieu presupposes a preliminary contraction of its elements, even if the latter remains implicit or concealed by representation, or by the urgency of the situation.[2]

What is this originary sensation? Contemplation is related to the affect, which implies a relation of forces. To contemplate is to capture one or several forces, as a tissue becomes an eye when it succeeds in capturing light. Capture [*capter*] is not the same as excitation, since it is a matter of relating excitations, of making a principle of them, of contracting their successive vibration. To capture is a habit, and habit is the positive product of a relation of forces. To contemplate, to contract, to inhabit is what characterizes the subjugated force that conserves the evanescent, that fastens a relation to it rather than letting it escape. A force is inseparable from its relation to at least one other force. Passive force, *habitus*, contemplates the relation from which it proceeds, conserving it. The objection does not appear to hold.

Sensation envelops "a constitutive difference of level, a plurality of constituting domains" (FB 27). *Disparity* is the name Deleuze gives to this system in which heterogeneous dimensions communicate, and which conditions every event: nothing would appear, nothing would exist, if there had not been unequal relations, if the calculations of "God" had always been correct (DR 222). A "thing" exists insofar as it appears, not necessarily to a human consciousness but as a force that affirms itself by exerting itself on something else (the power to affect) or else by capturing something else (the power to be affected). On what does the world and all that exists hang [*tient*]? . . . What is the *consistency* of the world, if we are to understand that what appears to us in representation presupposes a sensation, an affect, or that the perceptual givens presuppose an appearance, a difference "by which the given is given" (DR 222)? The world we represent to ourselves is formed in relations of forces, it consists—in the strong sense—in an overlapping of variable affects that are the events of Nature. A body is not a thing, or a substance, and does not really have a contour; it exists only insofar as it affects and is affected, it feels and is felt. What is a body if not a certain manner of pressing, of resisting, of opacifying, etc. (FB 48)? Representation disincarnates the body: we do not give form to the body without contorting it, stripping it of its outside, without situating it in an exterior, rather than implicating it. Representation isolates the body, separates it from what it can do; the contour-line designates angels rather than bodies. Likewise, the face takes on a body only and becomes visible only by effacing itself, by looking away, and never in the face-to-face (ATP 123 ff., 170; C1 101). In other words, the body does not hang on [*tient à*] anything: it is not, it only *insists* (FB 43–4). The regular homogeneous world of representation envelops *singularities* on the basis of which it deploys itself, and as diversity. Deleuze consequently indicates the role of sensation within science. There is no science without "partial observers" installed in the "vicinity of singularities," yet this does not render it subjective since they are "points of view on the things themselves." Science is itself perspectivist in the special sense defined by Deleuze: it does not merely arrive at a relative truth, but at a "truth of the relative" (WP 24–7).

What is a singularity? Singularity is distinguished from the individual or the atomic in that it is ceaselessly divided on either side of a difference in intensity that it envelops. Since singularity is a motif widely invoked in contemporary philosophy these days, it is important to specify its Deleuzian meaning, which is original and precise. The concept of singularity is based on the notion of the "differential

relation" or "disparate," which avoids any simple reduction to the
atomic, and consequently the confusion of the singular with the individual. Singularities correspond to the values of differential relations
(DR 176, 208–9, 278) or the distributions of potentials (DR 117–18,
220–1, 278). The concept has an origin that is at once mathematical
and physical. It comes from the theory of differential relations (and
from the role of "singular points" in the search for solutions), and
the study of "metastable" systems. But it is applied without metaphor
to the existential and even ontological field, since time itself implies
differences of intensity. In Deleuze's conception of it, singularity testifies to the paradox of difference, of being simultaneously one and
multiple, a "point-fold" (L 14). Singularity is at once *pre-individual*
and *individuating* (DR 246–7). Individuals themselves are not singular, even though they are constituted "in the vicinity" of certain singularities and therefore are in an originary relation with something
else (DR 117 ff.; LS 111; ATP 257–8, 262, 369 ff., 407 ff.). From
this follows an immanent definition of the individual according to its
affects rather than its form or its separated figure. To what am I sensitive? By what am I affected? It is only by experimenting that I can
come to know my own singularities (ATP 257; SPP 123–4).

Let us return to the constituent sensation, to the individuating
contraction. We now confront a latent dualism of active and passive
forces, as well as the difficulty of making the two ways of thinking the sign, or the two schemas of the disparate, coincide: forces
and points of view. Two differences enter into communication and
resonate together, on either side of their difference. Each envelops
the other, repeats it or replays it on its own level. The reciprocity
between them, even if it is unequal, is nonetheless a full reciprocity,
and it is therefore not enough to induce a cleavage between active
and passive. What is more, each difference is alternately implicating and implicated, which is to say affected and affecting. The only
logical issue is how to apply the cleavage to difference itself, and to
consider each difference as a system of action and reaction, the relation between differences establishing itself in both directions between
the activity of one and the passivity of the other. "At the same time,
each force has the power to affect (others) and to be affected (by
others again), so that each force implies power relations" (F 71):
force is divided, it is comprised of both an active and a passive pole.

We are now in a position to identify the circumstances under
which a point of view becomes reactive and reverses the hierarchy
at the center of the relation. It becomes reactive when it is isolated,

deprived of distances and perspectives (or—in another formulation—when a singularity is cut off from its prolongations). Force is thus "separated from what it can do" (NP 23, 112), it loses its mobility, its faculty of passing through other points of view and being affected by them: in short, its ability to become. The severed point of view now acts as a pole of identity or of absolute recognition, an affective minimum or zero intensity (a "black hole"); all that it is not becomes nothing, and is negated. There remains only a scrap of rage like a last glimmer, like the damned souls for Leibniz, "hardened in a single fold that it will not unfurl" (L 71–4). Power now relates to the act as to a suffering. It is at the same moment that unactivated force is condemned to react, and that its affects are crushed and reduced to ressentiment. Finally, active and reactive are the two poles of an essentially passive, sensitive force, the aptitude to affect being derived from the power to be affected (to love not as a result of being loved, but of sensing or being sensitive). Force perceives and experiences before acting, and introduces an effect in another only in accordance with what it experiences. Is it capable of *giving*, or only of competition (C2 141–2)? In any event, it is never violence that affects, since violence in itself is only ever terrorizing or paralyzing. The affect always issues from a force that affirms itself and from the will that it expresses, even if it is negative (will to violence)—effective violence is only ever the concomitant.

The dilemma of forces and points of view is therefore solved; however, the idea of a contemplative individuation presents yet another logical difficulty. Habit consists in the capture of a point of view (a sign); yet if it is true that an affect or a relation of forces is the encounter between two heterogeneous points of view, then this encounter presupposes that the capturing force already occupies a point of view. A prior individuality therefore seems to be presupposed. How can we avoid the problem of an infinite regression here? The rigorous consequence of contemplative individuation must be drawn: a subject appears only in the disjunction of two points of view, the disparate is in principle prior to their separation. Force becomes subject only by contracting a habit, in passing from one point of view to another: an isolated point of view is non-sensible [*n'est pas sensible*], in the double-sense of the term.[3] We are contemplative habits, but our contemplations take place between two milieus, at the point where something becomes sensible. We are born, we consist and become sensitive only *in the middle* [*au milieu*]. Origins and destinations are only illusory effects of representation that emerge once the affect has faded away. The event is always in the middle, and we appear as things only in its afterglow. This also shows how *ambiguous* the subject is (LS 114). Beneath the constituted cogito invested in his properties there is an "I inhabit" or an "I feel" that merges with them and with the points of view that they implicate: there is no "I feel" that is not an "I feel *that I am becoming-other*." Constituent habit is passage, transition.

Contemplative becomings are the very consistency of our existence, or what enables us to distinguish something in it, what ensures that salient or remarkable points as well as reliefs and singularities glimmer in it, rather than an undifferentiated night (the rest is action, the routine exploitation of a milieu). The affect is by definition interesting: the sign, or what which forces thought—*desire*. What is desire for Deleuze? Neither lack nor spontaneity (D 89, 97). Desire is local and singular, and merges with the contemplations themselves, these violent signs that draw the subject into a becoming-other and forge within him a will that seeks their return and their explication. Desire is itself a *passive synthesis*, rather than an empty drive seeking to exteriorize itself. It begins outside ("the Outside where all desires come from" (D 97), born from an encounter. The interior pressure, the claim related to the contemplative habit, is secondary in relation to the encounter; it refers to an impersonal will conquered in the encounter and which the subject obeys, a "One wants" that demands the return of the sign. Desire refers first of all to a joy in difference or in the affect (sense/sensation), a joy in discovery and not in relief, a joy in *learning* that wants its own return (PS 7; on the relation between desire and sense, cf. LS, 30th Series; AO 109; ATP 256–8). Desire is interpreted and lived as lack (or pleasure as the suppression of the desire-lack) only when we mistake the effect for the cause, as in the dialectical inversion. Desire is a *machine*, it is inseparable from a connection, from a variable assemblage of composing heterogeneities producing the affect (D 89, 97, 99–100, 103–5; ATP 154–5).

Disjunctive Synthesis and Ethical Difference

Heterogeneity, or the divergence of points of view, is affirmed as such only in the course of a becoming: each point of view originally presupposes at least one other point of view with which it is in relation. Only an encounter can make the points of view appear in their respective and constituent difference. A point of view is apprehended as what it is—pure difference—only in its difference from other points of view. Alone it is only a subjective manner of representing the world. Representation equalizes points of view and preserves only a relative divergence in relation to a common object seen from diverse angles. What renders the difference of points of view sensible is difference, disparity, the sign. Sensation (or the affect) presupposes this disparity, and the concrete emergence of such a point of view refers to such a system. A point of view becomes sensible only in its difference from at least one other point of view. Thus we have a new reason to state that every milieu always already presupposes at least one other, and appears only from out of its distance from the latter.

The disparate presides over differenciation. In what sense is there at the same time a becoming here? Each of the two points of view becomes sensible out of its difference from the other, but also at the same time by passing into the other, since the coexistence of points of view is a mutual envelopment (difference as a positive relation). The disparate puts representation into flight, and the difference between points of view traces a line of flight. A subject is born at the heart of the system, one that is ambiguous and immediately divided, since the distance that resonates in it is doubled and unequal. The subject is a coming-and-going [va-et-vient], a there-and-back [aller-et-retour], a dissymmetrical "survey" (WP 211). A point of view affirms itself by differentiating itself from another, and this process itself presupposes that it passes into the other, or becomes other "at a different level." The process of differentiation therefore refers to a *zone of indiscernibility* where points of view exchange places and pass into one another (C2 69–71, 81, 203; CC 71). The disparate is "distinct-obscure," which is also to say "distinct but indiscernible" (C2 70), "differentiated without being differenciated" (DR 214). It is a non-localizable liaison (DR 113, translation modified; C2 153). One does not know "where something ends, where something else begins" (C2 154), as in negotiations where "you do not know whether they are still part of the war or the beginning of peace" (N prefatory note). Here we rediscover Aion, and the insoluble overlapping of two questions: what happened (infinite speed of a result)?, what is going to happen (infinite slowness of an anticipation)? In the transition between perspectives we do not become sensitive without at the same time and through the same process becoming *imperceptible*. And yet it is in this way that we distinguish ourselves, that we are distinguished, that we attain a "proper name" and become "someone." "Loving those who are like this: when they enter a room they are not persons, characters, or subjects, but an atmospheric variation, a change of hue, an imperceptible molecule, a discreet population, a fog or a cloud of droplets" (D 66).

Deleuze's most profound idea is perhaps this: difference is just as much communication, contagion of heterogeneities; in other words, that a divergence never erupts without a reciprocal contamination of points of view. "Disjunction [is] no longer a means of separation. Incompossibility is now a means of communication . . . The communication of events replaces the exclusion of predicates" (LS 174). The conceptual encounter of the Outside and of Implication, the *in*-determination of time as complicated exteriority or internal difference, leads to the concept of *disjunctive synthesis* as the very nature of relation (Deleuze sometimes says "inclusive disjunction"; CC 110, 153–4, 156). To connect is always to communicate on either side of a distance, by the very heterogeneity of terms. An effective encounter is certainly not fusional—a "politeness" is always required, an art of distances (neither too close, nor too far).[4] The indiscernibility of points of view does not amount to an homogenization, as with the disparates found in physics which tend toward an equal redistribution once they enter into relation: the disparate makes points of view indiscernible, not indistinct.

The key idea is therefore that points of view do not diverge without mutually implicating each other, without each "becoming" the other in an unequal exchange that does not amount to a mere permutation. The idea is derived from a concept of multiplicity according to which a pure difference has with others only a relation of difference, and which is only affirmed as such precisely at a distance from them. A point of view affirms itself or becomes sensible only by measuring the distance that separates it from the others, by going all the way to the end of this distance, by passing into the other points of view. If it is true that one point of view only actualizes itself by eclipsing [*faisant passer*] another—since two points of view cannot coexist in actuality—the process nevertheless implicates the virtual coexistence of points of view, their envelopment and mutual reprisal: "point of view on a point of view" (LS 175), in both directions.

Virtual is here opposed not to the real but to the actual (DR 208). Virtual coexistence must be fully real since it conditions the affect, which is the very consistency of what exists. Yet how can this coexistence be experienced if there is no subject other than an individuated one? In other words, what is the consistency of the "larval subject" referred to above? The answer is contained in the recent notion of the *crystal of time*, which specifies the nature of the distinct-indiscernible

(C2 Ch. 4). It is not only points of view that cease to be discernible in becoming, but the very duality of the actual and the virtual. Deleuze describes an "image with two sides, actual *and* virtual" (C2 68), where the distinction between the actual and the virtual subsists but has become unassignable (e.g. in the cinema of Ophuls, Renoir, Fellini, and Visconti—cf. also CC 63). The actual does not disappear in favor of the virtual, for such a situation would be unlivable; it has, however, become unlocalizable. One thus sees how virtual coexistence can be experienced: in the incessant permutation of the actual and the virtual. The subject persists, but one no longer knows *where*. The subject of becoming is said to be larval because it is undecidable and problematic.

The possibility of conserving the affect as such and not merely its afterglow, of rendering it incessant, and consequently of attaining the interminable empty time of Aion—this defines the *practical* problem: creation, of art or of philosophy (even though Deleuze accords a creative component to science, owing to the fact that it "confronts chaos," he shows that it does not have as its object the conservation of the event). A philosophy is not a point of view, nor does it have as its goal the agreement of points of view. On the contrary, it disjoins them; it traverses distances and creates the signs capable of conserving them as such (concepts). The same is true of art, which does not represent the world, but disjoins it in its own way through percepts and affects. The thinker is not enlightened by a natural light; he disjoins necessarily, but disjunction does not produce a black hole so much as the light stuck to the black ("distinct-obscure")—glimmer, flash or a will-o'-the-wisp. Not autism and its collapse, but schizophrenia as a *process* or becoming (DR 28, 118, 146–7, 194–6; AO 5 and 75–8).

"A point of view on a point of view": such a statement, absurd within the world of representation, takes on a meaning at the virtual level. Points of view do not touch, and are not contiguous. There is no virtual panorama of the ensemble of points of view, for this would preserve all the traits of representation. There are only crystals of time where the actual is no longer assignable. The consistency of the virtual is the very mobility of points of view, each enveloping the others only by being enveloped by them in its turn, on either side of a fugitive frontier. This mobility, or this incessant overlapping, will vanish with the realization of becoming, that is to say, with the accomplished actualization of one of the points of view. The latter puts a stop to the positive distance rendering points of view sensible, and passes from the field of absolute differences to that of representation and action, where difference is no longer anything but the other side of a relative resemblance.

However, it is not enough to say that the subject is born in disjunction. Inseparable from an identification, the subject does not merge with this identity. I sense that I am becoming-other: the subject is always in the past tense [*au passé*], identifying with what he has ceased to be in becoming-other; rather than an "I am," the Cogito states "I was"—another way of saying that "I is an Other" (LS 310). The subject passes from the inclusive disjunction that inaugurates it to the exclusive identification that separates it from what it is becoming. The first-person is always retrospective, the subject is "without fixed identity, forever de-centered, *defined* by the states through which it passes": "So *that's* what it was! So it's *me!*" (AO 20). This philosophy—is it necessary to say this?—does not eliminate the subject, as is sometimes said by those who wish to reassure themselves by supplying a facile refutation. In fact, we pass our time saying "I," identifying ourselves, recognizing ourselves and listing our properties. What Deleuze shows is that the subject is an effect and not a cause, a residuum rather than an origin, and that the illusion begins precisely when we take it to be an origin—of thoughts, of desires, etc. Here begins the long history of the origin, as urgent to seek out as it is unobtainable: a history of anxiety and neurosis, a voyage in the black hole. It belongs to identity to be lost, and to identification to always begin too late, after the fact.

To draw the consequences of this is to present life as that "secret coherence which excludes that of a self," to present a "man without name, without family, without qualities" as he whom I become or do not cease to become, or who I am insofar as I become (DR 89–90). It is no longer only the crack that separates me from what I was (a matter of the past), leaving the subject suspended in the void, incapable of collecting himself [*se rejoinder*]. It is a *rupture* with the form of the past that renders us capable of loving (ATP 199). Aion, the empty ordinal time of the event, constantly causes an indefinite pronoun (*one*) to appear there where I was. A final formulation of the cogito could thus be "one thinks" or "it's thinking," as in the way we say "it's raining" and "it's windy" (D 64; ATP 265). The affect can only be experienced by a subject, but this in no way implies that it is a personal subject, or that it occupies the center. On the contrary, the subject experiences a swerve [*déportement*] of the self that does not leave him as he was before. It therefore becomes my affect, but inasmuch as I become other and as the intensity fades. That the form of the "I" does not coincide with the affect is not only a problem of its psychological description, but follows from its very logic. Consequently, the subject does not become other by departing from an identity that was originally his own. His only identities are concluded from his becomings, an undecided [*indécise*] and open multiplicity that ceaselessly displaces its center by differing with itself. Insofar as it refers to the constitutive alterity of points of view, the Other comes first in relation to the subject, and presides over the division of the ego [*le moi*] and the non-ego [*le non-moi*] (LS 307–11).

We now understand that the revelation of the hour is something other than a simple content revealed to a thinking subject. It dislocates the subject, opening onto a multiplicity of possible individuations; it puts the traditional model of truth founded identity and recognition into crisis (C2 130). For Deleuze, the affect is truth (sensation/sense), insofar as it puts heterogeneous possibilities of existence into perspective. It is the emergence of distance *within* existence, of divergence *within* the world. Truth is *ethical difference*, the evaluation of immanent modes of existence in their disjunctive synthesis.

Nothing shows better the incompatibility of the two conceptions of truth—recognition and the "art of distances"—than the rise of the *powers of the false* in narration. From Melville to Borges, from Orson Welles to Resnais and Robbe-Grillet, becoming emerges as such in literature and cinema by means of falsifying processes capable of producing in language and in the image an indecision proper to life and the body, and of maintaining "undecidable alternatives" and "inexplicable differences" (C2 Chapters 5–6 and 203; CC 132–3). It is at the exact same moment that "narration becomes temporal and falsifying" (C2 132). To the eyes of the "truthful man" who demands information and who counts on a unified and objective "reality" composed of extrinsic disjunctions (either . . . or), the immanent world must appear to be a gigantic fraud—as if a crooked, neo-baroque or neo-Leibnizian God had brought all the incompossible worlds into existence at once (L 63; on the forger who "imposes a power of the false as adequate to time," cf. C2 132). From the point of view of representation, the "truths of time" are falsifying.

Ethical difference distinguishes itself absolutely from moral opposition to the extent that it is no longer a question of passing judgment upon existence in general in the name of transcendent values, without perceiving the variety and inequality of its manifestations (EPS Ch. 16; SPP Ch. 2). It refers to an immanent evaluation: the emergence of value is not separable from an experience, and merges with it. Beyond the alternative of transcendence or chaos, an axiological cleavage still persists on the basis of an immanent criteria inherent to experience itself, one which rejects at once both moralism and nihilism: affective intensity, the sensed difference of at least two systems of affective intensities. Despite appearances, no criteria is less "subjective" than this, precisely because the affect implies the collapse of constituted interiority, delivering its verdict only along an unassignable threshold where persons no longer recognize themselves (cf. above, Ch. 2). No criteria is less arbitrary, once necessity is said to be conquered in an experience of the outside (cf. above, Ch. 1).

> There is not the slightest reason for thinking that modes of existence need transcendent values by which they could be compared, selected, and judged relative to one another. On the contrary, there are only immanent criteria. A possibility of life is evaluated through itself in the movements it lays out and the intensities it creates on a plane of immanence: what is not laid out or created is rejected. A mode of existence is good or bad, noble or vulgar, complete or empty, independently of Good and Evil or any transcendent value: there are never any criteria other than the tenor of existence, the intensification of life. (WP 74)

What affects, what possibilities of life emerge from such a mode of existence? Is it rich in affects, or does it enclose us in anxiety? Or inversely, which mode of existence for such and such affects? What would be the conditions of a mode of existence less likely to compromise becoming and the chance for new encounters, new affects? The immanent ethical criteria is consequently that of anger and social creation ("The powers that be need to repress us no less than to make us anxious"—D 61). However, the revolution is worth less by virtue of its future (estimated or effective) than by the power of life that it manifests here and now (becoming). When the immanent glimmers disappear under the radiant abstraction of an ideal or foundation subordinating practice, anger is put in the service of Judgment, and the damned have their hour of glory. Thus begins the interminable paranoiac calculus of splinterings [*écarts*] and deviations, fidelities and treasons—in short the degrees of participation in the Idea—in a rage of recognition opposed to the profoundly undecidable character of all social or revolutionary becoming (S 95; ATP 472–3; CC 136).

Simplifying things to the extreme, we might say that the intensive scale entails at the very least a minimum, which would be the isolated point of view separated from what it can do, a frozen existence surviving on opinions and clichés, anxious and vindictive (Leibniz's damned). But there is also a maximum: the point of view of the creator, an existence in absolute becoming, capable of apprehending and "preserving" distances, of experiencing the difference between the high and the low: *becoming-intense, becoming-imperceptible.* Between these two limits there is an existence in a relative becoming, experiencing distances in a fugitive manner, incapable of contracting and contemplating them, and of causing them to return. "Nothing is more distressing than a thought that escapes itself, than ideas that fly off, that disappear hardly formed, already eroded by forgetfulness or precipitated into others that we no longer master" (WP 201).[5]

In short, the "best" point of view is a limited one: it is not the best because it passes through all the others, or because it affirms and lives ethical difference. It does not ignore the base points of view, but lives them intensely, and considers the ensemble of existential possibilities from out of them, even at the cost of then inverting its perspective and ending up with the other kind of distance (baseness seen from on high). We always rediscover the idea that there are not many truths but one truth, itself multiple and differenciated. Truth is the test of ethical difference, a life that "does not divide without changing in nature" with each new distance it arrives at, with each new perspective it conquers. Ethical difference is rhythm. To become intense or imperceptible is to condense the successive periods, simultaneous lines and experienced possibilities in the disjunctive synthesis of a single and sole Event, in the open resonating system of a life.

Refrain, Haecceity, Free Indirect Discourse

Truth as hour is contemplative habit, sign, becoming. To develop the sign has nothing to do with searching for a hidden sense, since sense merges with the very dynamism of development; rather, it leads us to repeat it as a pure movement, to contract it in a sign that must be called a *refrain* [*ritournelle*]. By refrain we must understand a trait of expression corresponding to a case or a circumstance, and which strikes us only when the hour arrives (N 26; CC 157). This type of sign appears first of all in music, but it is not properly musical since nothing prevents the invention of literary, cinematic, or philosophical refrains, in conformity with the concept we have given it, i.e. a trait of expression related to an hour (ATP 11th Plateau).[6] If the immanent concept is the expression of an hour, we can define it without any metaphor as a refrain (WP 21). The expression of an hour must be understood here in the same sense as when we spoke of a "truth of time": not the content of the hour but the expression that corresponds to it, or which is expressed at that hour.

Truth is the hour captured by the refrain. However, if we recall that the subject is born from an hour and becomes other when the hour changes, then in turn it is clear that the hour merits the name *haecceity*, an original mode of individuation. Here Deleuze pays homage to Duns Scotus, who renewed the problem of individuation in the fourteenth century by refusing the traditional alternative: by matter / by form. He created the word "hæcceitas" in order to positively designate individual singularity. But the connivance stops there, for Scotus conceived haecceity as an individuation *of* form, whereas Deleuze thinks it as an intensive and evental individuation, as mobile and communicating. Earlier we called singularity pre-individual and individuating in relation to formed and separated individuals; here it amounts to the same thing to define it as the individuality proper to the event.

It is therefore a question of showing that becoming is at once a perfect individuality, and that this individuality is overlapping and never ceases to communicate with others. Haecceity refers to an evental individuality, and is opposed to the received idea according to which there can be no individuality without form (whether in existence, as a body or a person, or in art, as in the work). The informal principle of individuation is intensity:

> A degree of heat is a perfectly individuated warmth distinct from the substance or the subject that receives it. A degree of heat can enter into composition with a degree of whiteness, or with another degree of heat, to form a third unique individuality distinct from that of the subject. What is the individuality of a day, a season, an event? A shorter day and a longer day are not, strictly speaking, extensions but degrees proper to extension, just as there are degrees proper to heat, color, etc. (ATP 253)

The event is defined by an instantaneous coexistence of two heterogeneous dimensions in an empty time in which the future and the past perpetually coincide and encroach on one another, distinct yet indiscernible. Properly speaking, the event is what comes, what arrives, an emergent dimension not yet separated from those that precede it. The event is the coming intensity, one that has begun to distinguish itself from another (time is "a perpetual *self-distinguishing*"—C2 82). Intensity is simple and singular, but always related to at least one other intensity from which it detaches itself. As was the case for relations between forces, it is a question of an essential relation, although not internal to the nature of the terms, since intensity is in a relation with an *other* intensity, and relates itself to this other only insofar as it distinguishes itself from it. Intensity is birthing as much as vanishing. It is therefore possible to maintain on the one hand that intensity is the communication of heterogeneous terms, and on the other that the heterogeneous terms are themselves intensities: regardless of its appearance, there is neither a circle nor an infinite regression here. In this sense, the simplicity of the degree always envelops a difference of degrees or of levels, once it is said that difference of degree is here a difference in nature. In this we rediscover the double characteristic of singularity: to be simple and nevertheless to implicate a division, a differential relation.

Haecceity therefore consists in a passage or a change. Intensity arrives only in an in-between; an hour always implicates the difference between two hours (ATP 263). Haecceity is related to an atmospheric change in the mind or in nature: an hour is always crepuscular, *Zwielight* (distinct-obscure), "at dusk" (ATP 314, 340). Or Lorca's "'five in the evening,' when love falls and fascism rises" (ATP 261). The determinations overlap, the actual and the virtual become unassignable. The refrain is thus no less the crystal of time (ATP 349). Intensity is not a milieu, but it fades into the state of the milieu once it is differenciated or separated from that which it distinguishes itself from. It troubles the beaten-down regularity of a mode of existence by causing it to pass into other modes and to communicate with them: it is *rhythm*, or absolute speed. "To change milieus, taking them as you find them: Such is rhythm" (ATP 314). Truth is time *and* ethical difference, for ethical difference itself is rhythm, the disjunctive confrontation of variable and relative existential speeds (SPP 123). Haecceity is not a qualified space-time but a pure *spatio-temporal dynamism*: it does not combine two preexisting empirical space-times, rather it presides over their genesis. It is the putting-into-communication of heterogeneous dimensions of time from out of which space-times are derived. It is the birth of a space-time, "a beginning of the world" or the "birth of Time itself" in a spatializing dynamism (PS 44–5). Haecceity is thus a kind of inverted Kantian schema, since the dynamism no longer conforms to the concept but actually sustains its creation. The sign that forces thought induces a *drama* in the thinker which the latter must follow if he is to conserve it in a concept (DR 216 ff.).

One may object that the spatio-temporal drama that presides

over the formation of the concept is abstract and metaphorical. But perhaps we have a poor understanding of the nature of abstraction. If philosophy is abstract—necessarily and to its credit—this is because it takes up space-time in its genetic moment, rather than taking as its object qualified space-times that it would designate and comment upon in a general manner. A concept is the capture of a drama or a pure dynamism, and it is dynamism or becoming itself that is abstract: it traces a line of flight between points of view, a line that is quite precisely called abstract. A concept thus refers to a singularity that is indifferent to the distinction between the general and the particular (LS 67), and introduces an authentic abstraction into language.

The abstract is thus not a spiritual domain opposed to nature, even if it can only be gathered by the mind, or, more precisely, by language. Deleuze shows that sense is not reducible to signification, the latter always being associated with the designation of a concrete state of affairs [*état des choses*] (LS 3rd Series). The consistency of the world lies in the affect or sensation—in other words, in the event that renders a state of affairs distinct. But we have seen that this event is not of the body, even if it happens to bodies; it is at the limit of bodies, in the passage from one state of affairs to another (e.g. to grow). The event is incorporeal, vanishing in the actualization of the new state of affairs. Language is possible—which is to say, a proposition-thing relation is thinkable—only by virtue of this incorporeal element that must be attributed to bodies even if it is really distinct from them (LS 26th Series). It is because of the event that language is in a relation with things. The question of the truth or falsity of a proposition comes only later and presupposes this prior relation, since even a false proposition must have a sense (LS 3rd Series). Here Deleuze rediscovers the Stoic *lekton*: as the incorporeal effect of a mixture of bodies that renders language possible, the event is by nature the *expressible* (LS 2nd Series). Doubtless, a proposition designates and signifies a state of affairs, but it can do so only by enveloping an incorporeal event that it incarnates. The event is gathered in language by the verb, under the form of the *infinitive* (LS 26th Series). The infinitive expresses nothing other than a pure spatio-temporal dynamism. "To grow" is abstract, even if it can be said only of things. Abstraction is a process seized for itself in its singularity, a beginning of actualization interminably recovered [*repris*] and conserved in its commencement—in short, an *infinite movement* ceaselessly continued or accomplished without ever being concluded.

Such a movement has an absolute or infinite speed that is not to be confused with the relative speeds of milieus, but which does coincide, however, with an infinite slowness, in conformity with the empty time of Aion (WP 35 ff.).

To seize the world or Nature in its eventality [*événementialité*], to create signs in language that preserve its distinctions or singularities (concepts)—this is what is proper to philosophy. The philosophical hour is not that of general rather than particular questions, but that of singular questions that seize the event as such, or which seize things as events (DR 188).[7] A concept does not represent reality, it neither comments upon it nor explains it: it carves out pure dramas within what happens, independently of the persons or objects to which they happen. Thus the Other, space, time, matter, thought, truth, possibility, etc., can become concepts because they are treated as events.

The question "what use is philosophy?" is therefore especially poorly posed. Philosophy is not a discourse on life but a vital activity, a way life has of intensifying itself by preserving its passages, of testing and evaluating its own divergences and incompatibilities—in short, of *becoming-subject*, with all the ambiguity and instability characterizing the disjunctive synthesis (WP 209). In this respect, nothing is more painful than the spiteful jeremiads about the abstraction of philosophers and the little concern they show for explaining and giving a meaning to "lived experience" [*vécu*]. In fact, they have better things to do. They have to live, to become, and to live the becoming-subject of life. The philosopher thinks only by virtue of signs encountered, and we need not look elsewhere for his relation to his time, his untimely presence today. Untimely, because he thinks only by extracting the event in the present, by experiencing the Idiot's incapacity to act. Today, because the signs he captures are emitted by his time, and are those that are emerging and forcing thought now (novelty). Whence the strange relation between the philosopher and politics, so easily misunderstood: the philosopher—the inactive, the contemplative, the incompetent—conceives action only as *counter-effectuation*, and becomes capable of action again only by departing from signs, from his "habit" of the time (LS 21st Series). Consequently, he puts action in crisis, and conceives action only from out of such a state of crisis. He wants rhythm in action. The philosopher causes a crisis and knows nothing other than this; he has nothing to say about the rest, and testifies in his quasi-silence to a singular modesty, glorious and haughty—something like a Deleuzian modesty. And what is a crisis of action, a creation within the order of action, a "social power of difference," if not a revolution (DR 208; WP 98–101)? The philosopher's political opinions are about nothing if not about this social creation that echoes his own conceptual creation. The philosopher cries that "he is missing a people" (C2 215–24; WP 109–10). What are the signs today? We are always between dog and wolf, but perhaps the hour has come for us to think this way, since we no longer believe in these significations, in these true opinions, which we nevertheless ceaselessly lay claim to. Perhaps it is time to believe in this world, an immanent world that carries divergence within itself and, every now and then, the transitory glory of a "becoming-revolutionary."

Art, and even literature, cannot have the same object as philosophy. It preserves the event not as sense in concepts, but as sensation in percepts and affects (WP Ch. 7). The recent texts of Deleuze specify the difference between literature and philosophy by distinguishing between two manners of working the outside of language, in conformity with the two poles of the sign or the event: sensation/sense, affect/expressible. Literature frees nonlinguistic visions and auditions that nevertheless exist only in language (CC lv), whereas philosophy frees abstract expressible movements that obey the same conditions. Deleuze does not believe there to be less mind or thought in art than in philosophy. Feeling [*sentir*] is thought expressing itself in Images rather than in Expressibles. In both cases, to cause the outside to erupt forth and to preserve it—once it is acknowledged that it does not endure but repeats its beginning—is a matter of syntax. A philosophy is a *style* in the same way as a novelistic work or a poem, which pertains not to one or several propositions but to the rhythmic breaks that disjoin them even as they bring them into relation. Concepts are thus related to themes rather than to theses. As for propositions, once they become separated from the movement that sweeps them along they are left with no other object than mere states of things, even abstract states. Once separated from what they can do, philosophical statements can only give the illusion of *designating* abstract and unreal entities, as opposed to *making* the real abstract movement of bodies and persons.

To create is not to give form to a matter, to represent the given or to reflect upon it, but to *erect* [*dresser*] haecceities—refrains or crystals of time—in visual, sonorous or linguistic materials (taking advantage of the double possibility language offers). In Deleuzian parlance, to set up takes over the idea of explicating or developing:

131

"erect an image" (CC 171; C1 210), "to erect Figures" (FB 37 and 42–3: to erect a resonance), "to erect the event" (WP 33 and 160). This is because sense is less the object of an actualization than of a *refraction,* of a "continuous and refracted" birth in a second, created sign (PS 48–50). To set up means to suspend actualization by extracting its virtual part (drama, infinite movement), to repeat the very movement of explication.

Are there properly social signs? Can juridical signs claim the status of refrains or crystals? The response is as precarious as social becomings are fragile and transitory. Acquired and codified rights are certainly not refrains or crystals: rather, what interests Deleuze are the signs belonging to jurisprudence which, when it creates law, are not simply the acts of judges, but are principles or rules born out of cases. Jurisprudence does not have the form of a judgment, for it "proceeds by singularity, the extension of singularities" rather than by the subsumption of the particular under the general. The rule is no longer something one applies but something one creates, just as a concept is dramatized rather than schematized. Jurisprudence preserves encounters that are specifically juridical, repeating the emergence of problems within the law (L 67; N 153–4, 170; cf. also ES Chapters 2–3; ATP 461–73).

Finally, the concept of haecceity shows the extent to which individuality is necessarily mobile, overlapping, and communicating (DR 254 and 257). The word *communicating* occurs frequently in Deleuze's works (LS 24th Series; ATP 33, 238, 267, 313, etc.; C1 73, etc.). It expresses the implication of the outside in every phenomenon, in all of existence. The reason for this implication, for this insistence of the virtual in the actual, has already been examined: nothing consists, appears, affirms itself, exerts a force, produces an effect, without implicating a disjunction with something else, a virtual coexistence with that from which it separates itself, and consequently a contagion of points of view in reciprocal implication.

> Every individuating factor is already difference and difference of difference. It is constructed upon a fundamental disparity, and functions on the edges of that disparity as such. That is why these factors endlessly communicate with one another across fields of individuation, becoming enveloped in one another in a demesne which disrupts the matter of the Self as well as the form of the I. Individuation is mobile, strangely supple, fortuitous and endowed with fringes and margins; all because the intensities which contribute to it communicate with each other, envelop other intensities and are in turn enveloped. The individual is far from indivis-

ible, never ceasing to divide and change its nature . . . The fringe of indetermination which surrounds individuals and the relative, floating and
fluid character of individuality itself has often been commented upon . . .
The error, however, is to believe that this indetermination or this relativity
indicates something incomplete in individuality or something interrupted
in individuation. On the contrary, they express the full, positive power
of the individual as such, and the manner in which it is distinguished in
nature from both an I and a self. The individual is distinguished from the
I and the self just as the intense order of implications is distinguished from
the extensive and qualitative order of explication. Indeterminate, floating, fluid, communicative and enveloping-enveloped are so many positive
characteristics affirmed by the individual. (DR 257–8; cf. equally 254)

Nothing is experienced, nor does anything consist (in the strong
sense) except through the putting-into-perspective that displaces
points of view in making them reprise one another unequally. We
are alive, intense, and able to think only to the extent that at least
one other thinks within us. "There is always another town within
the town" (LS 174): a new neo-baroque or neo-Leibnizian way to
express the power of the false. The contagious insistence of the other
in becoming is a leitmotif of Deleuze's thought: "so many beings
and things think in us" (LS 298), "all the voices present within a
single voice, the glimmer of girls in a monologue by Charlus," "the
murmur from which I take my proper name, the constellation of
voices, concordant or not, from which I draw my voice" (ATP 80,
84, and 35–6), "always a voice in another voice" (C2 167). It is in
this way that Deleuze takes over the theory of *free indirect discourse*,
no longer defined as an empirical mix of direct and indirect that
would presuppose already constituted subjects, but as an originally
plural enunciation where distinct but indiscernible voices "com-
plicate" themselves, an impersonal enunciation presiding over the
individuation of subjects (ATP 77, 79–80, 84; C1 72–6; C2 149–50):

The dissolved self opens up to a series of roles, since it gives rise to an
intensity which already comprehends difference in itself, the unequal in
itself, and which penetrates all others, across and within multiple bodies.
There is always another breath in my breath, another thought in my
thought, another possession in what I possess, a thousand things and a
thousand beings implicated in my complications: every true thought is an
aggression. It is not a question of our undergoing influences, but of being
"insufflations" or fluctuations, or merging with them. That everything is
so "complicated," that I might be an other, that something else thinks in
us in an aggression which is the aggression of thought, in a multiplication

133

which is the multiplication of the body, or in a violence which is the violence of language—this is the joyful message. (LS 298)

Notes

1. This passage, which appears on page 189 of the French edition of *What is Philosophy?*, is omitted in the English translation—Trans.
2. Contraction would appear as such if reaction were to be deferred or paralyzed. Cf. the affection-image, and above all the pure optics and sounds that bring about the passage from *The Movement-Image* to *The Time-Image* through a "rupture of the sensory-motor schema."
3. Which is why the trajectory of a *line of flight* in Deleuzian perspectivism requires the coexistence of at least two points of view, and puts representation in crisis: it is becoming, it puts representation into flight (D 36–76; ATP 10).
4. Cf. the unforgettable homage to François Châtelet of November 28, 1987, of which *Périclès et Verdi* constitutes the summary. [An English translation appears in *Dialogues II*—Trans.]
5. For a theory of an immanent typology, cf. NP Ch. 4, and 49–52 (determination of the concept of will to power as immanent, "plastic" principle, "no wider than what it conditions," therefore already similar to an intensive multiplicity). Cf. also LS 21st Series; C2 137–47; SPP Ch. 4; CC Chapters 6, 10, 12, 15.
6. Under yet another aspect, the refrain is the mark of a "territory." We rediscover here the determination of the sign as difference: the refrain does not delimit a territory without at the same time enveloping the outside from which the latter distinguishes itself (without being detached from it). It therefore virtually implicates a movement of "deterritorialization" and refers the territory (which is consequently never originary) to an "Earth"—or a plane of immanence, or a body without organs—that it presupposes and on which it is inscribed. Hour and territory: the refrain expresses the double aspect of individuation, both a relation of exteriority as well as a temporal relation.
7. On the relation between such questions and those of children, and the "becoming-child" of philosophy, cf. ATP 256–60 and CC Ch. 9.

Conclusion

I have attempted to introduce a thought whose principal theme is the event, and to show the reasons for this theme as well as the overarching lines of its conceptual treatment.

In the articulation of the *outside* (heterogeneity, exteriority of relations) and of *implication* (fold, envelopment-development, virtual complication), I believe to have found the abstract motor of Deleuzian thought. The majority of its concepts are elaborated at the intersection of these two themes.

The general problem, the conditions of which are developed by the logic of the event, is that of *immanence*: the belief in this world, which is to say a world taking upon itself divergence, heterogeneity, and incompossibility. A philosophy not content to verbally refute transcendence and dualism, but which actually carries out their destitution by forging the appropriate concepts—how can we characterize such a philosophy? The philosophy of Deleuze is a *dual monopluralism*. The real-formal distinction (difference in nature) is established twice: between the dimensions of time, between time-sense and the body. But it is never numerical, so that the multiple never resolves itself in the One (multiplicity), while time-sense and the body never form a dualism (reciprocal immanence). The core of this response lies in the freeing of the category of the *event*: consistency of the virtual, exteriority of relations, and ultimately the identity of the outside, of sense, and of time.

It falls to the reader to decide whether the latter is indeed *our problem*, if it is indeed what is at issue in thought and existence today, and in this way.

Certain important aspects of Deleuze's thought were involuntarily neglected, unable to be integrated in this presentation. In particular, the concepts of earth-territory, of the rhizome, and of lines. I have sought above all to extract the logical movements of an oeuvre that seems to me to be one of the most important and most powerful of the twentieth century, my only fear being that I might have slightly diminished or ossified, or rendered confused by a will to clarify, a work nevertheless so "distinct-obscure."

THE VOCABULARY OF DELEUZE

François Zourabichvili

Contents

Literally . . .

1. *Literally . . .* what reader of Deleuze could forget this mania of language? And beneath its apparent insignificance, how can we not recall the tireless and nearly imperceptible memory of a gesture subtending the entire philosophy of "inclusive disjunction," of "univocity" and "nomadic distribution"? For their part, the writings everywhere testify to the same insistent warning:[1] do not treat as metaphors concepts which, despite their appearance, are nothing of the sort; understand that the very word metaphor is a trap [*leurre*], a pseudo-concept, one that enthusiasts of philosophy no less than its detractors have availed themselves of, and of which the entire system of "becomings" or the production of sense constitutes the refutation. Confronted with the strange and variegated chain that Deleuze's concepts deploy, readers with good sense can always oppose their own set of rules [*cadastre*] and consequently find nothing in it but the figurative. Nevertheless, they will still hear in a muted fashion the perpetual denial of this "literally," the invitation to the reader to place their ear prior to the established division between an original [*sens propre*] and a figurative meaning. In accordance with the meaning given to it by Deleuze and Guattari, must we not invoke the notion of the "refrain" for this discreet signature, this insistent call—always familiar and disconcerting—to "leave the territory" toward the immanent and undivided earth of literality? Let us therefore assume that to read Deleuze is to hear, if only by intermittences, the call: "literally . . ."

2. We do not yet know the thought of Deleuze. Too often, whether hostile or adoring, we act as if his concepts were familiar, as if it were enough that the concepts simply touch us in order for us to understand them without spelling them out, or as if we had already made a survey of their promises. Such an attitude is ruinous for philosophy in general: first of all, because the force of the concept risks being confused with an effect of verbal seduction, an effect which is certainly irreducible and belongs by all rights to the philosophical field, yet which cannot replace the need to follow the *logical movement* that the concept envelops; secondly, because it amounts to protecting philosophy from the Deleuzian novelty.

This is why we do not suffer from an excess of monographs on

Deleuze. On the contrary, we lack consistent monographs, books that *explain* his concepts. And by this we in no way exclude those books *with* Deleuze, or any usage—even aberrant—provided it has its own necessity. However, such uses can only multiply and diversify themselves to the extent that the Deleuzian concepts are better understood, taken seriously in their real tenor, which demands unusual movements of the mind that are never easy to carry out nor to foresee. It is sometimes thought that the explication of a concept is a question of scholarly replication, and consequently that it is a movement accomplished for oneself and through oneself. Perhaps philosophy today suffers too often from a false alternative—either to explain *or* to use—as well as a false problem: the impression that a too-precise approach would amount to canonizing a current author. Consequently, we are not surprised to occasionally find philosophical production divided on the one hand into disincarnated exegeses, and on the other into essays which, although ambitious, still seize their concepts *from above*. Assuming it is not merely decorative, the same applies to the artist, the architect, or the sociologist who at a certain moment in their work uses an aspect of Deleuze's thought, for they too are eventually led to explain it to themselves (that this meditation takes a written form is a different matter). Indeed, it is only in this way that things change, that the novelty of a thought can disturb us and lead us toward unforeseen lands, lands which are not those of the author but are *our own*. For it is true that we do not explicate the thought of another without having an experience that properly concerns our own thought, until the moment where we either take our leave of the commentary, or else pursue it under conditions of assimilation and deformation that are no longer discernible from a fidelity.

For there is another false problem, namely, that of the "external" or "internal" approach to an author. Sometimes it is the study of a thought for itself that we reproach as being internal, doomed to a sterile didacticism and proselytism; at other times we find the inverse suspicion, that of an incurable exteriority, of a point of view of presumed familiarity or an elective affinity with the intimate and ineffable pulsation of the thought in question. It will be readily admitted that the exposition of concepts is the only guarantee of an *encounter* with a body of thought. The exposition is not the agent of this encounter, but the possibility of its accomplishment under the double condition of the sympathetic and the strange, and which is the opposite of misunderstanding and an immersion that we might describe as congenital. For difficulties arise here: the necessity of replaying this thought in another life, as well as the patience to tolerate an aridity that becomes infinite. That the heart beats when reading the text is a necessary prelude, or better still an affinity that is needed in order to comprehend. *But this is only half of comprehension*; as Deleuze says, it is the "non-philosophical comprehension" of concepts (WP 218). It is true that this part deserves to be insisted upon, since the practice of philosophy in the university excludes it almost methodically, while a dilettantism believing itself to be cultivated confuses it with a *doxa* of the times. But the fact that a concept has no sense or necessity without a corresponding "affect" or "percept" does not prevent there being something else in addition: a condensation of logical movements that the mind must effectuate if it wants to philosophize. Otherwise we remain in the initial fascination of words and phrases that we mistake for the irreducible component of intuitive comprehension. For as Deleuze writes, "You need all three to *get things moving*" (N 165). We wouldn't need Deleuze if we didn't sense in his oeuvre something that has never been thought, something capable of affecting philosophy in still inestimable ways—which is a result of our *letting ourselves be affected philosophically by it.*

3. Nothing seems more propitious than a lexicon spelling out Deleuze's concepts one by one, while underlining their reciprocal implications. Deleuze himself endeavored to confer a weight and a precision on his concepts that he often found to be lacking in philosophy (WP Ch. 1). A concept is neither a theme nor a particular opinion pronounced on a theme. Every concept participates in an act of thinking that displaces the field of intelligibility, modifying the conditions of the problem we pose for ourselves; it thus does not let itself be assigned a place within a common space of comprehension given in advance for pleasant or aggressive debates with its competitors. But if there are no general or eternal themes except for the illusion of common sense, does the history of philosophy not become reduced to a long line of homonyms? It testifies rather to mutations of variables that explore a "transcendental empiricism."

Moreover, Deleuze himself wrote three lexicons: the "Dictionary of the Main Characters in Nietzsche's Work" (PI 92–101), "Index of the Main Concepts of the *Ethics*" (SPP 44–110), and lastly the "Conclusion" of *A Thousand Plateaus*. The echo between the latter and the introduction to the book ("Introduction: Rhizome") underlines the fact that the arbitrary character of the alphabetical order is the most certain way of not superimposing upon the multiple relations of imbrication between concepts an artificial order of reasons that would divert attention away from the true status of necessity in philosophy.

Each entry begins with one or several citations. In most cases it is less a question of a definition than of perceiving the problem to which a concept is attached, and of sampling in advance its lexical environment. The cited phrase, at first obscure, should be clarified and complemented in the course of the entry, which proposes a sort of sketch, drawn with words. As regards the choice of entries, some brief remarks may of course be made: why "complication" and not "abstract machine," a concept so essential to the problem of literality? Why "break-flow" rather than "code and axiomatic"? "War machine" and not "childhood block"? Doubtless, I cannot be exhaustive; certain entries, such as "plane of immanence," seem to deserve a closer examination; but I also counted on this provisional, abortive state of my reading of Deleuze (hence the most obvious lacunae: the cinematic concepts[2]). What I am proposing is a series of "samples," as Leibniz liked to say, but as Deleuze had also said of Whitman (CC 57).

Aion

* "In accordance with Aion, only the past and the future inhere or subsist in time. Instead of a present which absorbs the past and future, a future and past divide the present at every instant and subdivide it ad infinitum into past and future, in both directions at once. Or rather, it is the instant without thickness and without extension, which subdivides each present into past and future, rather than vast and thick presents which comprehend both future and past in relation to one another" (LS 164).

** Deleuze rehabilitates the Stoic distinction between *Aion* and *Chronos* in order to think the extra-temporality of the event (or, if one prefers, its paradoxical temporality). However, the ordinary translation of Aion as "eternity" risks rendering the operation equivocal: in reality, the eternity that belongs to the Stoic conception of the instant has only an immanent sense, which has nothing to do with what will later become the Christian eternity (this is equally what is at stake in Nietzsche's reinterpretation of the Stoic theme of eternal return). Aion is opposed to Chronos, which refers to the chronological or successive time in which the order of the before and the after is subject to the condition of an englobing present in which, as we say, everything happens [*tout se passe*] (here Deleuze competes with Heidegger who, under the name of "anticipatory resoluteness," had contested the primacy of the present from Augustine to Husserl[3]). According to a first paradox, the event is that which subsists in the world only by being enveloped in language, the latter being made possible only through this envelopment. But there is a second paradox: "the event is always a dead time; it is there where nothing takes place" (WP 158). This dead time, which in some respects is a non-time, or what is called an "in-between" [*entre-temps*][4]—this is Aion. At this level, the event is no longer only the difference of things or states of affairs, it affects subjectivity, it carries difference into the subject itself. If we call a change in the order of sense an event (what has made sense up till now has become indifferent or even opaque, whereas what we are now sensitive to did not make sense before-hand), we must conclude that the event does not take place in time, since it affects the very conditions of chronology. Better still, it marks a *caesura*, a *break* [*coupure*], such that time is interrupted in order to be resumed on another plane (hence the expression: "in-between"). In elaborating the category of event Deleuze shows the primordial relation between time and sense: a chronology is thinkable only by virtue of a horizon of sense common to its parts. The idea of an objective time exterior to lived experience and indifferent to its variety is therefore only a generalization of this relation: it is the correlate of "common sense," the possibility of spreading out the infinite series of things and experiences on a single plane of representation. As an "in-between," the event in itself does not pass—first of all, because it is a pure instant, a point of scission or disjunction between a before and an after; secondly, because the experience corresponding to it is the paradox of an "infinite waiting that is already infinitely past" (WP 158). This is why the distinction between Aion and Chronos does not reinstate the Platonic-Christian duality of eternity and time: we do not experience a beyond of time, but only a temporality worked-over by Aion, in which the law of Chronos has ceased to reign. This is the "indefinite time of the event" (ATP 262). An experience of non-time within time, of a "floating time" (D 92), a dead or empty time, which is opposed to Christian *presence*: "This dead time does not come after what happens; it coexists with the instant or time of the accident, but as the immensity of the empty time in which we see it as still to come and as having already happened, in the strange indifference of an intellectual intuition" (WP 158). It is also the time of the concept (WP 160).

*** Under the name of Aion, the concept of the event marks the introduction of the outside within time, or the relation of time to an outside no longer exterior to it (contrary to eternity and its transcendence). In other words, *the extra-temporality of the event is immanent*, and in this respect paradoxical. By what right can we maintain that this outside is *in* time, if it is true that it separates time from itself? We can immediately see that it will not suffice to invoke the necessity of a spatio-temporal effectuation of the event. The response has two moments: 1. The event is within time insofar as it necessarily refers to a spatio-temporal effectuation, and as such is irreversible (LS 151). A paradoxical relation between two incompatible terms (before-after, the second term causing the first "to pass"), it implies materially the exclusion that it suspends logically. 2. The event is within time insofar as it is the internal difference *of* time, the interiorization of its disjunction: it separates time from itself. There is no reason to conceive of the event as outside of [*hors*] time, even if it is not in itself temporal. It is therefore important to have recourse to a concept of multiplicity, so that the "thing" possesses a unity only through its variations and not in accordance with a common genre that could subsume these divisions (under the names of univocity and disjunctive synthesis, the concept of "internal difference" fulfills this program of an outside inserted inside, at the level of the very structure of the concept—LS 24th and 25th Series). This idea can also be expressed by saying that there is no event outside of [*hors*] a spatio-temporal effectuation, even if the event is not reducible to it. In short, the event is inscribed in time, it is the interiority of disjointed presents. Moreover, Deleuze is not content with a dualism of time and event, but seeks a more interior relation between time and its outside, so as to show that chronology is *derived from* the event, and that the latter is the originary instance that opens all chronology. As opposed to Husserl and his inheritors, the event or the genesis of time occurs only in a plural form. The important thing is therefore to maintain the inclusion of the outside in time, for without this the event remains what it is for the phenomenologists: a unique transcendence opening time *in general*, an instance logically situated *before* all time, and not—if one can say this—*between* time become multiplicity [*entre le temps devenu multiplicité*]. According to phenomenological reasoning, there is logically only one sole event, that of Creation, even if it ceaselessly repeats itself: the fundamental homogeneity of the world and of history is thus preserved (Deleuze's invocation of "one and the same Event" [LS 170, 179] refers to this immediate synthesis of the multiple he calls "disjunctive," or internal difference, and must be carefully distinguished from the One as a total and englobing signification, even where the latter is conceived prior to the distribution [*partage*] of the one and multiple, as is the case with Heidegger's "ontological difference"—cf. WP 95). For it is uncertain that the break between time *and something other than it* actually justifies the name event. Hence we return to the preliminary Deleuzian proviso, that there is no event apart from an effectuation in space and time, even if the event is not reducible to it.

Assemblage

* "On a first, horizontal, axis, an assemblage comprises two segments, one of content, the other of expression. On the one hand it is a *machinic assemblage* of bodies, of actions and passions, an intermingling of bodies reacting to one another; on the other hand it is a *collective assemblage of enunciation*, of acts and statements, of incorporeal transformations attributed to bodies. Then on a vertical axis, the assemblage has both *territorial sides*, or reterritorialized sides, which stabilize it, and *cutting edges of deterritorialization*, which carry it away" (ATP 88).[5]

** At first glance, this concept may appear to have a vast and indeterminate usage: according to the case in question, it refers to heavily territorialized institutions (judiciary assemblages, conjugal assemblages, familial assemblages, etc.), to intimately deterritorializing formations (becoming-animal, etc.), and finally, to the field of experience where these formations are elaborated (the plane of immanence as "machinic assemblage of movement-images"—C1 59, translation modified). As a first approximation, we can say that we are in the presence of an assemblage any time we can identify and describe the coupling of an ensemble of material relations and a corresponding regime of signs. In reality, the disparity of the cases of the assemblage can be ordered only from the point of view of immanence—hence existence reveals itself to be inseparable from the variable and modifiable assemblages that ceaselessly produce it. Rather than having an equivocal usage, the disparity refers to the poles of the concept itself which, we might add, prohibits any dualism of desire and institution, of the unstable and the stable. Every individual confronts these large social assemblages defined by specific codes, and characterized by a relatively stable form and a reproductive operation: they tend to collapse the field of experimentation of the individual's desire back onto a pre-established formal distribution. This is the *stratified* pole of assemblages (which we call "molar"). On the other side, the way in which the individual invests and participates in the reproduction of these social assemblages depends upon local or "molecular" assemblages in which he himself is caught up, whether he limits himself to effectuating available social forms and molding his existence upon the current codes of the day, introducing into them his little irregularity—or alternately, whether he proceeds to the involuntary and groping elaboration of *specific* assemblages that "decode" the stratified assemblages or "put them into flight": this is the pole of the *abstract machine* (among which we must include artistic assemblages). Since every assemblage refers in the last instance to the field of desire in which it is constituted, each is affected by a certain disequilibrium. Each of us concretely combines the two types of assemblages to varying degrees, the limit being schizophrenia as process (decoding or absolute deterritorialization), and the question therefore being that of the concrete relations of forces between the types (see "Line of Flight"). If the institution is a molar assemblage reliant on molecular assemblages (hence the importance of the molecular point of view in politics: the sum-total of gestures, attitudes, procedures, rules, spatial and temporal dispositions that bring about the concrete consistency or the *duration*—in the Bergsonian sense—of the institution, the bureaucracy of the State or the party), the individual for his part is not an originary form evolving in a world, like some exterior scenery or ensemble of data to which he must simply react. The individual is constituted only by being assembled [*en s'agençant*], it exists only insofar as it is caught up from the outset in assemblages. The field of individual experience oscillates between a retreat into preconceived (and consequently social) forms of thinking and behaving, and a spreading out across a plane of immanence where its becoming is inseparable from the lines of flight or the transversals it traces among "things," freeing their power [*pouvoir*] of affection and in this way recovering a power [*puissance*] to feel and to think (a mode of individuation by *haecceities* that is distinct from the individual's way of orienting itself by means of identifying characteristics—ATP 260 ff.).

Consequently, the two poles of the concept of assemblage are not the collective and the individual; rather these are two senses or two modes of the collective. For if it is true that the assemblage is individuating, it is clear that it is not expressed from the point of view of a preexisting subject who would attribute it to itself: its *specificity* [*propre*] is proportionate to its anonymity, and it is in this sense that one's becoming-singular concerns everyone in principle (just like the clinical picture of an illness can receive the proper name of the doctor who managed to gather together its symptoms, even if he is in himself anonymous; *id.* in art—cf. M 14; D 125–6). We must therefore make no mistake about the collective character of the "assemblage of enunciation" corresponding to a "machinic assemblage": it is not produced *by*, but is by nature *for* a collectivity (hence Paul Klee's expression, so often cited by Deleuze: "a people is lacking"). It is in this way that desire is the true revolutionary potential.

*** From *Kafka* onward, the concept of assemblage replaces that of "desiring-machines": "Desire exists only when assembled or machined. You cannot grasp or conceive of a desire outside a determinate assemblage, on a plane which is not pre-existent but which must itself be constructed" (D 96). Once again, an insistence on the *exteriority* (and not exteriorization) inherent to desire: all desire proceeds from an encounter. Such a statement is only apparently a truism: "encounter" is understood here in a rigorous sense (so many "encounters" are nothing more than tired songs that send us back to Oedipus), whereas desire does not wait for the encounter as if for an occasion to exercise itself, it assembles and constructs itself in it. However, the principle interest of the concept of assemblage is to enrich the conception of desire through a problematic of the statement, picking things up where *The Logic of Sense* had left them: there, every production of sense had as a condition the articulation of two heterogeneous series by means of a paradoxical instance, and language in general functioned only in accordance with the paradoxical status of the event that tied together the series of corporeal mixtures and the series of propositions. *A Thousand Plateaus* addresses the very plane on which the two series are articulated, and gives an unprecedented range to the Stoic duality between bodily mixtures and incorporeal transformations: a complex relation is woven between "content" (or "machinic assemblages") and "expression" (or "collective assemblages of enunciation"), redefined as two independent forms nevertheless caught up in a relation of reciprocal presupposition, each of which supports the other. The reciprocal genesis of the two forms refers to the instance of the "diagram" or the "abstract machine." There is no longer an oscillation between two poles, as was the case earlier, but a correlation of two inseparable sides. Contrary to the signifier-signified relation (which is considered to be derivative), expression is related to content, yet without being either a description or a representation of it: it "intervenes" in it (ATP 85–91, with the example of the feudal assemblage). From this emerges a conception of language that is opposed to both linguistics and psychoanalysis, and is distinguished by the primacy of the *statement* over the proposition (ATP 4th Plateau). Let us add that the form of expression is not necessarily linguistic: for example, there are musical assemblages (ATP 296–309). If we remain solely within the purview of linguistic expression, what are the logics governing content and expression on the plane of their genesis, and overseeing their reciprocal insinuation ("abstract machine")? First, that of the "haecceity" (intensive compositions, affects and speeds—a significant extension of *Anti-Oedipus'* conception founded on the disjunctive synthesis and "partial objects"); second, a logic of enunciation privileging the infinitive verb, the proper name and the indefinite article. Both communicate in the dimension of Aion (ATP 260–5, in particular the example of little Hans). Finally, it is with regard to the concept of the assemblage that Deleuze's relation to Foucault can be evaluated, the redirected appropriations made of him, the play of proximity and distance linking the two thinkers (ATP 66–7 and 140–1; the entirety of *Foucault* is constructed around the different aspects of the concept of assemblage).

Becoming

* "To become is never to imitate, nor to 'do like', nor to conform to a model, whether it is of justice or of truth. There is no terminus from which you set out, none which you arrive at or which you ought to arrive at. Nor are there two terms which are exchanged. The question 'What are you becoming?' is particularly stupid. For as someone becomes, what he is becoming changes as much as he does himself. Becomings are not phenomena of imitation or assimilation, but of a double-capture, of a non-parallel evolution, of nuptials between two reigns" (D 2).

** Becoming is the content proper to desire (desiring machines or assemblages): to desire is to pass through becomings. Deleuze and Guattari state this in *Anti-Oedipus*, but do not create a specific concept of it until *Kafka*. First of all, becoming is not a generality, there is no becoming in general: this concept, a tool belonging to the subtle clinic of existence, concrete and always singular, cannot be reduced to the exstatic apprehension of the world in its universal unfolding, a philosophically empty marvel. Secondly, becoming is a reality: becomings, far from being the province of dreams or the imaginary, are the very consistency of the real (on this point, see "Crystal of Time"). In order to understand this clearly, it is important to consider the logic: every becoming forms a "block"—in other words, the encounter or the relation of two heterogeneous terms that mutually "deterritorialize" each other. We do not abandon what we are to become something else (imitation, identification), but another way of living and sensing haunts or is enveloped within our own and "puts it to flight" [*fait fuir*]. The relation thus mobilizes not two but four terms, distributed in interlaced heterogeneous series: x enveloping y becomes x', while y, seized by its relation to x, becomes y'. Deleuze and Guattari constantly insist on the reciprocal and asymmetrical character of the process: x does not become something else (e.g. animal) without y for its part becoming something else (e.g. writing, or music). Two things are combined here that must not be confused: a) (general case) the encountered term is drawn into a becoming-expressive, the counterpart of new intensities (content) through which the encountering term passes, in accordance with the two sides of every assemblage (cf. the theme, "You become animal only molecularly"—ATP 275); b) (restricted case) the possibility that the term encountered also be encountering in turn, as in the case of co-evolution, so that a double becoming takes place on both sides (cf. the example of the wasp and the orchid—ATP 10). In short, becoming is one of the poles of the assemblage, where content and expression tend toward indiscernibility in the composition of an "abstract machine" (hence the possibility of maintaining the non-metaphoricity of formulations such as "write like a [dying] rat"—ATP 240).

*** *Kafka* and *A Thousand Plateaus* present a hierarchy of becomings. This hierarchy, no less than the list that it arranges, can only be empirical, proceeding from an immanent evaluation: animality, childhood, femininity, etc., have no *a priori* privilege, but the analysis acknowledges that desire tends to invest them more than any other domain. It will not suffice to describe them as so many alterities in relation to a *model* of majoritarian identification (white-adult-male, etc.), for they are not at all proposed as alternative models, as forms or codes of substitution. Animality, childhood, femininity have value only according to their coefficient of alterity or of *absolute deterritorialization*, opening onto a beyond of form that is not itself chaos but a "molecular" consistency: perception then harnesses intensive variations (compositions of speed between informal elements) rather than the partitioning of forms ("molar" ensembles), while affectivity is freed from its repetitive melodies and ordinary impasses (see "Line of Flight"). This is the case with the example of the animal: as such, it is not this domesticated individual rendered familiar and part of the family; inseparable from a pack that is itself virtual (*a* wolf, *a* spider), its value lies exclusively in the intensities, the singularities, and the dynamisms that it presents. The immediate relation that we have to it is not a relation with a person, with its identifying coordinates and its roles; it suspends the dichotomous division of possibilities, the recognition of forms and functions. However, the very possibility of establishing a familiar relation with the animal or of attaching mythological attributes to it reveals a limitation of the animal from the point of view of deterritorialization (K 36–7; ATP 240–1). Between the different types of becomings, the criteria of selection can only have an immanent aim: to what extent, and in which cases, does becoming will itself? In this respect, becoming-child or becoming-woman seem to take us further than becoming-animal, for they tend toward a third degree where the terminus of the becoming is no longer assignable, toward an "asignifiance"[6] that no longer admits the slightest recognition or interpretation, where the questions "what happened?" and "how does it work?" take on a definitive superiority over the question "what does it mean?": not the renunciation of sense, but rather its productivity, through a refusal of the sense-signification confusion and of the sedentary distribution of properties. This third degree—though there is neither a dialectical progression nor a closed series here—is called "becoming-intense," "becoming-molecular," "becoming-imperceptible," "becoming-everybody/everything" [*devenir-tout-le-monde*] (K Chapters 2 and 4; ATP 10th Plateau).

Body Without Organs (BwO)

* "Beyond the organism, but also at the limit of the lived body, there lies what Artaud discovered and named: the body without organs. 'The body is the body / it stands alone / it has no need of organs / the body is never an organism / organisms are the enemies of bodies.' The

body without organs is opposed less to organs than to that organization of organs we call the organism. It is an intense and intensive body. It is traversed by a wave that traces levels or thresholds in the body according to the variations of its amplitude. Thus the body does not have organs, but thresholds or levels" (FB 44–5).

** The distinction between two clinical ensembles that at first glance appear to be convergent—the "perversity" of Carroll and the "schizophrenia" of Artaud—enabled the isolation in *The Logic of Sense* of the category of the body without organs, which Deleuze had already criticized psychoanalysis for having neglected. Against the fragmentation of his body and the physical aggression of words reduced to phonetic values from which he suffers, the schizophrenic responds with "breaths-cries," a welding of words or syllables thereby rendered nondecomposable, to which there corresponds a new experience of a full body without distinct organs. The BwO, as *A Thousand Plateaus* will regularly abbreviate it, is therefore an active and effective defense, a conquest proper to schizophrenia. It operates in a zone referred to as "depth," in which the "surface" organization that shores up sense by maintaining a difference in nature between bodies and words is in every respect lost (LS 13th and 27th Series).

In this respect *Anti-Oedipus* represents a turning point: the notion of the body without organs is reworked in accordance with new clinical material from which the concept of "desiring machines" will emerge. The notion of the body without organs now acquires a complexity that enables Deleuze, following the theme of univocity and nomadic distribution, to confront for a second time the major problem of his thought: how to articulate, beyond Bergson, the two inverse yet nevertheless complimentary dynamics of existence—on the one hand, the actualization of forms, and on the other the involution that destines the world to incessant involutions?[7] (This problem will be confronted a third time with the concept of the refrain).

*** The rectification concerns this point: the BwO is opposed less to the organs than to the organism (the organizing function by which each organ has its place and is assigned a role identifying it). The BwO is not longer a specifically schizophrenic entity, but the very body of desire of which the schizophrenic has the most extreme experience, being he who is above all the man of desire, since, simply put, he suffers only from an interruption of his process (a large part of *Anti-Oedipus* is devoted to extracting this dimension of a schizophrenic *process* distinct from its clinical collapse). The BwO doubtless refers to a lived corporeal experience, but not to the ordinary lived experience described by the phenomenologists: it is no longer a question of a rare or extraordinary experience (even if certain assemblages can reach the BwO under ambiguous conditions: drug users, masochists). It is the "limit of the lived body," an "immanent limit" (ATP 150, 154) reached by the body when it is traversed by "affects" or "becomings" irreducible to phenomenological experiences. It is then no longer a lived body,[8] since its becomings demolish the interiority of the ego (ATP 156, 161, 164). Although impersonal, it is no less the means by which one conquers the *proper name [nom propre]*, in an experience that exceeds the ruled and coded exercise of a desire "separated from what it can do." If the BwO is not the lived body but rather its limit, this is because it refers to a power that is itself unlivable as such, that of a desire always on the move, never fixing itself in forms: *the producing-product identity* (AO 4–8; these pages can only be fully understood on the basis of their implicit polemic with Book IX, 6, of Aristotle's *Metaphysics*). Consequently, there is no experience of the BwO as such, except in the case of catatonia or schizophrenia. We can therefore understand what is at first view a disconcerting ambivalence of the body without organs: the condition of desire, it is no less the "model of death" enveloped in every process of desire (AO 8 and above all 329; it is also in this sense that every sensation envelops an intensity = 0—AO 330; FB 65–6). As regards the organs, the BwO is at once their "repulsion" (the condition without which the organs would become sedimented, and the machine would no longer function) and their "attraction" (the organ-machines inscribe themselves on the BwO as so many intensive states or levels that divide it *into itself*) (AO 330). Better yet: the instance of antiproduction at the heart of production (AO 8–9). Such is the fragile articulation of the two dynamisms evoked earlier—since by nature they risk self-destruction—an articulation named production of the real, of desire, or of life (we understand by the same token why a desiring machine "functions only by breaking down").

Break-Flow (or Passive Synthesis, or Contemplation)

* "Far from being the opposite of continuity, the break or interruption conditions this continuity: it presupposes or defines what it cuts into as an ideal continuity. This is because, as we have

seen, every machine is a machine of a machine. The machine produces an interruption of the flow only insofar as it is connected to another machine that supposedly produces this flow. And doubtless this second machine in turn is really an interruption or break, too. But it is such only in relationship to a third machine that ideally—that is to say, relatively—produces a continuous, infinite flux" (AO 36).

** In *Anti-Oedipus* flow and break form a single concept, as difficult as it is essential. There is no ontological dualism or difference of nature here: the flow is not only intercepted by a machine that breaks it, it is itself emitted by a machine. Ontologically there is therefore only one term, "machine," and this is why every machine is a "machine of a machine" (AO 1–2). Infinite regression is traditionally the sign of a failure of thought: Aristotle opposed to it the necessity of a first term ("there has to be a stopping point"), while the classical age accepted it only by subordinating it to actual infinity [*l'infini en acte*] from the point of view of God. With Deleuze, regression takes on a positive value because it is the corollary of the paradoxical immanentist thesis according to which relation is primary, origin is coupling: having become an object of affirmation, regression offers a methodological guarantee against the return of the illusion of grounding (the illusion of a real division within being functioning as a transcendent reference for thought). There is nothing *given* that is not a *product*—the given is always a difference of intensity that springs forth from a "disparate" coupling (DR 117–18, 222–3; AO 322; ATP 369 ff.). Even the two terms of perception, subject and object, derive from a coupling that distributes them in reciprocal presupposition: in this sense, an eye is merely one piece of a machine that has been abstractly separated from its correlate (light). Husserl misses the true definition of *passive synthesis*: for it refers precisely to couplings such as this, to these "contemplations" or primary "contractions" (DR 70–9); yet if coupling is at the point of genesis, the latter necessarily regresses to infinity, thus implying a rehabilitation of regression. The renovated concept of passive synthesis comes to the fore in *Anti-Oedipus* under the name "desiring machines," where the principle of instability or metamorphosis it envelops is concretized (AO 26; this principle is referred to as "crowned anarchy" in the discussions of univocity). Which means that the given is never composed of flows, but of break-flow systems . . . that is, of machines (AO 1; the expression "ontology of flows" by which the system of

Anti-Oedipus is occasionally summarized is an invention of hasty polemicists).

*** Why this duality of break and flow? 1. The break-flow system designates the "true activities of the unconscious" (AO 325), the complimentary functions constitutive of a coupling, whereas the "partial objects"—no longer relative to a fragmented and lost whole as they were for Melanie Klein—are the "ultimate elements of the unconscious" (AO 324) that reciprocally determine themselves in the coupling, one as the source or emitter of a flow, the other as the receiving organ. We therefore should not be surprised by the paradox that ensues: the object-source is drawn from the flow [*prélevé sur le flux*][9] that it itself emits. This is because the object emits a flow only *for* the object capable of cutting into it (cf. the emblematic case of the mouth-breast machine occurring throughout *Anti-Oedipus*, notably 46–7). In turn, the organ-object can be grasped as an emitter of flows for another object (cf. the recurrent example of the mouth—AO 3, 36, etc.—and particularly in the case of anorexia—AO 1, 325). The relativity of the flow to the break must always be recalled. 2. "Desire causes the current to flow, itself flows in turn, and breaks the flows" (AO 5): breaking is not opposed to flowing (damming), in fact it is the condition under which something flows. In other words, a flow can only flow provided it has been broken. What do we mean by "break"? Precisely the rate of flow [*régime d'écoulement*] in each case, its output [*son debit*], whether it is continuous or segmented, more or less free or constricted. Still, these excessively dualistic images are insufficient: a flow will be uniform, or else unpredictable and mutating, according to the mode of break characterizing it. The concept of the break is therefore differenciated: the code is one kind, the "schiz" is another. The elementary misinterpretation would be to think that the schizophrenic flow, "a flow that overcomes barriers and codes," that "flows, irresistibly" (AO 131, 133, translation modified), escapes each and every break: this would be to forget the primacy of the machine, and the very word schiz (the act of splitting, of bifurcation—AO 91, 133). To the code as a style of break proceeding by alternatives or exclusions is opposed the schiz as an *inclusive disjunction*, the characteristic of becoming or of the encounter (Deleuze and Guattari do not reduce schizophrenia to its clinical collapse, but extract from it a *process*, the free production of desire). By distinguishing between three types of "lines," *A Thousand Plateaus* will rework the concepts of break and flow (ATP 8th and 9th Plateaus).

Complication

* "Certain Neoplatonists used a profound word to designate the original state that proceeds any development, any deployment, any 'explication': *complication*, which envelops the many in the One and affirms the unity of the multiple. Eternity did not seem to them the absence of change, nor even the extension of a limitless existence, but the complicated state of time itself . . ." (PS 45).

** The concept of complication has two levels, which correspond to the two usages of the word. First, it expresses a state: that of differences (divergent series, points of view, intensities or singularities) enveloped or implicated in one another (LS 297–8). Complication in this sense means co-implication, reciprocal implication. Such a state is characteristic of the virtual, where disjunctions are "included" or "inclusive," and is opposed to the regime of the actual, characterized by the separation of things in their exclusive relation (either . . . or): it is therefore not governed by the principle of contradiction. Complication therefore qualifies a first kind of multiplicity, an intensive one. It is the very logic of the world as "chaos" (DR 57, 124–5, 280; LS 297–8).

*** But more profoundly, "complication" expresses the synthetic operation of two inverse movements from the virtual to the actual (explication, development, unrolling) and from the actual to the virtual (implication, envelopment, rolling-up—in the later period of his works, Deleuze will speak of crystallization) (PS 89–90; EPS 16; L 6). Deleuze constantly stresses that these two movements are not opposed to one another, but are always interlocking (PS 45–6; EPS 16; L 6). What links them to each other is complication, insofar as it assures the immanence of the one in the multiple and of the multiple in the one. We must not confuse the reciprocal implication of complicated terms with the reciprocal implication of the one in the multiple and the multiple in the one, such as it is brought about through complication. From this follows the relation of two multiplicities, virtual and actual, which testifies to the overcoming of any initial dualism in favor of a monism where a single Nature oscillates between two poles: the multiple implicating the one, insofar as it is the one in an *explicated* state; the one implicating the multiple, insofar as it is the multiple in a *complicated* state. The importance of the concept of complication is therefore clear: it is opposed—even in the history of Neoplatonism—to the secluded sovereignty of the One; it carries the multiple into the origin, under the condition of a special regime of non-separation or of co-implication (this feature distinguishes Deleuze from phenomenology, from Heidegger, and at the end of the day from Derrida as well). Equally clear is the importance of the operation that it expresses, which brings into relation the two movements of actualization and redistribution, of differentiation and repetition, whose interdependent functioning provides a complete picture of the world according to Deleuze. The Neoplatonic "conversion," as the inverse of the "procession" of the One toward the multiple, is in fact incapable of carrying a movement of redistribution to the heart of the multiple; this is not its objective, since its return is directed toward the plenitude of the One, whose indifferenciation and indifference to the multiple signals a transcendence. The ascent toward the one *as* complication is totally different (a unity or immediate synthesis of the multiple, a pure "differenciator"), working-over all of the actual from the inside and opening it onto a complicated virtual totality that it implicates. Here the logic of complication intersects with the thesis of univocity of being, while the name of being tends to recede [*s'effacer*] before the differenciable name of becoming.

Crystal of Time (or of the Unconscious)

* "The crystal-image may well have many distinct elements, but its irreducibility consists in the indivisible unity of an actual image and 'its' virtual image" (C2 78). "At the limit, the imaginary is a virtual image that is interfused with the real object, and vice versa, thereby constituting a crystal of the unconscious. It is not enough for the real object or the real landscape to evoke similar or related images; it must disengage *its own* virtual image at the same time that the latter, as an imaginary landscape, makes its entry into the real, following a circuit where each of the two terms pursues the other, is interchanged with the other. 'Vision' is the product of this doubling or splitting in two [*doublement ou dédoublement*], this coalescence. It is in such crystals of the unconscious that the trajectories of the libido are made visible" (CC 63). "What constitutes the crystal-image is the most fundamental operation of time: since the past is constituted not after the present that it was but at the same time, time has to split itself in two at each moment as present and past, which differ from each other in nature or, what amounts to the same thing, it has to split the present in two heterogeneous directions, one of which is launched

toward the future while the other falls into the past. Time has to split
... in two dissymmetrical jets, one of which makes all the present
pass on, while the other preserves all the past. Time consists of this
split, and it is this, it is time, that we *see in the crystal*" (C2 81).

** This concept, one of Deleuze's last, presents the difficulty of con-
densing just about all of his philosophy. The crystal is the ultimate
state of the problematic of "real" experience, and is presented as a
deepening of the concept of becoming. First, it confirms that in any
becoming (becoming-animal, becoming-woman, etc.) it is not the
terminus that is sought-after (the animal or the woman that one
becomes) but the becoming itself, which is to say the conditions for
the continuation of desiring production or experimentation. It is not
Moby Dick, the huge sperm whale from Melville's novel, that interests Ahab: he pursues it only as a means to confront the excess of his
own life, and this is the true reason, the true logic, the true necessity
of his irrational conduct (CC Ch. 10). For his part, little Hans—so
poorly understood by Freud—has a "vision" of an omnibus horse
that falls and struggles under the lashes of a whip, but this vision is
doubled, crystalline: what the child sees in his relation to the horse
are the trajectories of his own libido. In this way he actively accedes
to his own *problem* (TR 89–113, and ATP 259–60). In both of these
cases, becoming means inhabiting a plane of immanence where existence is not produced without making itself into its own clinician,
without tracing the *map* of its impulses and its outlets.

But the reader can't help stumbling upon a difficulty here. The
pure given to which the "becomer" [*le devenant*] accedes seems to be
selected in advance due to its special resonances with a certain situation of life. Certainly, the mirror does not refer him to a narcissistic
image of himself; his situation is repeated or reflected in it, but in the
non-redundant element of an evaluative contemplation of himself.
What we need to understand then is how one's intimate life and
the spectacle are tied together; why, if real experience presupposes
the violence and chance of an encounter, we do not encounter just
anybody, or anything? It is in order to confront this problem that
Deleuze forges the concept of the crystal.

The decisive terms are *splitting* [*dédoublement*], *exchange*, and
indiscernibility. At first sight, the structure of exchange that defines
the crystal is established between the two terms of a becoming, instituting a relation of doubling or mirroring that frees a *vision*. The
relation of the subject to the object (little Hans seeing the horse)

proves from the start to be insufficient to describe the situation, which entails a moment of indiscernibility in which the little boy sees *himself* suffering in the horse and reflects his own affects in the singularities and the accidents of the latter (and vice versa). Such are the conditions of a real experience: the pure given is not relative to a preexisting subject that would open the field, nor to the forms or functions that would enable him to identify its parts. This illusion of preexistence comes only from the fact that the preformed givens of possible experience precede the access to the pure givens of real experience, which in truth is composed only of movements and the differences between movements, relations of speed and slowness, "movement-images." Henceforth, there is no longer affectivity exterior to the given, in the form of a constituted subject who would react to what he sees according to his feelings or convictions: affectivity is no longer distinct from powers that correspond to movements on the plane. It becomes not only possible but necessary to say—and without the risk of any anthropomorphism, nor any recourse to empathy of whatever sort—that the affects are those of the plane: in other words, that they are the things in themselves (for it is only from a derivative point of view that we can say: they are the *effects* of things *upon* us). "The trajectory merges not only with the subjectivity of those who travel through a milieu, but also with the subjectivity of the milieu itself, insofar as it is reflected in those who travel through it. The map expresses the identity of the journey and what one journeys through. It merges with its object, when the object itself is movement" (CC 61).

We misinterpret the affective investments of the child when we regard them as the coupling of an objective perception and an imaginary projection, rather than the splitting of the real between its actuality and *its own* virtual image (the privilege of the child and its exemplarity in the analysis of becomings is due solely to the fact that its experience is not yet organized by clichés or sensory-motor schemas). The crystalline structure of experience is this: the actual is given in its purity only insofar as it is immediately reflected in the psychism that traverses the plane: for example, the horse as seen by Hans in his becoming-horse. There is no neutral given, independent of our becomings. The opposition of the real and the imaginary (and of cognition and delirium) is secondary, and does not withstand the immanentist turn of critical questioning.

This crystalline splitting of the real institutes an "internal circuit" where the actual and *its* virtual are in a continual exchange, running from one to the other, "distinct but indiscernible" (D 150; C2 70, 81–2). Larger circuits then come to be grafted upon it, constituted by objective traits or evocations: they comprise the various thresholds of problematization through which—under the condition of the smaller circuit—the respective assemblages of Hans and the omnibus horse enter into communication: horse falls in the street / prohibition of the road and danger; power and domestication of the horse / desire proud-humiliated; biting / resisting-being naughty; etc. The mistake would be to think that the vision gives rise to the evocation: on the contrary, it is the vision that proceeds from the coupling of an ensemble of objective traits and a mental image that are mutually selected. It deepens itself by successively returning to the object, a new aspect of the object being revealed or passing to the first plane by resonating with a new psychic layer [*couche*] (C2 44–7, 68–9). This is why the haunting of the horse is active, and does not play the role of a simple representation: it is by exploring what the horse can do, the way in which it carries out the circulation of its affects, that the child contemplates and evaluates all the variable heights of his situation.

The crystal is this series of circuits that proliferate from out of the fundamental splitting of the real, properly understood: and as was already said, we see in it the trajectories of desire and their redistribution from one map to another. Why, however, do we see time in it? From one end of his oeuvre to the other, Deleuze insists on the coexistence or *contemporaneity* of two fundamentally heterogeneous temporalities: the chronological series of our trajectories or effectuations within an englobing present, and the virtual past or paradoxical eternity (Aion) of the becomings that correspond to them. Bergson has shown the impasses we are led to by conceiving the present and the past in a relation of succession, the past succeeding the present that is no more, or preceding the actual as a *former* present: the present can only be a static entity that does not pass, one that we imagine nevertheless to be ceaselessly replaced by another. We must thus assume, to the point of paradox, the evidence given by the passing of the present: if it passes all the while remaining itself present, this is because the present is contemporaneous with *its own* past (B 58; DR 81; C2 79; the same theme of contemporaneity can be found in the extraordinary concept of the "childhood block"—K 78 ff.; ATP 164, 294). The doubling of the real is consequently a doubling of time. However, it does not suffice simply to show the impossibility of constituting the past beginning from a single present, and the necessity of conceiving the past as a second temporality doubling the present (which, following one of Bergson's arguments, conditions the reactualization of former presents in the form of memories). The passing of the present is fully accounted for only when we explain this doubling through an incessant scission of time: presents align themselves one after the other only because the past multiplies its layers in depth; our effectuations all appear to follow one another without collision in a single englobing present, but their apparent continuity carries out redistributions of problems or situations that cause the present to pass. Here we discover the multiplicity of psychic layers implicated in the plural discovery of the object, which are so many successive maps glimpsed in the crystal. To say that the crystal makes us see time is to say that it draws us into its perpetual bifurcation. It is not the synthesis of Chronos and Aion, since Chronos is only the time of abstract actuality, separated from *its own* virtual image, the order of an always-already-given. The synthesis is rather that of Aion and Mnemosyne, of the temporality of the pure given, of absolute movements on the plane of immanence, and of the multiplicity of layers of the pure past where this temporality becomes terraced and multiplies itself. (Likewise, in his books on cinema Deleuze does not say that the movement-image is abolished by the time-image or the crystalline regime of the image, since cinema remains by definition a "machinic assemblage of movement-images," but rather that it continues to persist within the time-image as the first dimension of an image that expands dimensionally; on the other hand, and in accordance with the everyday subordination of experience to the sensory-motor schema, he describes the cinema of the movement-image as one that detaches the actual from its virtual double.) Finally, Deleuze names this synthesis Cronos, the titan who devours his children, since time ceaselessly re-launches and recommences its division, linking itself only through ruptures (C2 81–2).

Why invoke the name "pure past" for this temporality elsewhere described as an instantaneous synthesis of expectation and observation [*l'attente et du constat*], the infinitive of a caesura (Aion)? "Pure" qualifies a past that is only past, which is to say that is not a former present, a "past that was never present" (DR 81). It is not defined relatively in relation to an existing present, but absolutely, in relation to a present of which it is the past or the having-been (this is how we must understand the statement that "the past does not follow the present that it is no longer, it coexists with the present it was" (C2 79). Bergson called it the "memory [*souvenir*] of the present": not the past that this present will become, but the past *of this* present. It is past as the element in which the present passes, and not because it would refer to an anteriority in a chronological relation. It is important to see clearly that this invocation of the pure past in Deleuze refers to a problematic of becoming, not one of memory. In the name of becomings, Deleuze dismisses back to back the preoccupations with history and with the future (N 152–3).

*** The concept of the crystal envelops a devaluation of metaphor, and is inseparable from a critique and a reworking of the concept of the imaginary. Let us recall the basic schema: not a second image that would come to redouble the first, but the splitting of a single image into two parts that originally refers the one to the other. Freud was certainly right to think that little Hans' relation to the horse concerned something other than the horse; but it was not what he thought it was. The world in all its complexity and richness is not the resonance chamber of a single and same story (Oedipus), but the proliferating crystal of unforeseeable trajectories. For the metaphorical interpretation of psychoanalysis must be substituted a "schizoanalytic" process of *literal* deciphering. "Literal" does not mean adhesion to the pure actual (as if, for example, the non-metaphoricity of Kafka's writings was sufficient to exhaust its fictional content). However, the identification of the imaginary with the unreal prevents us from seeing that a literary fiction—beyond the alternative of a metaphorical representation of the real and the arbitrary escape into dreams—can be an experiment, or a field of experimentation. Inversely, the real that is opposed to the imaginary appears as a horizon of pure recognition where everything is already familiar, no different from a *cliché* or a simple representation. On the other hand, once we relate the imaginary as production or creation to the actual-virtual couple in its crystalline regime, it becomes a matter of indifference whether the actual is experienced or forged (imagined). The conceptual division is no longer the same: what we see on the cinematic screen, what a writer recounts or describes, what a child imagines in the exploration of his pleasures and his frights, is actual—or given—in the same way as a "real" scene. What matters is the type of relation that the actual entertains with a possible virtual element. There is metaphor when the actual is assumed to receive its true meaning from another image actualized in it, but which could be actualized on its own (such as the primitive scene or fantasy—the ground of metaphor is recollection [*souvenir*]). There is dreaming when the sensations of the sleeper do not actualize themselves in an image without the latter in its turn actualizing itself in another, and so on, in a continuum in becoming overflowing all metaphor (C2 57). Lastly, there is a crystal when the actual, whether lived or imagined, is inseparable from a virtual that is co-originary with it, such that one can speak of "its own" virtual image. The image is split in itself rather than being actualized in another, or being the actualization of another.

This displacement of the real-imaginary couple (or real-unreal) toward the virtual-actual couple strips any consistency from the objections raised by those surprised by the fact that Deleuze can pass without any transition from children to artists ("In its own way, art says what children say" [CC 65]—which, as he constantly reminds us, does not mean that children are artists). If the crystal dissolves the false opposition of the real and the imaginary, it should at the same time give us the genuine concepts of both the imaginary and the real; for example, literature as *effective fiction*, a production of images but also a real production, a production of the real, a delirium of imagination linked to the reality of a becoming, guided and sanctioned by it (cf. *Kafka*). For if the imaginary is no longer opposed to the real, except in the case of metaphor or arbitrary fantasy, then for its part the real is no longer pure actuality but, as Bergson put it, the "coalescence" of the virtual and the actual. It is along the paths of the imaginary that the crystal of a work or of a childhood haunting reveals the real in person.

Perhaps we can now better understand the meaning of literality. Once again, it is entirely a question of the intrinsic or extrinsic nature of the relation between the actual and the virtual: the representation of a scene versus the trace of a becoming. This is because literality is not literal meaning [*sens propre*] ("There are no literal words, neither are there metaphors"—D 3): the crystal, having rejected the real-imaginary duality as an abstraction, at the same time undermines the presumed separation of the literal and the figurative. Just as for the subject-object couple, we must say: properties are not distributed in advance, the distinction between the literal and the figurative is established only within the given (sedentary distribution, wrongly taken to be original). Far from extolling an obtuse fixation on the literal usage of words, commitment to literality takes us prior to the distinction between the literal and the figurative—the plane of immanence or of univocity, where discourse, prey to its becomings, has little to fear from the "sedentary" minds who take it to be metaphor.

Desiring Machines

* "In desiring-machines everything functions at the same time, but amid hiatuses and ruptures, breakdowns and failures, stalling and short circuits, distances and fragmentations, within a sum that never succeeds in bringing its various parts together so as to form a whole" (AO 42). "Desiring machines constitute the non-Oedipal life of the unconscious" (BS 95).

** A desiring machine is defined first of all by a coupling or a "break-flow" system, where the terms determined by the coupling are "partial objects" (yet no longer in Melanie Klein's sense of the term, since they no longer refer to the anterior integrity of a whole): from this point of view, it is already composed of machines, to infinity. *Anti-Oedipus* begins with the univocal or immanent plane of a Nature conceived of as process of production (this text should be placed alongside the beginning of the first chapter of *Matter and Memory*, cited elsewhere as an example of the installation of a plane of immanence: C1 Ch. 4; WP 48–9). Next, the break-flows are inscribed, recorded, or distributed following the law of the disjunctive synthesis on a full body without organs (AO 9–16). Finally, a subject that never preexists the machine but is produced in it as a "remainder" or a "residue" circulates across the disjunctions and consumes-consummates them as so many states of itself (AO 16–22; for a recapitulation of the three aspects, 36–41). Desiring machines are paradoxical: they function "only when they are not functioning properly" (AO 31). However, once we realize that the word machine is not a metaphor here, we see that it is only paradoxical in appearance. In fact, the typical sense of the word is the result of an abstraction by which one isolates the technical machine from the conditions of its emergence and of its functioning (from men or possibly even animals, from a particular type of society or economy, etc.). The machine is social before being technical, knows nothing of the distinction between production and its functioning, and is in no way confused with a closed mechanism (K 81–2; AO 36 ff.; BS 91). Lastly, there is no difference in nature between the "social machines" (the capitalist market, the State, the church, the army, the family, etc.) and "desiring machines," but rather a difference of regime or of logic: the latter "invest" the former and constitute their unconscious, which is to say at once that they feed off of them and render them possible all while putting them into "flight" (AO 340 ff.; BS 111–12).

Desiring Machines

In *A Thousand Plateaus*, the concept of the desiring machine disappears in favor of the concepts of assemblage and abstract machine (where one again finds this paradoxical function of a conditioning destabilization).

*** We are not surprised to find a divergence between the conventional meaning of the word "desire" and the Deleuzo-Guattarian conception of it: in fact, the divergence is within the word itself, between the experience it refers to and which it is a question of raising to the level of a concept, and the interpretation of it that is circulated in accordance with the exigencies of the conscious representations of a constituted subject. Desire is typically opposed to its realization, which pushes it back onto the side of the dream, of fantasy, of representation. Here, however, we see it brought back onto the side of production, where its model is no longer the theatre—the eternal representation of the story of Oedipus—but the factory, and "if desire produces, its product is real ... the objective being of desire is the Real in and of itself" (AO 26–7). Desire is not the representation of an absent or missing object, but an activity of production, an incessant experimentation, an experimental montage. The famous statement "desire is a machine" (AO 26) assumes here a twofold polemical significance: 1) it challenges the psychoanalytic idea that dreams are the "royal road" to the unconscious; 2) it competes with Marxism more than it agrees with it, by raising in turn the problem of the *production of existence* and by asserting that "desire is part of the infrastructure" (AO 104; the factory model of the unconscious is substituted for that of the theatre).

However, to break with the habitually idealistic conceptions of desire implies contesting their logic: when we imagine desire as the tension of a subject in relation to an object (the logic of the representation of desire) we subordinate it to an end distinct from it— *possession*; by doing so, not only do we not account for the reality of desire as such or of its formation, but desire is deluded. It is of course necessary that I have at my disposal the beings and things from which I draw the singularities that enter into the machinic composition of my desire, and which establish my "territory"—but precisely in order for me to able *to desire*, or, put differently, to pursue an affective adventure on this machinic plane. In this sense, desire is not lack but process, a vagabond apprenticeship; it suffers only from being interrupted, and not from that part of the "object" that escapes it again and again. In this it is also distinguished from pleasure: the

164

explorations of pain belong no less to desire; it is not a question of wanting to suffer and taking pleasure in it, but of a becoming, an affective journey (cf. the examples of courtly love: D 99–101 and ATP 156–7; of masochism: ATP 152, 156). The other deception is that of the subject: desire represented as a faculty ready and willing to express itself, knowing only external hindrances (a bridled subject prevented from exteriorizing himself). In reality, desire is never given in advance, and its movement does not go from inside to outside: it is born from the outside, from an encounter or a coupling (D 52, 97). Explorer, experimenter, desire goes from effect to effect or from affect to affect, mobilizing beings and things not for themselves but for the singularities that they emit and that it draws [*prélève*] from them. This extraction [*prélèvement*] of singularities does not imply that things parcel themselves out in the Kleinian sense, since things and "partial objects" do not operate in the same plane, and because the plane on which the latter are "machined" is not composed of things. The usual representation of desire—a tension toward something or someone—refers therefore to the formation of a "desiring machine" that precedes the subject-object division and accounts for it.

Deterritorialization (and Territory)

* "The function of deterritorialization: D is the movement by which 'one' leaves the territory" (ATP 508). "The territory is not primary in relation to the qualitative mark; it is the mark that makes the territory. Functions in a territory are not primary; they presuppose a territory-producing expressiveness. In this sense, the territory, and the functions performed within it, are products of territorialization. Territorialization is an act of rhythm that has become expressive, or of milieu components that have become qualitative" (ATP 315).

** The term "deterritorialization," a neologism first appearing in *Anti-Oedipus*, has since been widely utilized in the humanities. But it does not form a concept when taken solely by itself, and its meaning remains vague so long as it is not related to three other elements: territory, earth, and reterritorialization—the ensemble of which forms, in its accomplished version, the concept of the *refrain*. We distinguish between a *relative* deterritorialization, which consists of reterritorializing oneself differently, in changing territories (yet *becoming* is not change, since there is no term nor end to becoming—here there could perhaps be a certain difference with Foucault); and an *absolute* deter-ritorialization, which is equivalent to living on an abstract line or a line of flight (if becoming is not change, all change nevertheless envel-ops a becoming which, when seized as such, releases us from the grip of reterritorialization: cf. the concept of the "counter-effectuation" of the event—LS 21st Series—and the question "what happened?"—ATP 8th Plateau). Such is more or less the schema prevalent in *Anti-Oedipus*, where "deterritorialization" is synonymous with "decoding." Yet the problem of reterritorialization is already posed here, leading to the polemical theme of the "new earth," always to come and above all to construct, against every promised or ancestral earth as fascist or archaic forms of reterritorialization (AO 315–22, 257–8).

In *A Thousand Plateaus* the schema becomes more complicated and more refined through an accentuation of the ambivalent rela-tion to the earth—the depth of the Natal and the smooth space of nomadism—which, consequently, also affects the territory. Not only does the rigidity of the code no longer account for every type of ter-ritory, but reterritorialization is now fully accepted as the correlate of all deterritorialization, once it is said that deterritorialization is no longer effectuated on a territory properly speaking, but, when it is absolute, upon an unlimited earth: a nomadic assemblage, desert or steppe as paradoxical territory, where the nomad "reterritorializes on deterritorialization itself" (ATP 381; the relative-absolute dis-tinction corresponds to the opposition between history and becom-ing, absolute deterritorialization being the moment of desire and of thought—WP 88). This shift of emphasis opens the way to the concept of the *refrain*.

*** Borrowed from ethnology more than from politics, the concept of territory certainly implies space, but it does not consist in the objective delimitation of a geographical location. Territory has an existential value: it circumscribes for a given person the field of the familiar and the captivating, marks distances from others, and protects against chaos. The intimate investment of space and time implies this delimitation, inseparably material (the consistency of an "assemblage"—see the entry on this word) and affective (the problematic frontiers of my "power" [*puissance*]). The territorial layout distributes an outside and an inside, sometimes passively per-ceived as the untouchable contour of experience (points of anxiety, of shame, of inhibition), sometimes actively haunted by its own line of flight, and thus more like a zone of experience. In *Anti-Oedipus*, the territory was indistinguishable from the code, because it was above all an index of fixity and closure. In *A Thousand Plateaus*, this fixity expresses only a passive relation to the territory, which is why the latter becomes a distinct concept in this work (ATP 321–2): "the constituting mark of a domain, an abode" and not of a subject, the territory marks out the relations of propriety or of appropriation (and concomitantly, of distance) in which all subjective identification consists—"a having more profound than being" (ATP 316). The proper name and the ego make sense only as a function of a "mine" or of a "home" [*chez moi*] (ATP 319, 504). This value of appropriation is linked to the becoming-expressive of sensible qualities, which enter like inseparable variables into the composition of a *refrain*, a marking of distances, which—and this is decisive—even in the case of animals proves to be anterior to all functionality (ATP 315–23; WP 183). The territory is thus the subjectivizing dimension of the assemblage, which means that there is intimacy only on the outside [*au-dehors*], in contact with an exteriority, born out of a contemplation prior to any division of a subject and an object (see "Break-flow" and "Plane of Immanence"). This primordial having is first thematized by Deleuze under the name "habit" or "contemplation" (DR 72–9). The concept then changed, as is seen in the distinction between *milieus* and *territories* (ATP 313–15). Once it becomes part of the logic of the assemblage and the refrain, the motif of having contributes to the definition of the essential practical problem, that of *leaving the territory*: what relation to the strange, what proximity to chaos, can the territory tolerate? What is its degree of closure, or, inversely, of permeability (screen) to the outside (lines of flight, points of deterritorialization)? Not all territories are of equal value, and as we have seen, their relation to deterritorialization is not a simple opposition.

Disjunctive Synthesis (or Inclusive Disjunction)

* "The whole question is to know under what conditions the disjunction is a veritable synthesis, instead of being a procedure of analysis which is satisfied with the exclusion of predicates from one thing in virtue of the identity of its concept (the negative, limitative, or exclusive use of disjunction). The answer is given insofar as the divergence or the decentering determined by the disjunction become objects of affirmation as such" (LS 174). "The disjunction has become *inclusive*: everything divides, but into itself" (CC 153).

** 1. By inclusive disjunction we typically understand a complex such that, two propositions being given, *at least* one or the other is the case (for example, "it is nice out or it is cold"): here "inclusive" does not have a positive sense, but signifies only that the disjunction envelops a possible conjunction. There is no exclusion here, but we can see that the exclusion of the two propositions disappears only at the point where their disjunction is cancelled. Consequently, in a strict sense every disjunction is exclusive: a non-relation in which each term is the negation of the other. With Deleuze the notion takes on an entirely different sense: the non-relation becomes a relation, disjunction becomes a relation. Was this not already the originality of the Hegelian dialectic? But the latter had paradoxically relied on negation in order to affirm disjunction as such, and was able to do so only by the mediation of the whole, by elevating negation to contradiction (B is everything that is not A—DR 45); even when raised to the infinite, there is a disjunctive synthesis here only under the horizon of the readsorption or "reconciliation" that distributes each term its place at the end of the day. In reality, even opposites or relative terms (life-death, parent-child, man-woman) are not destined to a dialectical relationship: "The disjunction, being now inclusive, does not closet itself inside its own terms. On the contrary, it is non-restrictive" (AO 77—an essential page; cf. also the illustration of this account through the theory of *n* sexes, 294 ff.); it causes each term to pass into the other following an order of asymmetrical reciprocal implication that does not resolve itself into an equivalence, nor into a higher-order identity. A Nietzschean perspectivism confers a positive consistency upon disjunction: a *distance* between nondecomposable *points of view* that are nonetheless not self-identical, since the route is not the same in each direction (according to a well-known Nietzschean example, sickness as a point of view upon health differs from health as a point of view upon sickness—LS 173–5; AO 76–7).

2. Why does Deleuze conclude that "everything divides into itself" (AO 19, 76; CC 153; CC 110)? It is here that the term *inclusive* disjunction takes on a positive sense. Take the couples life-death, parent-child, man-woman: the terms have only a differential relation, and the relation is first, for it is that which distributes the terms between which it is established. As a result, the test [*épreuve*] of sense lies in the double trajectory of the distance that relates them: one is not a man without becoming-woman, etc.; and where psychoanalysis sees an illness, there is on the contrary the living adventure of sense or of desire on the "body without organs," the superior health of

the child, the hysteric, the schizophrenic (AO 75 ff.). Each time, the opposing terms are so many points of view or solved cases in relation to a "problem" from which they derive (their condition, their generation, or their sex) and which is logically described as *internal difference*, or an instance of that which "differs from itself" ("Bergson's Conception of Difference" DI 32 ff.; NP 51; B 102; LS 262). And what of the objection that the examples chosen are equivocal, since their terms are in a relation of reciprocal presupposition from the start? Consider the disjunctive syntheses of the anorexic: they form an open series (speaking-eating-shitting-breathing) that defines a problem of the mouth as an organ, and beyond the fixed function assigned to it by the organism (AO 1, 38, and particularly the inclusive disjunction of the mouth-anus, 325). Moreover, it is the whole of nature, the ramified multiplicity of living species that testifies to a spacing [*echelonnement*] or a free communication of problems and resolving divisions that refer in the last instance to univocal being as Difference [*LA différence*]: "the univocity of being does not mean that there is one and the same being; on the contrary, beings are multiple and different, they are always produced by a disjunctive synthesis, and they themselves are disjointed and divergent, *membra disjuncta*" (LS 179; cf. also DR 39). Each being in principle implicates all the others, each concept opens onto every predicate: the world, unstable or chaotic, is "complication" (LS 174 and 294–301).

3. From the practical point of view, the disjunctive synthesis is the suspension, neutralization, or exhaustion of the always derived distribution that nature and society submit us to by "stratifying" the undivided reality of univocal being or the body without organs: "Whereas the 'either/or' claims to mark decisive choices between immutable terms (the alternative: either this or that), the schizophrenic 'either ... or ... or' refers to the system of possible permutations between differences that always amount to the same as they shift and slide about" (AO 12; cf. also CC 153–5). This play of permutations clearly has a defensive value in relation to identitarian fixations, but precisely by safeguarding becoming or the desiring process; the same to which everything returns here "is said of that which differs in itself," meaning that which divides into itself and does not exist outside of its divisions (the principle of inclusive disjunction). The desiring process consists in a trail of intensities which, far from being equivalent, give rise to an immanent evaluation. Disjunctive synthesis merges in the last instance with this evaluation, and with the interpretation of the Nietzschean Eternal Return

as selective. Once we understand that it does not select modes of existence that return "once and for all," careful attention must be paid to the radicality of the mode that is opposed to the latter and which passes the test, proving itself capable of returning "for each and every time" (LS 301). It is not a question of an existence that changes modes, but of an existence whose mode is to suspend every mode: the principle of a nomadic ethics characterized by a "becoming-everyone," "becoming-imperceptible" (ATP 279–80). This existence should not be seen as withdrawn or even contemplative in the banal sense—on the contrary, it is a matter of being equal to the world in order to live it in the reality of its intensities, which implies the highest level of "machinic" activity, an incessant construction of "assemblages" under the rule of the involuntary.

*** Disjunctive synthesis (or inclusive disjunction) is the principal operator of Deleuze's philosophy, his signature concept above all others. It matters little whether it appears monstrous in the eyes of those who call themselves logicians: defining his own work as the elaboration of a "logic," Deleuze criticizes the discipline institutionalized under this name for abusively reducing the field of thought by restricting it to the puerile exercise of recognition, and for justifying a self-contented and obtuse good sense under whose gaze everything in experience that threatens to undermine the two principles of contradiction and the excluded middle is branded a pure nothingness, any attempt at a discernment therein being regarded as fruitless (WP Ch. 6). The thinker is first of all a clinician, a sensitive decipherer and a patient of the regimes of signs that existence produces, and according to which it itself is produced. His task is to construct logical objects capable of accounting for this production, and thus to raise the critical question to its highest point of paradox: where "conditions no broader than the conditioned" are envisaged (this program leads directly to the concept of inclusive disjunction). Thus Deleuze vehemently protests against the confusion of irrationalism and illogicism, calling for a "new logic, definitely a logic, but one that . . . does not lead back to reason," an "extreme and nonrational logic," an "irrational logic" (CC 82–3; FB 83). Deleuzian irrationality must not remain a vague label, ripe for every malicious misunderstanding. It is comprised of at least two powerful elements, which equally form the program of "transcendental empiricism": the refutation of grounding (conceptual necessity is to be sought in the involuntary character of the encounter), and the logic of the disjunctive synthesis

or inclusive disjunction, or complication (the principles of contradiction and the excluded middle have their jurisdiction only in a
derivative domain).

Event

* "We will not ask therefore what is the sense of the event: the event is
sense itself. The event belongs essentially to language; it has an essential relationship to language. But language is what is said of things"
(LS 22). "With every event, there is indeed the present moment of its
actualization, the moment in which the event is embodied in a state
of affairs, an individual, or a person, the moment we designate by
saying '*here*, the moment has come.' The future and the past of the
event are evaluated only with respect to this definitive present, and
from the point of view of that which embodies it. But on the other
hand, there is the future and the past of the event considered in itself,
sidestepping each present, being free of the limitations of a state of
affairs, impersonal and pre-individual, neutral, neither general nor
particular, *eventum tantum* ... It has no other present than that
of the mobile instant which represents it, always divided into past-
future, and forming what must be called the counter-effectuation. In
one case, it is my life, which seems too weak for me and slips away
at a point which, in a determined relation to me, has become present.
In the other case, it is I who am too weak for life, it is life which
overwhelms me, scattering its singularities all about, in no relation to
me, nor to a moment determinable as the present, except an impersonal instant is divided into still-future and already-past" (LS 151,
translation modified).

** The concept of the event is born out of a distinction made by
the Stoics: "the event is not to be confused with its spatio-temporal
effectuation in a state of affairs" (LS 22, translation modified). The
statement "the knife is cutting the flesh" expresses an *incorporeal
transformation* that differs in nature from the corresponding *mixture
of bodies* (the moment when the knife actually materially cuts the
flesh) (ATP 86). The effectuation within bodies (the incarnation or
actualization of the event) only gives rise to the succession of two
states of affairs—before/after—in accordance with the principle of
exclusive disjunction, whereas language gathers together the difference between these two states of affairs, the pure instant of their
disjunction (see the entry on "Aion"): it is up to it to accomplish the

disjunctive synthesis of the event, and it is this difference that creates *sense.*

But we should not conclude from this that the event sheltered within language is linguistic in nature, as if it were merely the equivalent of the mixture of bodies on another plane: the frontier is not between language and the event on one side and the world and its states of affairs on the other, but between two interpretations of the relation between language and the world. According to the first, required by the logicians, this relation is established between the propositional form to which language is reduced, and the form of a state of affairs to which the world is consequently reduced. The distribution with which Deleuze proposes to repair this double denaturation *passes both within language and within the world*: the paradox of the event is that, purely "expressible," it is no less an "attribute" of the world and its states of affairs, so that the dualism of the proposition and its corresponding state of affairs is not found on the plane of the event, which subsists only in language, all the while belonging to the world. The event is therefore both sides at once—in language, it is that which distinguishes the proposition; in the world it is that which distinguishes states of affairs. Even better, it is the double-differenciator of significations on the one hand, of states of affairs on the other. Hence the application of the virtual-actual couple (and to a lesser degree the problem-solution couple) to the concept of the event. Hence also the two directions to which this primacy of the event leads: a theory of signs and of sense, and a theory of becoming. On the one hand, Deleuze opposes the conception of signification as a complete entity or explicit datum, one still pregnant in phenomenology and every other philosophy of "essence" (a world of things or of essences would not make sense by itself, as it would be missing sense *qua* difference or event, and it is this alone that renders significations perceptible and engenders them within thought). From this emerges the interest in *style* or *syntactical creation*, as well as the thesis that, properly speaking, the *concept* is not composed of propositions, but is rather the event freed for itself in language (WP 22–3, 33–4). On the other hand, he sketches an ethics of *counter-effectuation* or *becoming-imperceptible* (LS 21st Series; ATP 8th and 10th Plateaus) based on the liberation of the evental or "ineffectuable" [*l'ineffectuable*] part of every effectuation. In sum, the event is inseparably both the sense of statements and the becoming of the world; it is that of the world which allows itself to be enveloped in language, thereby enabling the latter to function. Consequently, the event is explicated in a *Logic of Sense*.

*** Are we justified in opposing the thought of the event to the thought of being or, on the contrary, should they to be merged together? The event occurs at two levels in Deleuze's thought: the condition under which thought thinks (the encounter with an outside that forces thought, a sectioning of chaos by the plane of immanence), and the special objecticities [*objectités*] of thought (the plane is populated solely by events or becomings, and each concept is the construction of an event on the plane). And if there is no way of thinking that is not also a way of experiencing, of thinking *what is*, then philosophy cannot assume the evental condition that guarantees its specific necessity without at the same time putting forward a description of a pure given that is itself evental. If one likes, and *par provision*,[10] let us call this an experience of *being*—although neither in its style nor in its reasons does the Deleuzian approach have anything to do with that of Heidegger; and even though being is a deceptive notion in this case, provided it is true that there is givenness only in becoming (it will be noted that Deleuze avoids the word "being" as much as possible). Any talk of a Deleuzian ontology must therefore come with heavy precautions, if only out of consideration for a thinker who did not readily wield such a category. These precautions are of two sorts. On the one hand, we must be attentive to what, for Deleuze, makes the conversion of critical philosophy into ontology possible—mainly, the fact that the pure given is not *for* a subject (the division of the reflexive subject and the intended and recognized object is carried out only *within* the given, whereas the pure given refers to a paradoxically "adjacent" subjectivity, which is to say not transcendental but always situated on the plane of immanence). On the other hand—and this is the aspect we will develop here—it is a question of thinking a *heterogenesis*, according to Guattari's splendid term, where "genesis" is no longer understood in its traditional sense as engendering, as birth or constitution (this is the true relation between fact and law, which Deleuze claims can be found neither in Kant nor in Husserl, since both "trace" the conditions from the conditioned, the form of the transcendental from the empirical: the recognitional form of an indeterminate object, one relative to a conscious subject). "Genesis" is consequently understood in relation to a new concept of "becoming," and this is undoubtedly what distances Deleuze most from phenomenology and its heirs, even its

ungrateful ones. Phenomenology "fails" to think the heterogeneity that is fundamentally at stake in becoming (in strict Deleuzian
terms: this is not its problem, it poses a different problem). In fact,
it thinks only a *becoming-same* (the form in the process of being
born, the appearance of the thing), and not what really should be a
pleonasm—a *becoming-other*. Is this not precisely what is expressed
by the dislocation of the Heideggerian word *E r e i g n i s* (event)
in *Ereignis* (appropriation)? Hence the equivocation that arises
when the phenomenology outliving Deleuze attempts to take up the
theme of the event and to rediscover it as the very heart of what it
had always endeavored to think. For, considering its fundamental
problematic, it can only ever obtain *advents* [*avènements*], births
and arrivals (but then again, its problem being different, perhaps this
is what it wants, or what its "plane" brings back from "chaos"). Its
theme is the beginning of time, the genesis of historicity, and not, as
for Deleuze, the caesura or rupture irrevocably cutting time in two
and forcing it to begin again in a synthetic capture of the irreversible and the immanent, the event occupying the strange position
of a still-there-and-already-past, still-to-come-and-already-there (see
"Aion"). Consequently, for Deleuze historicity itself is in becoming,
affected from within by an exteriority that undermines it and causes
it to diverge from itself. This duel between two thoughts of the event,
of genesis, and of becoming—the one reclaiming "being," the other
seeing there nothing but a screen or a word—is this not ultimately a
duel between a Christian and a non-Christian conception of the new?

Line of Flight (and Minor/Major)

* "The line of flight is a deterritorialization. The French do not
understand this very well. Obviously, they flee like everyone else,
but they think that fleeing means making an exit from the world,
mysticism or art, or else that it is something rather sloppy because
we avoid our commitments and responsibilities. But to flee is not to
renounce action: nothing is more active than flight. It is the opposite
of the imaginary. It is also to put to flight—not necessarily others,
but to put something to flight, to put a system to flight as one bursts
a tube . . . to flee is to trace a line, lines, and a whole cartography"
(D 36).

** This concept defines the practical orientation of Deleuze's philosophy. We may begin by taking note of a double equality: line = flight,

to flee = to put to into flight. What defines a situation is a certain distribution of possibilities, the spatio-temporal division of existence (roles, functions, activities, desires, tastes, varieties of joy and pain, etc.). It is less a question of rituals—a dreary repetition, regulated alternation, an excessive narrowness of the field of options—than of the same dichotomous form of possibility: either/or, exclusive disjunctions of all kinds (masculine-feminine, adult-child, human-animal, intellectual-manual, work-leisure, black-white, heterosexual-homosexual, etc.) that *striate* in advance our perception, affectivity, and thought, imprisoning experience within ready-made forms, even forms of refusal and struggle.

There is an oppression that coincides with this striation, one that is visible in these binary couples, each of which envelops a hierarchy: each disjunction is at base that of a *major* and a *minor*. And if we were to say that dichotomous gridding [*quadrillage*] interrupts desire as a process or an incessant autoproduction, the question may of course be asked: is it desire that takes refuge in minor states once domination is established, or does minorization not rather affect those regions of existence where desire escapes all assignation and all segmentation? The second option would be tantamount to declaring desire to be intrinsically feminine, infantile, etc. In reality, if becomings have a privileged relation to femininity or childhood, this is because these relations tend to bring about flight within situations dichotomized around the state of (qualitative) majority defined by the adult male. Hence the artificial character of an emancipation consisting in the affirmation of an identity of the woman, since the latter can have no other content than the characteristics drawn from the distribution of roles, attitudes, etc., instituted through domination. From this point of view, even "women must become-woman" (ATP 291), which is to say, a woman must rediscover the point where her self-affirmation, far from being that of an identity inevitably defined by reference to a man, is rather this elusive and essenceless "femininity" that never affirms itself without compromising the established order of affections and mores, since this order implies its repression. This is also why becoming-woman concerns men as much as women: the latter do not cultivate the line of flight that they *are* within a given situation (and not the identity that the situation imposes upon them) without putting the ensemble of the situation into flight, and thus "contaminating men, sweeping them up in that becoming" (ATP 275–8, 292, 469 ff.).

For Deleuze and Guattari, the solution lies less in a change of

175

situation or in the abolition of all situations than in the vacillation, fluctuation, and disorganization of any given situation. This does not mean that all situations are of equal value; their respective value lies in the degree of disorganization they can withstand without bursting apart, and not in the intrinsic quality of order to which they testify. However, expressed in these terms, Deleuzo-Guattarian practice would fall prey to another infamous dichotomy: order-disorder. Yet disorder properly understood is not nothingness or chaos, but rather a "sectioning" [*coupe*] within chaos, a confrontation with it rather than its denial in the name of forms presumed to be natural (see the entry on "Plane of Immanence"). These vectors of disorganization or of "deterritorialization" are precisely called *lines of flight*. We can now comprehend the double equality of which this complex expression is comprised. To flee is here understood in both senses of the word: something loses its impermeability [*étanchéité*] or its closure; evasion, escape. If to flee means to put into flight, this is because flight does not consist in exiting the situation and going somewhere else, changing your life, escaping into dreams, or even transforming the situation (the latter case is more complex, for to put the situation into flight necessarily implies a redistribution of possibilities that—barring obtuse repression—open onto an at least partial transformation, entirely unprogrammable, related to the unforeseeable creation of new space-times and original institutional assemblages; nevertheless, the solution lies in the flight, in the pursuit of a desiring process, and not in the transformation, the result of which would for its part only be as valuable as its own lines of flight, and so on). It is nevertheless still a question of an exit, but the latter is paradoxical. Deleuze analyzes cases of all different natures, the family, society, institutions; let us restrict ourselves to philosophy, which has its own situation—not because it is somehow more important than the other cases, but because comparatively speaking it is instructive regarding the Deleuzian approach. "To leave philosophy, by means of philosophy" (ABC, "C comme culture"): everything happens as if philosophy enveloped its own outside, as if its true outside were not external to it [*hors*] but was to be found rather at its center (to leave philosophy by becoming a sociologist, an anthropologist, a psychoanalyst, or a militant is only to leave the situation intact so as to leap into other situations one judges to be intrinsically better). Here we would have the grounds for a possible confrontation with Derrida: where the latter defines the situation as the "closure of metaphysics" and, far from dreaming of another *logos* than the *logos* (defined as speech and presence), proposes to "deconstruct" it beginning with the exclusion that has always undermined it (writing and its effect of "différance"), Deleuze proceeds by a method one could call *perversion*, which proceeds sometimes by discerning and cultivating a line of thinkers "who seemed to be part of the history of philosophy, but who escaped from it in one respect, or altogether: Lucretius, Spinoza, Hume, Nietzsche, Bergson" (D 14–15), sometimes by diverting pieces from all different varieties of theory so as to use them for other ends (DR, LS, AO, ATP, *passim*), sometimes by relating a concept to its true conditions, which is to say to the forces and intuitive dynamisms that subtend it (DI 98 ff.—the method of "dramatization"), and finally, rather than launching a frontal critique of a theme or an idea, by approaching it from a "thoroughly twisted conception" (the juridical contract in Sacher-Masoch—N 142–3 and M 93 ff.). An approximation of this opposition between the two approaches can be found in the text "To Have Done With Judgment" (CC Ch. 15): the one carried in the direction of an interminable analysis as the only possible Justice, the other operating by a series of "finite processes" (for this is indeed Deleuze's way of making use of the history of philosophy—some examples of finite processes: his interpretation of the Kantian Cogito, of the paradoxical contemporaneity of the past and the present in Bergson, etc., as so many fixed pieces whose sense-effects are nevertheless ceaselessly renewed as a function of the assemblages in which they are taken up).

Instead of criticizing, always put into flight (K 46–7) . . . But why speak of perversion? Here I am thinking not only of the usual definition—a deviation with respect to object or aim—but of a text describing the attitude Freud had isolated as the distinctive trait of perversion: "It might seem that a disavowal is, generally speaking, much more superficial than a negation or even a partial destruction. But this is not so, for it represents an entirely different operation. Disavowal should perhaps be understood as the point of departure of an operation that consists neither in negating nor even in destroying, but rather in radically contesting the validity of that which is: it suspends belief in and neutralizes the given in such a way that a new horizon opens up beyond the given and in place of it" (M 31). If it is not a question of taking flight "out-of" but of putting into flight, there is indeed still something from which one flees, and which merges with this putting-into-flight: the absolute reign of the yes and the no, of the alternative as law of the possible, choice as the pseudo-liberty of a desire subjugated to pre-established divisions (LS

320; CC Ch. 10, not only the way Bartleby scrambles this division, but the "metaphysical perversion" of Captain Ahab, the man who is "fleeing from everywhere" CC 77–9; finally CC Ch. 18, *passim*). Contrary to the dialectic, which claims to overcome the alternative through a synthetic reconciliation, and in doing so admits and conserves the premise (we don't reach becoming by combining being and nothing), the line of flight is placed under the sign of the indiscernible and of *inclusive disjunction*. Finally, and in an almost etymological sense, the pervert is the man of surfaces or of the plane of immanence (LS 133). For we trace this line only crookedly [*de travers*]—the other aspect of the double equality. It is through a free usage of the organ that we deterritorialize it, that we cease to live it as if it were originally bound to the function ascribed to it by the organism, so as to assemble it differently on a "body without organs" or a plane of immanence, according to encounters with other "partial objects" themselves extracted [*prélevé*] or diverted. Which is to say that the line of flight is always *transversal*: it is by being transversally related that things lose their face, cease to be pre-identified by ready-made schemas, and acquire the consistency of a life or a work—in other words, of a "non-organic unity" (PS 161–9). The transversal is like a sectioning of univocity within constituted forms, a pure plane of experience on which all communicates with all (and is composed or not), beyond the barriers of form, of function, or of space.[11]

*** With this, our two equalities are surpassed in the direction of a third: drawing a line of flight = thinking in terms of lines. Not that there is anything else on the plane of immanence than these lines of flight on which "non-organic life" constructs itself, and transversally in relation to constituted forms. But drawing a line on the plane yields a new point of view on the ensemble of a situation, an immanent criteria that enables the analysis of assemblages according to their two poles, deterritorialization and stratification (institutions). Immanent since, in conformity with the primacy of the plane of immanence from the critical point of view (conditions of experience), every form or organization must be constituted beginning from it. Thus there is not a world of fixed forms and a world of becoming, but different states of the line, different types of lines, the intricacy of which constitutes the modifiable *map* of a life. This geographical theme of the map is opposed to the archeological approach of psychoanalysis (cf. ATP 12, 203; N 33; CC Ch. 9).

What, at bottom, is a line? It is a sign that envelops time, the basic element of a semiotic of duration, of a clinic of existence (Deleuze only arrives at this concept beginning with *Dialogues* [D 119–40]; *Proust and Signs*, which described the "worlds of signs" deployed "according to lines of time" [PS 25], had sought the synthesis of the two terms but still maintained their separation). A given assemblage or a situation is analyzed by means of a differentiation of the concept of the line, as opposed to the "system of points and positions" characterizing structuralist thought (D 37). Three different types are distinguished, which define so many relations to space and time: besides the lines of flight, which refer to Aion and to smooth space, there are lines of "rigid segmentarity" (binary cycles and striated space), and between the two poles there is a line with an ambiguous status, a line of "supple segmentarity" (fragmentary deductions, thresholds of affective redistribution) (ATP 195–207, 222–31).

Why does Deleuze affirm the primacy of lines of flight (D 125, 135; ATP 204–5), when they appear to be so fragile, so uncertain, sometimes absent or else dried up, and whereas the situation seems at first to be defined by its regularities and the periodic movements from which it is precisely a matter of leaving? We must not let the factual order obscure the principle: if it is true that the transversal is first in experience, it is upon lines of flight that forms and subjects are constructed, which must be constituted *within* the given. Hence, inversely, the lines of flight that originally traverse the latter from within, the multiple internal exteriorities that work them over even as they constitute them, and which justify a "joyful pessimism," an immanent faith, the serene anticipation of better days even though things necessarily go badly. For if our forms are constructed first of all on deterritorializations, and if we suffer from their severity, we no less need them in order to *reproduce* our existence. "Dismantling the organism has never meant killing yourself, but rather opening the body to connections that presuppose an entire assemblage ... You have to keep enough of the organism for it to reform each dawn" (ATP 160)—since, here again, the problem is not to flee (the organism) but to put into flight.

Multiplicities

* "Multiplicity must not designate a combination of the many and the one, but rather an organization belonging to the many as such, which has no need whatsoever of unity in order to form a system" (DR 182).

** Having its origin in Bergson, this concept carries out a double displacement: on the one hand, the opposition of the one and the multiple loses its pertinence; on the other hand, the problem now becomes one of distinguishing between two kinds of multiplicity (one that is actual-extensive, divided into *parts* external to one another, such as matter or extension; and one that is virtual-intensive, dividing itself only into *dimensions* enveloped in one another, such as memory or duration). Moreover, the old opposition appears to be relative to one of the two types, mainly the actual-extensive type, which is derived by means of "actualization" from the virtual-intensive type. Which is why the invocation of one or several multiplicities without any further specification always refers in Deleuze to the virtual-intensive type, which alone realizes the immediate unity of the multiple, the reciprocal immanence of the multiple and the one.

On the one hand, Deleuze remains profoundly faithful to the Bergsonian idea according to which the concrete is always a mixture in which the thinker must distinguish two tendencies or two types of multiplicities: hence the series of great dualities, Chronos-Aion, striated and smooth space, molar-molecular, etc. (cf. B 21–35; ATP 474–5). We can already see that it is not a question of two worlds, nor even of two separate options between which existence would have to make a choice: generally speaking, for Deleuze there are only bodies, and the event at their surface, the mind merging with the "crystalline" adventures of the plane of immanence or the body without organs (FB 34). Though it haunts it and exceeds it, in no case does the virtual transcend the actual or exist beyond it.

On the other hand, Deleuze constantly reworks the concept of multiplicity, carrying it along paths foreign to Bergson. From the initial concept he retains above all a remarkable trait to which he gives an unprecedented scope: "what divides only by changing in nature" (B 40; DR 237, 257–8; ATP Plateaus 1, 2, 10, 14; C1 Chapters 1–2). This raises once again all the equivocation regarding the primacy of the One for Deleuze.[12] In *Difference and Repetition*, multiplicity belongs to a theory of the problem or the Idea (DR 182 ff.); already, under the name "perplication," Deleuze evokes non-hierarchal, lateral transitions between Ideas of every nature, according to the "crowned anarchy" of being affirmed in its univocity (DR 187, 280); nevertheless, the logical description of multiplicities here remains somewhat static. It is in *A Thousand Plateaus* that the consequences of the remarkable trait are the most clearly stated: once it is joined directly to the idea of the encounter, we understand better in what respect every multiplicity is from the outset a "multiplicity of multiplicities" (ATP 34—moreover, the composition of the book explicitly obeys this logic). In parallel fashion, the concept of multiplicity supplies the logic of the parts that compose desiring machines or assemblages: "partial objects" whose detachment [*prélevement*] does not imply the fragmentation of a whole as in Melanie Klein, for when we abandon the plane of constituted totalities (the objects of empirical givenness, organized according to the exigencies of representation) in order to reconnect with a plane on which fragments that are in a certain respect absolute are assembled, without any horizon of totalization, we can only attain the conditions of "real" experience. Having neither form nor individuality, the assembling of these nondescript fragments of reality gives rise to intensive individuations (or "haecceities"—ATP 260 ff.): as "pre-individual singularities," they constitute the intensive dimensions of a multiplicity (LS 297; AO 309 note, and 324). From this point of view, the logic of multiplicities completes that of inclusive disjunctions, and the concepts of multiplicity and singularity prove to be strictly interdependent.

At this point, the reader may have the unpleasant sense of racing out of control from one thing to the next [*emballement*], or even of a reciprocal neutralization between concepts: the dimensions of a multiplicity are themselves multiplicities, therefore singularity = multiplicity, etc. The feeling dissipates when we remember that a multiplicity is composed of dimensions that envelop themselves in each other, each reprising all the others at a different degree, according to an open list that can always increase dimensionally; while, for its part, a singularity is never isolable, but is always prolonged "as far as the vicinity of another singularity" (DR 201), according to the principle of the primacy of couplings or of relations. It is in this way that a multiplicity transforms itself by "dividing itself" on a body without organs that is never equivalent to a "lived body" [*corps propre*] (on the contrary, the concept of the "lived body" presupposes a halting of the primary play of desiring machines, and the "sedentary" distribution of an organism).

*** Another difficulty awaits the reader, mainly, the apparent equivocation that arises when we take into account two levels of pre-individuality in certain passages of *A Thousand Plateaus*. The same word, "multiplicity," sometimes seems to designate a "complication" of intensive dimensions (or singularities), and other times an extensive "mass" or "pack" of elements said to be abstract. In reality, the two aspects are joined: their distinction, one foreign to Bergson, is based on an original interpretation of the Spinozist theory of the body (ATP 253–60). Just as with inclusive disjunction, the second aspect makes it possible to do justice to a clinical material disfigured by psychoanalysis (ATP 2nd Plateau *in extenso*: the case of the "wolf man"). The dimensions still retain their primacy (ATP 244–5, 249), for it is by virtue of them that the mass or the pack is not confused with an aggregate of already-formed individuals, with an actual-extensive type of multiplicity. This key moment in *A Thousand Plateaus* is where the phenomena of "becoming-animal" take on their importance: a transition toward the "molecular" takes place here, defined as the regime where nondescript unities acquire their determination only when grouped in masses according to relations of speed and slowness. As art and psychotic "delirium" both testify, the intensive cuts a paradoxical path through representation. For its part, and in light of the intimate relation tying concepts to space, it is therefore important that philosophy take up this reversion of the intensive within the extensive—for it is here that the strict interdependence of the "molecular" and of nomadic distribution within the determination of "smooth space" appears (ATP 381–2).

Nomadic Distribution (or Smooth Space)

* "It is an errant and even 'delirious' distribution, in which things are deployed across the entire extensity of a univocal and undivided Being. It is not a matter of being which is distributed [*se partage*] according to the requirements of representation, but of all things being divided up [*se repartir*] within being in the univocity of simple presence (the One – All)" (DR 36–7, translation modified).

** The difference between distributing [*partager*] a closed space and dividing things up in an open space, between distributing to people a space divided into parts and distributing people in an undivided space, has first of all a pastoral sense (before signifying the law, the Greek word *nomos* first referred to the activity of grazing—DR 36 and ATP 557 fn.). Is it by means of metaphor that Deleuze applies this word to the difference between two states of thought, creative and representational? Certainly not, since for their part the two socio-historical values of the *nomos* (*nomadic* versus sedentary modes of existence) imply this difference. This is because thought is in itself affected in the most intimate way by space, and elaborates itself in accordance with abstract spaces that are sometimes "smooth" and sometimes "striated," or according to a variable mixture of the two (cf. the rehabilitation of the Leibnizian distinction between *spatium* and *extensio*, the first rough sketch of the two spaces which will then be expanded into the concept of the "body without organs"—DR 228–44; ATP 153). An open-ended list will then be drawn up of concrete "models" where the distinction is at work: technological, musical, mathematical, etc. (ATP 14th Plateau).

*** Why is philosophy so first and foremost concerned with this?

Some people imagine there to be eternal problems, and concepts already given, situated in some sky where we would simply have to go and retrieve them: such people reason according to a fixed or sedentary distribution. Or else, we believe that thought advances according to an order of progressive unfurling; we imagine all the great philosophers since Plato being compared before the tribunal of Truth [*LA vérité*], as if there existed an objective distribution outside of all singular distribution: such a belief implies a transcendence. On another hand, ideas appear to belong to domains, and significations to objects that indicate their "literal" usage and the possibility of a "figural" usage (as if, for example, the sense of the words "illness" or "prison" were exhausted by their reference to the physical states of things they serve to designate). Failing to appreciate the intrinsically nomadic character of sense, refusing it the right to a *literal* drift, we *enclose* it, and our acts of comprehension are entirely penetrated by an implicit set of rules [*cadastre*] which at best leads us to judge weakly (at worst, dishonestly) the semantic migrations that lay claim to philosophy, which are driven by a necessity and a rigor specific to it: for example, the non-scientific usages of a scientific idea (as if science itself in its moments of invention does not assiduously and legitimately practice such importations . . .)

The thought that resolutely affirms *chance* is entirely different: not that it opposes to necessity the right to arbitrary fantasy (no one was more sensitive than Deleuze to the theme of necessity, seeking to push the concept beyond all of its received versions, cf. PS 16–17, 95 ff.; DR 138–9); on the contrary, this affirmation is the test that frees thought from the illusion of a necessity sought within the relation to an originary and transcendent distribution, which thought can only postulate (sedentary illusion of grounding) (LS 10th and 12th Series). The undivided space of the *dice-throws* of nomadic distribution also indicates how the One according to Deleuze must be understood: without distantiating itself from the multiplicity of distributions, it prevents each from closing upon itself and giving in to the mirage of an isolated and divided One—a line of flight or of deterritorialization intimately affecting every mode of being or particular existence (there is no basis to claim any primacy of the One over the multiple in Deleuze). It is in this sense that the nomad is defined less by his displacements—like the migrant—than by the fact of inhabiting a smooth space (desert or steppe—ATP 381). Ultimately, smooth space is the plane of immanence or of the *univocity* of being (WP 36).

Nonorganic Life (or Vitality)

* "There is a profound relationship between signs, events, life, and vitalism: the power of nonorganic life that can be found in a line that is drawn, a line of writing, a line of music. It is organisms that die, not life. Any work of art points a way through for life, finds a way through the cracks. Everything I have written is vitalist, at least I hope it is, and amounts to a theory of signs and events" (N 143)

* It is rare for the word "vitalism" to be invoked with the rigor of a concept. Like everyone else, philosophers have their less glorious moments where they reveal, without admitting it, their interest in cultivating a *doxa* of their own, in maintaining the ambiguity of certain words so as to be able to hurl them at the figure of the adversary like a testament to their infamy. So why not *denounce* Deleuze's vitalism, seeing as how he himself never ceased to avow it? When it comes to such infra-philosophical maneuvers, it is decisive that one not know what one is talking about. When vitalism is spoken of, it refers more or less to two things: to a certain mistake of the eighteenth-century natural sciences grounded in a sort of mysticism that evaded every effort at a real explication (the postulation of a "vital principle" as the final reason of the living), and to the cult of vitality that propagated itself diversely across Europe at the end of the nineteenth century, and which was later claimed by various political movements, fascism among others (the invocation of the spirit of a race, of a people or of the individual, and the superior rights of life in its combat against forces regarded as being degenerate). The rejection of the idea of spontaneity that is the corollary of the theory of the desiring-machine should suffice to render ridiculous every insinuating exploitation of the Deleuzian use of the word "vitalism." It is true

that for this one must ascend to a philosophical plane. You will never find a concept of life in general in Deleuze. If he took an interest in the Nietzschean concept of "will to power," and if he identified it in the last resort with Bergson's duration-memory, this is first and foremost because he extracts from them a differentiated-differenciable characteristic, which excludes any recourse to life as a transcendent value, independent of experience, preexisting the concrete and trans-individual forms in which it invents itself (NP Chapters 2–3, notably 49–52, 100–1; C2 137–47). There is no life in general—life is not an undifferentiated absolute but a multiplicity of heterogeneous planes of existence, classifiable according to the type of evaluation they command or that animates them (their distribution of positive and negative values); and this multiplicity traverses individuals rather than distinguishing them from each another (or: individuals are distinguished only according to the type of life dominant in each of them). Secondly, Deleuze seeks within this concept a problematic by means of which to overcome the alternative between a morality grounded in transcendent values and a nihilistic or relativistic immoralism which, under the pretext of the facticity of all transcendent values, concludes that "everything is equal." More precisely, we must distinguish two kinds of relativism, only one of which is nihilism: "It is not a variation of truth according to the subject, but the condition in which the truth of a variation appears to the subject" (L 20). It is one thing to affirm that truth depends on one's point of view, and it is something else to say that truth is indeed relative to a point of view but that this does not make all points of view equivalent. How can a point of view have arrogated a superiority to itself in the absence of any objective criteria enabling one to measure its claims from without? Precisely by assuming this condition, and consequently by posing the problem of an *immanent evaluation* of points of view or of the evaluations conditioning each mode of existence (EPS 269–70; C2 141–2; WP 75; CC Ch. 15). Superior is the mode of existence that consists in the mutual test of modes of existence, or that devotes itself to making them resonate amongst themselves. True is the distance or the ensembles of distances tested, and the immanent selection that effectuates itself therein. Which means that *truth is creation*, not in the sense that God could have created it otherwise (Descartes), but rather where it is relative to the perspective that a thinker or an artist has been able to take on the variety of modes of existence and the systems of available values (C2 146). But the question again arises: by virtue of what can the point of view that orders points of view be considered superior to others? How can we even say that points of view are ordered in experience? Is it because the creative point of view is the only one that is open, the only one to problematize itself and to live existence as a problem? This response risks introducing a finality that would compromise the condition of immanence. It must be asked why thinking is worth more at the end of the day than not thinking. The Deleuzian answer is that *to think is more intense*. The objection that comes to the fore here must be weighed carefully: certainly, it must be within experience that we learn the intensive superiority of *affects* (by which we mean, through the encounter with the heterogeneous or the outside through which every affectivity finds itself shaken and redistributed) upon our ordinary affections . . . but, under the guise of an ultimate statement, does this not function as an external criteria of judgment, as the surreptitious reintroduction of a transcendent value—intensity—thereby signaling the failure of the program of immanent evaluation? In the last resort, intensity is an immanent criteria because the auto-affirmation of our faculties coincides with the affirmation of the new, of a result [*issue*], of the affect, and it is in this way that intensity is determined—whatever the terrors that may accompany it—as *joy*.

*** Consequently, Deleuze can reserve the more specific name of life or vitality not for the multiplicity of forms of life, but for those amongst these forms in which life—the very exercise of our faculties—affirms itself: a paradoxical form, one that is in fact closer to the formless. Here again a Nietzschean inspiration is recognizable, and we must reaffirm, although from another angle, the absence in Deleuze of any concept of life or vitality in general: on the one hand, because life as he conceives it is always and inseparably *nonorganic* (or *impersonal*; cf. LS 151; D 49; etc.), on the other hand owing to the fact that, since what is proper to nonorganic life is its creativity and consequently its unpredictability (certainly not a natural or originary wealth that it would suffice to simply exteriorize), we would seek in vain for its standard form (even if nothing prevents one from aping in the most painful and sad way the *image* that Deleuze inevitably gives of nonorganic vitality, which is nevertheless "imageless"; in just the same way is it possible to venerate the rhizome without even the shadow of a rhizomatic inspiration). Nonorganic life is an expression that originally comes from Worringer (ATP 411, 496–500; FB 46 and 108; C1 50–5), and is overdetermined by the concept of the "body without organs" taken from Artaud (FB 44–5;

186

CC 131) and by the thought of Bergson (C2 81). Care must be taken regarding this relation to Bergson. "Life as *movement* is alienated in the material *form* that it creates" (B 104); life is creation but the living is closure and reproduction, so that *élan vital*—like duration—dissociates itself at each moment in two movements, one in which the actualization-differenciation of a species or an organic form takes place, the other by which it is pulled together as a virtual totality always open to each of its differenciations; consequently, "it is not the whole that closes like an organism, it is the organism that opens onto a whole, like this virtual whole" (B 105). It is by refusing to circumscribe life within the limits of living forms (thereby defining life as organization), that the creative or progressive *tendency* traversing the living can be thought, beyond the unsatisfying alternative of mechanism and formalism. When properly understood, this refusal leads either to a conception of life as a principle distinct from matter, or else to a conception of matter itself as life: not by housing within matter souls that govern it, which would only testify to an incapacity to abandon the image of life as organization or as constituted subjectivity, but rather by naming life the anonymous creative activity of matter which, at a certain moment in its evolution, becomes organization: this second path leads to a fundamentally inorganic conception of life. There is no terminological fantasy here, much less a mystical fantasmagoria—except if one avoids logical reasoning and if we allow ourselves to be intimidated by the prejudices of the *doxa*. Once again, what is at stake in this redefinition of life is the attempt to think the way in which living forms exceed their own organization, the sense in which evolution traverses and overflows them (this logic contests and competes with that of Darwinism—we know that, in his studies of becoming, Deleuze had particularly reflected on the case of mutualism or co-evolution, clover and bumblebee, wasp and orchid, for which the theory of evolution has never supplied a sufficient answer; cf. ATP 10). Finally, if life is to be conceived of as prior to organization, as the pure creation of nature, there is no reason to suspect a metaphorical usage when we invoke it to describe phenomena beyond organization, such as psychic life and creation of thought. Every process refers to nonorganic life inasmuch as it escapes constituted forms rather than leading back to them, sketching one anew only to already slip off elsewhere toward other sketches: what we call "life" here depends not on the nature of the elements (material, psychic, or artistic formations, etc.) but rather on the mutual deterritorialization that draws them toward unforeseen thresholds (for example, and simplifying enormously, organization is a threshold crossed by matter; and in the wasp-orchid example we see the nonorganic life of a "block of becoming" that sweeps the two forms of organized life along, interlacing them up to the point where they cross a threshold of existence and enter into mutual presupposition). Nonorganic life is a typical example of a Deleuzian concept: its irreducibility to any assignation of a proprietary domain renders it susceptible to a *literal* usage in whatever domain one approaches, as well as a "transversal" usage that is itself no less literal, and which combines a multiplicity of domains, irrespective of their degree of heterogeneity. With this, we come closer to understanding not only the Deleuzo-Guattarian conception of nature, which no longer recognizes the distinction between the natural and the artificial, but also the concept of the plane of immanence, and, naturally, the experience of the body as it is thought under the condition of its relation to a body *without organs*.

Plane of Immanence (and Chaos)

* "We call this plane, which knows only longitudes and latitudes, speeds and haecceities, the plane of consistency or composition (as opposed to the plan(e) of organization or development). It is necessarily a plane of immanence and univocality. We therefore call it the plane of Nature, although nature has nothing to do with it, since on this plane there is no distinction between the natural and the artificial. However many dimensions it may have, it never has a supplementary dimension to that which transpires upon it. That alone makes it natural and immanent" (ATP 266) "The plane of immanence is not a concept that is or can be thought but rather the image of thought, the image thought gives itself of what it means to think, to make use of thought, to find one's bearings in thought" (WP 37). "The plane of immanence is like a section of chaos and acts like a sieve. In fact, chaos is characterized less by the absence of determinations than by the infinite speed with which they take shape and vanish. This is not a movement from one determination to the other but, on the contrary, the impossibility of a connection between them, since one does not appear without the other having already disappeared, and one appears as disappearance when the other disappears as outline. Chaos is not an inert or stationary state, nor is it a chance mixture. Chaos makes chaotic and undoes every consistency in the infinite. The problem of philosophy is to acquire a consistency without losing

the infinite into which thought plunges (in this respect chaos has as much a mental as a physical existence)" (WP 42). "Immanence is not related to Some Thing as a unity superior to all things or to a Subject as an act that brings about a synthesis of things: it is only when immanence is no longer immanence to anything other than itself that we can speak of a plane of immanence. No more than the transcendental field is defined by consciousness can the plane of immanence be defined by a subject or an object that is able to contain it" (PI 27).

** In a certain sense, what comes first is chaos (WP 200 ff.): an incessant influx of punctualities of every sort—perceptive, affective, intellectual—whose only common trait is to be aleatory and unrelated. And as Hume pointed out, the reign of pure chance can have no other effect on the mind than indifference ("The depth of the mind is indeed delirium, or—same thing from another point of view—chance and indifference" (ES 23).[13] Every life is therefore first engulfed by "data" of every sort.

And let us add: this is the case today more than ever, given that the media daily invites each of us to be interested in ever more numerous and disparate collections of data, and to register it all in light of the action it serves to orient, it being understood that to get around within such a complex world as ours implies being informed. The starting point (among others) for Deleuze's analysis of this regime of information or of order words is a cinema of action: a situation being given, the character begins by permeating himself with its constitutive data so as to arrive at the appropriate reaction capable of modifying it (C1 Ch. 9, ATP 75 ff.). Thus the presupposition of information is life as the perpetual activation of sensory-motor schemas: the data is useful, you sift it and "negotiate" it according to your vital interest or your customary usage; literally, information is the occurrence put-in-form, the form of use that in the strict sense makes it a "datum" once it comes to be seized by such a schema and recognized in advance as being useful, even if we're not sure what for.

But as this cumbersome profusion of putative utilities has something comically chaotic about it, we might think that it is only being opposed to a derisory screen, itself contaminated by what it claims to avert: what Deleuze calls the bankruptcy of "clichés," the rupture of these codes and sensory-motor schemas that at the same time assure the organic relation between man and the world. According to *Anti-Oedipus*, the modern age is defined by a "generalized decoding" inherent to capitalist societies; a relaxation, even a disappearance of the hold exerted over us by the ready-made forms of comprehension and of life, of the "processing" of data and of action (after the Second World War, according to *Cinema 2*). This fact, which pertains not to psychology but to civilization, leaves us with no defense against the excessive afflux of data we're delivered over to daily, and modern man is overcome with vertigo—fascination or nausea.

Such is more or less what Deleuze understands by chaos, the "modern fact" that reveals a situation that exists in principle. For never has the urgency of a different relation to chaos been imposed with such clarity and necessity, a relation which would no longer consist in protecting oneself from chaos with codes and ready-made schemas. It is therefore at the same moment that, faced with this new and nevertheless unassignable appearance of data, thought demands specific relations that can tell us which world it is that we are entering . . . but also, faced with the collapse of the old interpretive or informative schemas, it demands a new form of relating or deciphering, one distinct from the transcendent interpretive totalization that leads us to always already recognize that which takes place, instead of providing us the means by which to pursue its becoming. (The answer lies in the definition of the *clinical* as the evaluation of a becoming, sliding from one organization of signs to another along a "surface"—the first sketch of the plane of immanence—which is precisely the surface of sense [LS 83]; the two books of *Capitalism and Schizophrenia* are devoted to this undertaking, drawing up the plane of immanence on which the shift from a social regime of "codification" to a regime of "axiomatization" can then be evaluated; or, according to a more recent evaluation, the shift from the "disciplinary societies" defined by Foucault to the "control society" defined by Deleuze himself; cf. N 177–82.) We hardly "react" to the data anymore—we no longer have any faith in the habitual sequences or in the tradition that would bring us to recognize within the aleatory punctualities of individual and collective life any data capable of being extended into action, yet which we nevertheless maintain in a lackadaisical manner, for lack of anything better. We return to a sort of indifference, which the debris of old schemas continues to deny, albeit with more difficulty every day. We have a presentiment that there is something important to be drawn from chaos, but we loath the customary forms of its exhortation, and we imagine that the conditions of an immanent discernment are not themselves given but dependent upon a special act. In short, we lack a *plane* that could section chaos in a new (or different) way, we lack the conditions that would enable us to *relate* this data and discover its sense, in a problematic rather than an interpretive mode. Thinking begins by the effectuation of such a sectioning [*coupe*], or the installation of such a plane. The plane of immanence is the condition under which sense occurs, chaos itself being this nonsense inhabiting the very ground of our lives. Nevertheless, the plane is entirely distinct from a grid of interpretation, which refers to ready-made forms of thought, to the clichés that cover over chaos rather than confront it: the plane is not subjacent to the given, like a *structure* that could render it intelligible by giving us recourse to a dimension "supplementary" to those included within it.

What is the nature of this plane? It necessarily has two sides, each being the mirror of the other: a plane of thought and a plane of nature, for "movement is not the image of thought without being also the substance of being" (WP 38). From a "formal" point of view, as Spinoza would say, the act consists in selecting certain chaotic determinations—those that we referred to above as occurrences, punctualities, or data that is *unprocessable* [*intraitable*], so to speak—in order to "preserve" them as so many "infinite movements" folded into one another. "Infinite" here means: abstracted from all spatio-temporal coordinates, restored to their pure sense, expressible by the infinitive verb. These retained determinations are those which thought identifies as belonging to it in principle: consequently, a division of fact and principle is carried out—a singular and modifiable division, not an originary one (we will return to this below)—that frees an *image of thought*, whose correlate is one or several *conceptual personae* effectuating its constitutive movements. These personae are not to be confused with the author nor with the fictional interlocutors with whom he may enter into dialogue, although the latter may occasionally incarnate them: drawn from chaos (Judge, Officer, Idiot, Stutterer, etc.), they are so many postures that the thinker assumes insofar as he thinks, and which become pure determinations of thought through him. The plane-personae ensemble defines the *problem(s)* that a thinker poses in his attempt at a resolution that is the creation of concepts (WP Ch. 3).

This indicates the extent to which *intuition* plays a role in philosophy, at least "if intuition is thought of as the envelopment of infinite movements of thought that constantly pass through a plane of immanence" (WP 40), and not as the accessing of superior realities, of essences independent of thought. It is in this sense—and in this sense alone—that the thinker has visions, which merge with the becoming-philosophical of certain determinations of the world,

with the gesture of orienting thought without reference points, of inventing one's own system of orientation (WP 37; N 147–8): "they are not outside language, they are the outside of language" (CC 5). It is in this sense as well that philosophical concepts, which receive their sense only from the problems to which they are attached, are subject in part to a non-conceptual comprehension, which concerns the non-philosopher—since it indicates the extent to which philosophy addresses itself to him in principle—just as much as it does the philosopher, who would be wrong to dismiss from his work that part of himself that does not philosophize. What Deleuze calls Reason is precisely this purely intuitive moment of the plane (WP 76). Neither a joke nor a provocation, this is intended to mark the fact that we cannot conceive of a unique originary reason: if there is reason, it refers entirely to something instituted, or rather to multiple acts of institution, called "processes of rationalization" (D 154–5, 161–2). Perpetually bifurcating, it does not exist outside of the distinct rationalities that each refer to a necessarily irrational act of foundation, but which testify at the same time to an entirely different sort of necessity. A thought that believes itself to be in possession of itself or that projects such an ideal into an indefinite future cannot help but fall back on a transcendence and on beliefs that exceed the given and shirk away from the true test of the thinker (cf. AO 373, 378–9 and DI 262: "Reason is always a region carved out in the irrational. . .").
Finally, in the adaptation of concepts on the plane that calls them, intuition is always accompanied by a *taste*. As one might have guessed, the ultimate consequence of the concept of the plane of immanence is that there is no *truth* that is not *created* (WP 27–8, 54; C2 147). So that, here again, the criteria of truth, which functions only in relation to a plane of immanence, from the problem to its solution, is subordinated to that of the *interesting*, the *important*, the *remarkable* (DR 189; WP 82–3; what Deleuze elsewhere referred to as "applying the test of the true and the false to the level of problems themselves"—B 15; DR 153–64). Deleuze's critique and subordination of the concept of truth must therefore not be confused with an indifference to the question of truth (cf. C2 Chapters 5–6).

But why are there *planes*, rather than a single and sole plane that could be called THE plane, which those rare thinkers seem to have approached for themselves (Spinoza, and Bergson briefly; cf. WP, 48–9)? The response can be schematized as follows: 1. If the ensemble of data or determinations is a chaos, this is because it carries in it images of rival thoughts, so that a thinker who tried to retain all of them would collapse, his plane being indistinguishable from chaos. 2. Yet in the other direction, by its very coherence and its relative cadence [*repos*], every selection risks resulting in an identification of the thinker's plane with a unique and universal plane that could substitute itself for chaos, thus re-enthroning transcendence at the same time as it devalues its own concepts and opinions (cf. the opposition between nomad and sedentary distribution). 3. The thinker can ward off this return of transcendence and opinion only if he draws up his plane in such a way as to envelop as much as possible THE plane of immanence, meaning the unthinkable that would lead the thought that identifies with it back to chaos, but whose affirmation is no less necessary in order to avoid another identification, mainly that of the created and the originary. 4. It must retain as in-principle determinations of thought those which affect infinite movements expressing an advance by perpetual recommencement and bifurcation, or the insistence of another thinker within the thinker (stuttering, glossolalia, searching like a dog sniffing in a random manner, etc.) (on all of this, cf. WP 50, 55, 59, 68, etc.).

Is this concept first in the "order of reasons"? The question apparently presents itself since, as the concept of the conditions of experience, the plane of immanence nonetheless appears to be preceded by chaos. Thus an ambiguity arises: there cannot be an experience of chaos, since it would be nothing but the collapse of the thought that let itself be seized by it without finding any schemas to oppose to it, lacking any intuition of a plane that could re-section it and enable it to take on the consistency of a clinical table. Which is why the punctualities from which we departed fully become "data" only under the condition of the schemas that inform them. However, these conditions prove to be too large in relation to what they condition: if they "give"[14] anything, it is only under the form of recognition [*reconnu*], or the already-known [*déjà-connu*], allowing us to speak of experience only in a hackneyed sense. "Real" experience begins with a sectioning or the installation of a plane. As a result, chaos is something thought rather than something given: it is *virtual*. Only the plane of immanence can deliver us over to a pure, immediate given, of which chaos offers us only a fading outline. By virtual we should not understand a state that would oppose itself to the real, which would have to realize itself in the manner of the possible: what corresponds to the virtual is actualization (and the inverse movement of crystallization). Moreover, if real experience envelops or implicates chaos, the proper understanding of the real no longer confuses it with a pure actuality, but includes within it a virtual component (B 96–7; DR 208 ff.). This is why to become, to create, or to think always implies a dynamism that is the inverse of that of actualization: *crystallization* (D 150–2).

*** This pure given is the other side of the plane of immanence: an image of thought does not emerge without at the same time putting forward the conditions under which something is; a new form of thought *is* a new way of envisaging experience, or of thinking *what is*. It is thus possible to retrace the discontinuous history of the given in philosophy, without ever attaining the immanence of a pure immediate given, even in Husserl. According to Deleuze, only two philosophers ever drew up a picture of this pure given, and stated its logic: Spinoza in the *Ethics*, and Bergson in the first chapter of *Matter and Memory* (and perhaps we should add: Deleuze and Guattari, in the brilliant opening of *Anti-Oedipus*).

But didn't we just claim that THE plane is not sayable? Then what does it mean that Spinoza "showed, one time, the possibility of the impossible" (WP 60—this theme at least indicates that it is by installing THE plane that the immanentist conversion is carried out, to believe in the earth, as Nietzsche said, or to believe in this world, as Deleuze put it)? By re-sectioning (*recoupe*) the chaos without imposing the slightest *a priori* cut (*découpe*) in its determinations, by bringing them into relation without enframing them within preconceived forms subtracted from experience, he produced a plane of experience that implicates its own potentially infinite redistribution. Spinoza allows himself nothing but the movement. Given a field of indeterminate material particles, perception is carved out [*se découpe*] only according to their variable redistribution in distinct compositions, defined by relationships of movement and rest, speed and slowness, but always exposed to encounters, to the migrations of sub-compositions, to compositions of compositions or else to decompositions ("longitudes"); as far as affectivity goes, it differenciates itself, enriches itself, reorganizes itself according to the becomings that correspond to these more or less joyful encounters (augmentations and diminutions of an anonymous power of action distributed on the plane, or "latitudes"). Aside from the movement that alone constitutes it, let us note the acentered character of the plane: these two traits are common to the description of the plane of immanence drawn from Spinoza (SPP Ch. 6; ATP 253–7), as well as the one Deleuze will elsewhere draw from Bergson (C1 Ch. 4). Otherwise it would hardly be possible to understand the fact that the concept of *haecceity*, which presents a mode of immanent individuation distinct from the organic individual forms that cut up [*découpe*] *a priori* the empirical field, is linked to a Spinozist account (ATP 260 ff.). The-animal-stalks-at-five-o'clock, a-horse-falls-in-the-street: these compositions in which beings do not detach themselves from the scenery or the atmosphere but are composed immediately and originally with them, already correspond closely to the concept of the *movement-image*. And as he says in his reading of Proust, we do not love someone apart from the landscapes, hours, and circumstances of all kinds that they envelop. For it is in this way that we are affected, or that the *affect* uproots us from the melodies of ordinary affections, that the *percept* wrenches us away from the usual expectations and spontaneous divisions of ordinary perception: by rejoining the plane of immanence on which everything is not always composed with everything else—since it also contains death as decomposition or absorption—but communicates with everything on the same plane (which is also named the plane of *univocity*) independently of the assignations of form, species, or of the organ (it is in this respect that, from the point of view of the pure given or of real experience, a plow horse is closer to an ox than to a racehorse—SPP 124). On this plane experimentation and encounters are always possible without running into any barriers; that it be pleasing is another question. Consequently, the conceptual personae that haunts Spinozism is the child (ATP 256; WP 72).

Let's pursue the analogy a bit further, so we may see to what extent the two approaches converge toward the same concept, despite the different accents placed on them. Turn to the first chapter of *Matter and Memory*: the pure given (the indistinction of the image, of movement and matter) precedes the consciousness I have of myself and of being this "I" that opens absolutely the field of perception, who knows himself to be situated in a point of space but who, not himself being in *his* field, displaces it with him. The error would be to confuse the field of perception with the plane of immanence: if it is true that there is something prior to any assignation of a subject intending an object, the plane on which the given is deployed does not open at any one point in particular, and there is no sense in claiming that it varies according to the angle of vision. It is there immediately, acentered, fixed so to speak, although not tied down to anything, like the cinematic images that pass across an imperturbable screen at the same time as they incite changing perspectives in the spectator. If there is a subject, it is constituted *in* the given, in accordance with the problem posed by Deleuze in his first book, *Empiricism and Subjectivity*, in 1953; and it is constituted there in each of its points. Consequently, to speak of a subject who perceives and experiences that he is "adjacent" is not to subtract it from the given by reintroducing *in extremis* the transcendental Ego; on the contrary, it is to make it circulate through all the points on the plane as so many *cases* of itself, in order to conclude it from this series of becomings (the Deleuzian cogito would be something like: "I feel I am becoming other, so I was, so it was me!"; cf. LS 310 and AO 16–22). If we return to the Spinozist description, we can now understand that it can be a question of a "fixed plane" (D 94; ATP 254) and of the "intensive states of an anonymous force" (SPP 127). In fact, there is no need of a fusion or a special empathy in order for each of the points on this plane of pure experience, which never give rise to a constituted subject, to correspond to an affect: for example, the distance that separates the racehorse from the draft horse, from the immanent point of view of what they can do, the dynamisms or rhythms of which each are capable; and on the contrary the proximity of the draft horse and the ox—all are immediate objects of a percept and an affect upon the plane of immanence.

Lastly, if we ask in what sense this plane of Nature or of univocity can be equivalent to THE plane of immanence of all thought, and consequently in what sense Spinoza demonstrates the "possibility of the impossible," we understand that even beyond the "dogmatic image of thought" to which his philosophy may seem from the outside to adhere (the natural affinity of thought with the true, a model of truth that preexists the act of though; cf. DR Ch. 3), his plane sets up *the paradoxical image of a thought without image*, of a thought that does not know in advance what it means to think and which can only incessantly return to the act that engenders it (the sectioning of chaos). If it can be said that Spinoza showed THE plane, this is insofar as thought reflects itself in this "smooth space" occupied only by unequal movements, composable or not, always recomposable differently, and lives them as so many dramas of itself, tests or hallucinations of what it can mean to think.

I will conclude with a few points of reference. The concept of the plane of immanence replaces that of the "transcendental field" drawn from the philosophies of Kant and Husserl (on these two authors, cf. LS 14th–17th Series and WP 46–7).

"Plane" and no longer "field": because it is not *for* a subject assumed to be outside of the field, or at the limit of a field that opens itself beginning from him according to the model of a field of perception (cf. the transcendental Ego of phenomenology—on the contrary, the subject is constituted in the given, or more precisely on the plane); and also because what comes to fill the plane accumulates or is connected only laterally, on its edges, since we find here only slippages, displacements, *clinamen* (LS 6–7, 270–1), even a "clinic," not only in the sense invoked above of a "slippage from one organization to another," but in the sense of a "formation of a progressive and creative disorganization" (which reflects the Deleuzian definition of *perversion*—see "Line of Flight"). The movements on the plane are opposed to the verticality of a foundation or to the rectilinearity of a progress (it is in *The Logic of Sense* that the transcendental field begins to be thought as a plane, even if the word is not pronounced [LS 109]; and the triad depth-surface-height—which is to say mixtures of bodies interacting and composing, events, forms—will be replayed or repeated differently as chaos-plane-transcendence or opinion in *What is Philosophy?*).

"Immanence" and no longer "transcendental": because the plane *does not precede* what comes to populate it or fill it, but is constructed and reorganized within experience, so that there is no longer any sense in speaking of *a priori* forms of experience, of an experience in general, applicable to every place and time (just as we can no longer be content with the concept of a universal and invariable space-time). In other words, such conditions are "no broader than the conditioned," which is why a critical philosophy radicalized in this way can claim to state the principles of a veritable *genesis* and no longer of a simple external conditioning indifferent to the nature of what it conditions (Foucault's *epistemes* or "historical *a prioris*" give an idea of this exigency, even if Deleuze's planes of thought refer rather to authors and to works).

There is no contradiction in the fact that Deleuze does not simply renounce the discourse of the "transcendental": the necessarily general concept of the conditions of real experience (which is to say always singular, inseparable from a production of novelty) is not to be confused with the supposed conditions of experience *in general*. Yet there is undeniably a difficulty to resolve, a philosophical mutation to accomplish, since it is a question of thinking the concept of something that is never given all at once nor once and for all, nor is it given progressively part by part, but which is differenciated or redistributed, and only exists in its own variations (cf. the opposition of "once and for all" and "for all times"—DR 95, 115; LS 60). Ever since his first article in 1956, "Bergson's Conception of Difference," Deleuze has pleaded for a new type of concept, which he found the outline of in Nietzsche (Will to Power) and in Bergson (Duration, Memory): a concept obeying a logic of *internal difference*, which is to say in which the object "does not divide without changing in nature" at each moment of its division, which differs with itself in each of its self-affirmations (see the entry on "Transcendental Empiricism"). It is in this way that we arrive at the concept of conditions of experience that differentiate themselves *with* experience, yet without merging with it and rejoining the empirical through a confusion of fact and principle. Such a concept no longer expresses a universal: as a result, Deleuze speaks sometimes of a plane of immanence in general, and sometimes of a plane established by this or that philosopher. These are variations of a single and same plane, once it is said that "single and same" no longer expresses anything having to do with a permanence or an identity to self (*The Logic of Sense* does considerable work with this notion of "single and same" in the sense of what exists only by differing from itself: the notion of the "common" undergoes something parallel—see "Univocity of Being").

Finally, we may note that the Deleuzian use of the word "immanence" is not derived from Husserl, even though it surfaces within the frame of a critical and non-metaphysical questioning. Deleuze extracts from Spinoza the tools for an anti-phenomenological radicalization of critical philosophy, through an operation that is not without analogy to post-Kantianism, whose importance he frequently celebrates. Here immanence becomes "pure" or "its own," as opposed to the immanence to consciousness that Husserl had made the criteria of his method (and when Deleuze repeats [*refaire*] the operation a second time in his interpretation of the first chapter of *Matter and Memory*, this is in order to parody [*contrefaire*] the famous formula of intentionality: every consciousness *is* something, and not consciousness *of* something; cf. C1 Ch. 4). Are we overstepping our rights of interpretation by making the Spinozist logic of the finite modes of *substance* the statement of a plane of *experience*? Not if one takes account 1. of the reasons for thinking that the concept of a unique substance, in the first part of the *Ethics*, is obtained under the exigency of immanence and not the reverse, which is to say beginning from the "attributes" of thought and extension (on the one hand, they have no outside; on the other hand they are not distinguished ontologically, being only two expressions of a single and sole reality); 2. of the rupture in tone that occasions the abrupt insertion of the theory of bodies within the deductive course of the second part (the passage is found after the scholium of proposition 13); 3. of the expressly ethical scope of this theory (cf. IVp39 and dem). "The author had to actually say all that I had him saying" (N 6): under the pretenses of a joke, could the history of philosophy wish for a more rigorous and profound maxim (except by taking a vacation from philosophy)?

Pre-individual Singularities

* "We cannot accept the alternative which thoroughly compromises psychology, cosmology, and theology: either singularities already comprised in individuals or persons, or the undifferenciated abyss. Only when the world, teaming with anonymous and nomadic, impersonal and pre-individual singularities, opens up, do we tread at last on the field of the transcendental" (LS 103).

** The elaboration of the concept of singularity proceeds from a radicalization of critical or transcendental interrogation: the individual is not first in the order of sense, it must be engendered in thought (the problematic of individuation); sense is the space of nomadic distribution, there exists no originary division of significations (the problematic of the production of sense). Even though at first glance it may seem to be the ultimate reality as much for language as for representation in general, the individual presupposes the *convergence* of a certain number of singularities that determine a condition of closure under which an identity can be defined: that certain predicates are retained implies that others are *excluded*. Under the conditions of representation, singularities are from the outset predicates attributable to subjects. And yet by itself sense is indifferent to predication ("to green" is an event as such before becoming a possible property of a thing, "being green"); consequently, it communicates in principle with every other event, independently of the rule of convergence that appropriates it for a potential subject. The plane on which sense is produced is therefore populated by "nomadic" singularities, at once unattributable and non-hierarchical, and constituting pure events (LS 50–2, 107, 113). Between these singularities are relations of divergence or disjunction, and certainly not convergence since the latter already implies the principle of exclusion governing individuality: they communicate only through their difference or their distance, and the free play of sense and production resides precisely in the course of these multiple distances, or "disjunctive synthesis" (LS 172–5). As the individuals that we are, we are derived from this nomadic field of individuation that knows only couplings and disparities, a perfectly impersonal and unconscious transcendental field, and we reconnect with this play of sense only by testing its mobile borders (DR 254, 257). At this level, a given thing is itself no longer anything but a singularity that "opens itself up to the infinity of predicates through which it passes, as it loses its center, that is, its identity as concept or as self" (LS 174, 297–8).

*** Pre-individual singularities are thus always relative to a multiplicity. It is possible to say, however, that Deleuze wavers between two possible treatments of the term. Sometimes singularities designate the intensive "dimensions" of a multiplicity (LS 298; AO 309 fn., 324), and on this account could also be called "intensities," "affects," or even "haecceities"; their redistribution thus corresponds to the affective *map* of an assemblage (ATP 203; CC 61), or to the continuous *modulation* of a material (ATP 369–70, 405–9). Other times they are distributed at the level of each dimension and are redistributed from one dimension to another: such are the "outstanding" or remarkable points at each degree of the Bergsonian cone of memory (B 62, 100), the "points on the dice" with each throw of a nomadic distribution (DR 197–8; LS 60–1), the "singular points" whose redistribution determines the conditions of a solution in the theory of differential equations (DR 176–8; LS 54–5), etc. However, it is not clear that these two treatments do not converge. It will be noticed that Deleuze passes easily from *a* singularity to *singularities*, as if each singularity were already several (LS 52, 297): this is because the singularities that compose a multiplicity "penetrate one another across an infinity of degrees," where each dimension is like a point of view on all the others, reprising them all on its own level. This is the law of "sense as a pre-individual singularity, or an intensity which comes back to itself through others" (LS 299—the logic of the disjunctive synthesis). This "complication," which is only *de jure*, demands to be effectuated: as a result, the creative throw of the dice effects a redistribution only if the "reprisal of singularities by one another" is carried out under the conditions of an encounter between distinct "problems" (DR 200) or heterogeneous series (LS 53). From here to the theory of the apprenticeship (DR 22–3, 192) and of what it means to "have and Idea" (DR 182–200 —an extremely difficult text, the comprehension of which is nonetheless decisive; compare it with F 84–91), one is already well underway on the path toward what *A Thousand Plateaus* will explore in terms of a "multiplicity of multiplicities" (the theory of "becomings").

Problem

* "The failure to see that sense or the problem is extra-propositional, that it differs in kind from every proposition, leads us to miss the essential: the genesis of the act of thought, the operation of the faculties (DR 157). "All concepts are connected to problems without which they would have no meaning and which can themselves only be isolated or understood as their solution emerges" (WP 16). "We are led to believe that problems are given ready-made, and that they disappear in the responses or the solution. Already, under this double aspect, they can be no more than phantoms. We are led to believe that the activity of thinking, along with truth and falsehood in relation to that activity, begins only with the search for solutions, that both of these concern only solutions" (DR 158). "True freedom lies in a power to decide, to constitute problems themselves" (B 15).

** The importance of the concept of the problem for Deleuze, and the precision that he conferred upon it both by following and going beyond Bergson, must not be overlooked. It is banal, at least in France, that professors of philosophy require above all from their students a "problematic"; it is rare, however, that they make any effort to define their status, with the result that the whole thing becomes surrounded with an aura of initiatory mystery that never fails to produce its usual effects of intimidation. The whole of Deleuze's pedagogy resided in this methodological and deontological insistence on the role of problems (among other places, a convincing example may be found by consulting the recordings or transcriptions of his courses, which are largely available today): *statements and concepts have a sense only according to the problems to which they are related*. The philosophical problem, which must be stateable, is not to be confused with the ordinary dramaturgy of the dissertation, the contradictory juxtaposition around a single topic of theses that are at first glance each equally admissible as the next (for what one calls a problem is only the artificial tracing of responses to a question plucked from the sky). What is this sense that the problem confers on the conceptual statement? It is not a question of the immediate signification of propositions: the latter are related only to situational data (or states of affairs) which themselves precisely lack the orientation and the principle of discrimination of the problematic that enables them to enter into relation, which is to say, to make sense. Problems are acts that open a horizon of sense, and which subtend the creation of concepts: the appearance of a new questioning opening up an uncommon perspective on that which is most familiar, or creating interest in something that had been up till then regarded as insignificant. Certainly, everyone is more or less inclined to acknowledge this fact; but it is one thing to admit it, and another to draw from it its theoretical consequences. If questioning is the expression of a problem, its directly stateable side (even if philosophical questions sometimes remain implicit), at least two equally stateable constituents are also derived from it, of which it falls to the philosopher to be the "portraitist" or "historian," in the sense of a natural history: a taxonomist or a clinician, an expert in the tracking and differenciation of regimes of signs (N 46, 136; WP 55). First, a *new image of thought*, defined by the selection of certain "infinite movements" (a new sectioning in chaos, a new plane of thought); second, the *conceptual personae* that effectuate it (WP Chapters 2–3 and particularly 54, 74, 80–3).

First consequence: the horizon of sense is not universal (see "Plane of Immanence" and "Univocity of Being"). Second consequence or deontological aspect: philosophical *discussion*—which is to say, putting forth objections to an author that are necessarily conceived from the point of view of a different problem and on a different plane—is perfectly futile, and only the frivolous or vindictive part of intellectual activity. Not that exchange is to be banished, nor is thought to be autarchic—there is in Deleuze the whole theme of the "populous solitude" (ATP 377)—but dialogue has an interest only in a diverted mode of collaboration, as in Deleuze *and* Guattari, or else in the mode of a free conversation, whose ellipses, discontinuities and other foldings serve to inspire the philosopher (D 1st part; WP 28–9, 139–40, 144–5). Third and final consequence: even if we have every right to demand argumentation from the philosopher, this still remains subordinated to the fundamental act of *posing* a problem.

*** This act of posing [*acte de position*] is the irreducibly *intuitive* component of philosophy, which does not mean it is arbitrary, nor lacking in rigor: simply put, necessity responds to other criteria than that of rationalism, which is to say a thought in full possession of itself; and rigor has other virtues than those of valid inference. The latter is the object of a secondary preoccupation, one that is subordinate and non-facultative. Were it facultative, the demonstrative character of the Deleuzian statement would be poorly understood, including its allusive and digressive aspects, whether it takes the polyphonic, heterogeneous and discontinuous form of *Capitalism and Schizophrenia*, or else when it takes on an uneven and elliptical appearance, as in the taut texts of the final years (on the allusive and digressive as positive traits of philosophical enunciation, cf. WP 23 and 159–60). Yet if the validity of its reasoning were its primary criteria, the entirety of philosophy would fall prey to the trap of apparent contradictions: a collection of untenable paradoxes whose sense or necessity we would be incapable of comprehending. Philosophy is therefore a choice, or, what amounts to the same thing, it is irrational, the founder of heterogeneous rationalities. Irrational: the word can incite fear, or justify regrettable amalgams, only from the point of view of a rationalist nostalgia, which is to say a thought that has not traversed the circle of grounding and which consequently would not be convinced to draw its necessity only from the *outside*, from an *encounter* with that which forces thought (PS 16, 97; DR 139). The criteria demanded by such an encounter entails that thought be constrained to think what it can not yet think, having no ready-made schema by which to recognize it, nor any form at its disposal that would enable it to pose it *a priori* as an *object*. At this point philosophy proves to be inseparable not only from a properly immanent belief, but from a *non-conceptual* component of comprehension, which is also the precise means by which philosophy can claim to address itself to everyone (rather than being content with the general and vague claim that "everyone" yields before it by claiming in return to judge it with their own criteria). Doubtless, philosophy could give itself this universal form of the possible object, but only by assuming a role altogether too large for it, which rather than confronting singularity, would in fact erase it. This is why the thought that thinks its own act thinks at the same time the conditions of "real experience," however rare this may be; which is to say, the conditions of a mutation of the condition commensurate with what it must condition—not the universal form of the possible object but irreducible singularities, effractions of the non-recognizable to which, each time in the course of a "groping experimentation" (WP 41), there responds an original redistribution of traits that define what thinking means, and a new posing [*position*] of the problem. The posing of the problem is not justifiable by arguments: arguments are indispensable, but logically internal to the problematic. Moreover, if they serve to display its coherency, to trace paths within the concept or from one concept to another, it would be illusory to separate them from the act of posing the problem, for the *consistency* they provide comes only negatively from the rules of logical validity that they respect, just as logical possibility conditions what happens only by default. It's obvious that if one contradicts oneself one says nothing: there's hardly any interest even in pointing this out. On the other hand, the conditions of the truth of a proposition, the validity of a reasoning, in other words, its *informational* character, in no way guarantees that it has any sense or interest, which is to say that it be related to a problem. Which means that logic's point of view is not safeguarded from *stupidity*, from the chaotic indifference of valid remarks that solicit our minds every day under the name of "information": philosophy cannot content itself with the logicians' criteria of consistency (on the question of stupidity as the negative of thought, more essential than error, cf. NP 103 ff.; DR 148 ff., 159–60, 275–6; N 129–30). Consistency may thus be defined in a positive way by the inseparability of conceptual constituents of a strictly evental nature, which refer to the act of problematization [*l'acte de position de problème*] whose grounds it deploys (which a strictly formal point of view would be unable to ground, even though it never actually attempts to do so) (WP 19–20, 140). In short, there is no real difference between conceptualization and argumentation: in both cases it is a question of the same operation, which specifies and resolves a problem. There is no place in philosophy for a problematic autonomous from argumentation. The reader thus begins to understand why Deleuze can say that "the concept is not discursive" (or that philosophy "does not link propositions together") even if "philosophy proceeds by sentences" (WP 22–4). In the final analysis, the Deleuzian position is this: *irrationalism, not illogicism*; or better, the *logic of the irrational*. "Irrational" refers on the one hand to the encounter in which the act of thinking is engendered (in this sense, it is the correlate of the "necessary"), and on the other hand to becoming, to the lines of flight that belong to every problem, in itself and in the undefined object that is apprehended through it. "Logic" refers to the coherency of the system of signs or of symptoms—and in this case, specifically of concepts—that philosophy invents in order to respond to this challenge.

Refrain (Difference and Repetition)

* "The refrain moves in the direction of the territorial assemblage and lodges itself there or leaves. In a general sense, *we call a refrain any aggregate of matters of expression that draws a territory and develops into territorial motifs and landscapes* (there are optical, gestural, motor, etc., refrains). In the narrow sense, we speak of a refrain when an assemblage is sonorous or 'dominated' by sound—but why do we assign this apparent privilege to sound?" (ATP 323). "The great refrain arises as we distance ourselves from the house, even if this is in order to return, since no one will recognize us any more when we come back" (WP 191).

** The refrain is defined by the strict coexistence or contemporaneity of three mutually implicated dynamisms. It forms a complete system of desire, a logic of existence (an "extreme logic without rationality"). It involves two slightly different triads. First triad: 1. Seeking to rejoin [*rejoindre*] the territory, in order to ward off chaos. 2. Drawing up and inhabiting the territory that filters chaos. 3. Leaping out of the territory or deterritorializing oneself toward a cosmos distinct from chaos (ATP 299–300 and 311–12; N 146–7). Second triad: 1. Seeking a territory. 2. Leaving or deterritorializing oneself. 3. Returning or reterritorializing oneself (WP 67–8). The discrepancy between these two presentations hinges on the bipolarity of the earth-territory relation, and on the two directions—transcendent and immanent—in which the earth exercises its deterritorializing function. The earth serves at once as this intimate home toward which the territory naturally bends but which, seized as such, tends to infinitely repel the latter (such is the Natal, always lost—ATP 311, 325, 338 ff.—we are reminded of the catatonic pole of the full body in *Anti-Oedipus*, which rejects every organ); and, as this smooth space that every *limes*[15] presupposes and envelops, opening it up in principle, it is the irreducible destabilization of the territory, even those most closed (e.g., WP 180–1; one notices here a sort of wavering around the term "deterritorialized earth," since it sometimes is so in principle, as "chaosmos," whereas other times it is so as a result of its relation to the cosmos, as in ATP 345). The refrain merits its name in two ways: first, as a line that keeps coming back, keeps beginning again, keeps repeating itself; next, as the circularity of the three dynamisms (to find oneself a territory = to seek to rejoin it) [*se chercher un territoire = chercher à le rejoindre*]. Thus every beginning is already a return, but the latter always implies a divergence, a difference: reterritorialization, the correlate of deterritorialization, is never a return to the same. There is no arrival, there is only ever a return, but returning must be thought of as the reverse or the flipside of departing, and it is at the same moment that we both depart and return. Consequently, there are two distinct ways of departing-returning, and of infinitizing this couple: as the wandering of the exile and the call of the groundless, or else as nomadic displacement and the call of the outside (the Natal is only an ambiguous outside—ATP 326). These are two forms of diverging from the self: being torn away from a self to which we ceaselessly return as if to a stranger, since it is lost (the relation of the Exile to the Natal belonging to the second moment of the first triad); tearing a self out, a self that we keep coming back to only as a stranger, unrecognizable, having become imperceptible (relation of the Nomad to the Cosmos, the third moment in the second triad). There is neither an incompatibility nor even an evolution between the two triads, but only a difference of accent. What is at issue is the existential sense of the *return* as a problem (the word "refrain" [*ritournelle*] evokes the Eternal Return [*Retour Eternel*] in the manner of a portmanteau): what happens to this line that, returning to itself, differenciates an interior from an exterior (installation of a territory)? Does it ruin itself in a mad whirling around this origin the simulacra of which it secretes (Natal)? Or by doing so does it repeat the outside that it envelops, and which it overlaps even as it distinguishes itself from it (the limit is at the same time a screen)? This logical tension reveals the way in which the line, the mark, and the sign of the territory merge with the refrain. The two senses of returning make up the "small" and the "large" refrains: territorial, or closed in on itself; cosmic, or swept along by a semiotic line of flight. And it is through the relation of these two states of the refrain, small and large, that music (ATP 302, 349: "deterritorialize the refrain") and then art in general (WP 184–6) become thinkable. And if it concerns the concept as well, this is insofar as the latter passes again and again through the various singularities that compose it (WP 20) in accordance with an earth that is sometimes natal and immutable (thus it is *a priori*, innate, or even an object of reminiscence), sometimes new and to-come [*à venir*] (constructed on a plane of immanence: when the philosopher draws up his territory on deterritorialization itself) (WP 41, 69, 88).

Rhizome

* "Subtract the unique from the multiplicity to be constituted; write at *n* - 1 dimensions. A system of this kind could be called a rhizome" (ATP 6). "Unlike trees or their roots, the rhizome connects any point to any other point, and its traits are not necessarily linked to traits of the same nature; it brings into play very different regimes of signs, and even nonsign states. The rhizome is reducible neither to the One nor the multiple ... It is composed not of units but of dimensions, or rather directions in motion. It has neither beginning nor end, but always a middle [*milieu*] from which it grows and which it overspills. It constitutes multiplicities" (ATP 21).

** This concept, undoubtedly Deleuze and Guattari's most famous, is not always well understood. It is a manifesto unto itself: a new image of thought intended to combat the age-old privilege of the tree that disfigures the act of thinking and diverts us away from it (the introduction to *A Thousand Plateaus*, entitled "Rhizome," was published separately several years before the book; the notion appears for the first time in *Kafka*). It is glaringly obvious that "many people have a tree growing in their heads" (ATP 15): that it is a question of seeking out roots or ancestors, of locating the key to existence in the most remote childhood, or of binding thought to a cult of origins, of births, of appearance in general. Traditional genealogists, psychoanalysts, and phenomenologists are not friends of the rhizome. Furthermore, the arborescent model at least ideally submits thought to a progression from principle to consequence, sometimes leading it from general to particular, sometimes seeking to ground it, to anchor it forever in a soil of truth (even today's multimedia applications, struggling to install a transversal navigation, most often settle with a back-and-forth between a table of contents and dead-end sections). For Deleuze, this critique in no way prevents us from maintaining the distinction between fact and principle that emerges from critical or transcendental questioning. Careful attention must be paid here: if *transcendental empiricism* consists in thinking "conditions no broader than the conditioned," it is by no means obvious that we are required to treat the law as originary and the fact as derived. But we can also formulate this differently: the origin, itself affected by difference and the multiple, loses its *a priori* and englobing character, while the multiple escapes the ascendency of the One (*n*-1) to become the object of an immediate synthesis named "multiplicity"; henceforth it designates what is first in "real" experience (which is never "in general" or simply "possible"), as opposed to representational concepts. The rhizome means: no point of origin or first principle commanding all of thought; no significant progress that is not forged by bifurcation, unforeseeable encounters, and the reevaluation of the ensemble from new angles (which distinguishes the rhizome from a simple communication network—"to communicate" no longer has the same meaning; see "Univocity of Being"); no principle of order or privileged entry point to the path through a multiplicity (on these last two points, see "Complication" and the definition above: "it is composed not of units but of dimensions").

The rhizome is therefore an anti-method, which may appear to mean that all is permitted—and in fact it does, for this is its rigor, the ascetic character of which the authors frequently stress, under the heading of "sobriety," to their hasty disciples (ATP 6, 99, 279, 308–9). Not to know in advance the ideal path for thought, to begin again through experimentation, to install a benevolence in principle, and finally, to regard method as an insufficient defense against prejudice since at very least it preserves its form (first truths): a new definition of seriousness in philosophy, against the puritanical bureaucracy of the academic spirit and its frivolous "professionalism." This new philosophical vigilance is, moreover, one of the meanings of the phrase "conditions no broader than the conditioned" (the other sense is that the condition is differentiated along with experience). The least one can say is that it is not easy to maintain such a position: in this respect, the rhizome is the method of the anti-method, and its constitutive "principles" are so many cautionary rules against every vestige or reintroduction of the tree and the One within thought (ATP 6–15).

*** Thought gives itself over to experimentation. This decision involves at least three corollaries: 1. To think is not to represent (it does not seek an adequation with a supposedly objective reality, but a real effect that revitalizes both life and thought, displacing their stakes, sending them further and in different directions). 2. There is a real beginning only in the middle [*au milieu*]—the word "genesis" recovers here its full etymological value of "becoming," without any relation to an origin. 3. If every encounter is "possible," insofar as there is no reason to disqualify *a priori* certain paths rather than others, encounters are not for all that selected by experience (certain arrangements and couplings neither produce nor change anything).

This last point requires more elaboration. The apparently free play that the method of the rhizome calls for should not be misunderstood, as if it were a matter of blindly practicing any old collage in order to arrive at art or philosophy, or as if every difference was fecund *a priori*, following a *doxa* commonly held today. Certainly, anyone who hopes to think must consent to a certain degree of blind groping without support, to an "adventure of the involuntary" (PS 95–7); and despite either the appearance or the discourse of our teachers, this *tact* is the aptitude least evenly distributed, for we suffer from too much consciousness and too much mastery—we hardly ever consent to the rhizome. Vigilance of thought is no less requisite, but at the very heart of experimentation: besides the rules mentioned above, it consists in distinguishing the sterile (black holes, impasses) from the fecund (lines of flight). It is here that thought conquers both its necessity and its efficacy: by recognizing the signs that force us to think because they envelop what we are not yet thinking. Which is why Deleuze and Guattari can say that the rhizome is a problem of *cartography* (ATP 12–13), which is to say a clinical problem, one of immanent evaluation. It can happen that the rhizome is aped, *represented* and not produced, that it serves as an alibi for assemblages without effect or for tiresome logorrhea: as if it sufficed for things to be unrelated for it to warrant an interest in relating them. But the rhizome is as benevolent as it is selective: it has the cruelty of the real, and spreads its shoots only where determinate effects take place.

Transcendental Empiricism

* "The transcendental form of a faculty is indistinguishable from its disjointed, superior or transcendent exercise. Transcendent in no way means that the faculty addresses itself to objects outside the world but, on the contrary, that it grasps that in the world which concerns it exclusively and brings it into the world. The transcendent exercise must not be traced from the empirical exercise precisely because it apprehends that which cannot be grasped from the point of view of common sense, that which measures the empirical operation of all the faculties according to that which pertains to each, given the form of their collaboration. That is why the transcendental is answerable to a superior empiricism which alone is capable of exploring its domain and its regions . . . Contrary to Kant's belief, it cannot be induced from the ordinary empirical forms in the manner in which these appear under the determination of common sense" (DR 143).

** Deleuze's most general problem is not being but experience. It is from this critical or transcendental perspective that Bergson and Nietzsche are taken up. The two studies have in common the following diagnosis: Kant was right to create the question of the conditions of experience, but the conditioning he invokes is that of possible and not real experience, and remains external to that which it conditions (NP 91; B 27). They both call for the same radicalization of the question: to think "conditions no broader than the conditioned," which is the concern of a "superior empiricism" (NP 91; B 27, 30; and already in "Bergson's Conception of Difference"—DI 36). In a parallel fashion, by way of Nietzsche and Proust, Deleuze puts forward a "new image of thought" oriented around the idea that "thinking is not innate, but must be engendered within thought" (DR 147): from this emerges the themes of the involuntary, of the violence of signs or of the encounter with that which forces thought, and the problem of a stupidity raised to the level of the transcendental (NP 103–10; PS 94–102). All of these themes are taken up again in *Difference and Repetition*, bolstered by a new argument: Kant's mistake was to have "traced the transcendental from the empirical" by giving it the form of a conscious subject correlated to its object (DR 142, 143; LS 97–8). As a result, the doctrine of the faculties is rehabilitated (cf. the quotation we opened with above, as well as PS 99), at the same time as the idea of an impersonal transcendental field is announced, one composed of pre-individual singularities (LS 99, 109).

And what of Deleuze's Spinozism? Does he not proceed from an entirely different inspiration, an ontological one, since it is here that the famous thesis of the univocity of being intervenes? Deleuze observes that the paradox of Spinoza consists in placing empiricism in the service of rationalism (EPS 149), and constructing a pure plane of experience which, under the name "plane of immanence," coincides with the revised transcendental field (ATP 253–4; SPP Ch. 6; WP 48–9; the logic of univocal being, according to which each being, a pure difference, measures itself against others only in relation to its own specific limit, is affiliated with the doctrine of the faculties). Deleuze can thus return to Bergson and read the beginning of the first chapter of *Matter and Memory* as the installation of such a plane of immanence (C1 56–61; WP 48–9). But why does he seem to slip so easily from the transcendental style to the ontological style, invoking, for example, the "pure plane of immanence of a Being-thought, of a Nature-thought" (WP 88)? The impression arises from the fact that there is no longer an originary Ego to mark out a frontier between the two discourses.[16] It is nevertheless not a question of returning to a dogmatic theory of the in-itself of the world [*l'en-soi du monde*], still less to a form of intellectual intuition in the Kantian sense: simply put, immanence has abandoned the frontiers of the subject, while the in-itself is no longer anything but difference, the degrees of which are traversed by a drifting and nomadic subject (logic of the inclusive disjunction—on this conversion, cf. C2 82; and on intuition, see "Plane of Immanence"). It has become a matter of indifference to speak in one or the other style: the ontology of the virtual or of singularities is nothing other than a tool for the description of "real" experience.

*** 1. Transcendental empiricism means first of all that the discovery of the conditions of experience itself presupposes an *experience* in the strict sense: not the ordinary or empirical experience of a faculty (for the data of empirical lived experience doesn't inform thought about what it can do), but this very faculty taken to its limit, confronted by that which solicits it in its own unique power (where, for example, philosophy discovers itself to be bound solely to the concept, rather than to opinion or reflection). For this reason, not only must critical philosophy become an empiricism, but empiricism, which "treats the concept as object of an encounter" (DR xx), accomplishes its vocation only by elevating itself to the transcendental. We can therefore understand why the use of clinical or literary material tends to replace the first-hand experience of phenomenology: this kind of experience is inherently rare, not available in an everyday way, and demands an appropriate semiotic invention.

2. Transcendental empiricism implies consequently that the conditions are never general, but are declined according to the *case*: hence the crucial claim that they are never broader than that which they condition. This statement seems at first glance to annul the distinction between fact and law by aligning the latter with the former (which would be paradoxical coming from someone who denounces the "tracing" of the transcendental from the empirical). What it really means is that we can never speak in advance of *every* experience, except by missing its essential variation, its inherent singularity, and by applying to it a discourse so general as to leave the concept and the object in a relation of mutual indifference. A special kind of concept is therefore necessary, a "plastic principle," following the example of the Will to Power (NP 50) or of Duration-Memory ("Bergson's Conception of Difference"—DI 37, 43–4), a differential

principle or a principle of internal differentiation where each degree specifies a mode of existence and of thought, a possibility of life (see "Plane of Immanence").

Univocity of Being

* "In effect, the essential in univocity is not that Being is said in a single and same sense, but that it is said, in a single and same sense, *of* all its individuating differences or intrinsic modalities" (DR 36). "The univocity of being does not mean that there is one and the same being; on the contrary, beings are multiple and different, they are always produced by a disjunctive synthesis, and they themselves are disjointed and divergent, *membra disjuncta*. The univocity of being signifies that being is Voice, that it is said, and that it is said in one and the same 'sense' of everything about which it is said" (LS 179).

** Foregrounding the medieval thesis of the univocity of being is without a doubt Deleuze's most important contribution to the history of philosophy (EPS Chapters 6 and 11; DR 35–42; LS 25th Series). This thesis, the history of which includes three stages, Duns Scotus, Spinoza, and Nietzsche, subverts the entirety of ontology, Heidegger included; deployed in its full consequences, it calls into question the very pertinence of the name of being. What is essential is that it carries within it the *affirmation of immanence*. 1. Univocity is the immediate synthesis of the multiple: the one is no longer said except *of* the multiple, as opposed to the latter being subordinated to the one as to a superior and common genre capable of englobing it. This means that the one is no more than the differenciator of differences, internal difference or disjunctive synthesis (as Deleuze notes, Spinoza's unique substance still preserves a certain independence in its relation to its modes, hence "Substance must itself be said *of* the modes and only *of* the modes" [DR 40], a reversal that will be carried out only by Nietzsche with the concept of Eternal Return; yet, returning to Spinoza for a second reading, he shows how the theory of bodies tends toward an entirely different conception of unique substance, by promoting a pure plane of immanence or body without organs—AO 309 fn.; ATP 153–4, 253 ff.; SPP Ch. 6). The word "differenciator," which appears often in Deleuze's writings has the unfortunate disadvantage of allowing us to suppose a separate instance lodged in the heart of the world ruling internally over its distributions; yet it is clear that it designates nothing other than the edge-to-edge of differences or the multiple and mutating network of their "distances" (the thing, restored to the originary or "transcendental" plane of the disjunctive synthesis, exists only as a singularity or a point of view enveloping an infinity of other points of view). 2. The corollary of this immediate synthesis of the multiple is the deployment of all things upon one and the same common plane of equality: "common" does not have here the sense of a generic identity, but of a transversal and nonhierarchical *communication* between beings that only differ. Measure (or hierarchy) also changes its meaning here: it is no longer an external measure of beings in relation to a standard, but the internal measure of each being in relation to its own limits ("the smallest becomes equivalent to the largest when it is no longer separated from what it can do" [DR 37]—a concept of "minority" will emerge from this later on [ATP 291 ff.], as well as a theory of racism [ATP 178] and a concept of childhood, e.g. CC 133: "The baby is combat"). This ethics of being-equal and of power is drawn from Spinoza but even more so from Nietzsche and his Eternal Return (DR 41 and 294–end). Ultimately, "univocal being is at one and the same time nomadic distribution and crowned anarchy" (DR 37). What sense is there in preserving the notion of unity here, even if it were only in the non-englobing mode of *a* multiplicity (immanence of the one to the multiple, immediate synthesis of the multiple)? The answer is that a pluralism that was not *at the same time* a monism would lead to a fragmentation of scattered terms, indifferent and transcendent to one another: difference, novelty, and rupture would amount to a brute and miraculous upsurge (creation *ex nihilo*—but from where would the power of this *nihil* come from? And what would this "coming" be?) In this respect, the one of univocity conditions the affirmation of the multiple in its irreducibility (WP 195–6). That everything comes from the world, even novelty, *without the latter being drawn from the past*, such is the lesson of immanence emerging from the solidarity of the concepts of univocity, disjunctive synthesis, and the virtual, when these are well understood.

*** The affirmation of the univocity of being, whose constant formula is "ontologically one, formally diverse" (EPS 66; DR 35, 301; LS 59), culminates in the equation "pluralism = monism" (ATP 20). There is therefore nothing that permits us to conclude a primacy of the one. It seems that this thesis, maintained by Alain Badiou,[17] does not sufficiently weigh the import of the statement according to which being is that which is said *of* its differences and not the inverse, the unity "is that of the multiple and is said only of the multiple" (NP 85–6, translation modified). Furthermore, the fact that a concept of simulacra applied to beings in general is the inevitable consequence of the thesis of univocity by no means appears to us to confirm a primacy of the one. The application of the simulacrum to beings signifies only that the vocabulary of being has ceased to be pertinent in the universe of the disjunctive synthesis, owing to what it still preserves from the fixed and identitarian horizon. For when Deleuze announces the overturning of Platonism and the universal through the ascension of the simulacra, what is simulated is nothing other than *identity*, the impermeable delimitation of forms and individualities, and not at all the play of inclusive disjunctions or becomings that produces this effect: "all identities are only simulated" (DR ix), "the simulacra makes the Same and the Similar, the model and the copy, fall under the power of the false (phantasm)" (LS 263). For Deleuze, all that is real is the mobile play of the disjunctive synthesis as the immediate synthesis of the multiple, or the Eternal Return interpreted as the "being of becoming" (DR 41); not the withdrawal of the one, for there is only Difference [*LA différence*] that diverges immediately from itself. I was about to say that the withdrawn one is not a pole in Deleuze's thought; in fact it is, but it is death, the pure and naked body without organs willed as such. This pole is doubtless implicated in vitality and desire, but precisely as the ultimate refusal to allow the multiple a self-organization or a self-unification. That the relation to death is the condition of the real does not mean that death is the real and that becomings are merely its simulacra (this illusion is repeatedly highlighted in *A Thousand Plateaus* as the risk inherent to desire). It is significant that of all of Deleuze's concepts, the simulacrum is the only one to be completely abandoned after *The Logic of Sense* (we find no trace of it except in the "Natal"—see "Refrain"). Two reasons for this can be put forward: it lent itself to too many misunderstandings; but above all, it still partook in the negative exposition of "crowned anarchy," focused entirely upon the critical demonstration of the produced or derived character of identity. The vacancy left by this concept will be filled in by the concept of becoming.

Virtual

* "The virtual is opposed not to the real but to the actual. *The virtual is fully real in so far as it is virtual* . . . the virtual must be defined as strictly a part of the real object—as though the object had one part of itself in the virtual into which it plunged as though into an objective dimension" (DR 208–9).

** Why does Deleuze's thought invoke the virtual? The virtual is the insistence of that which is not given. Only the actual is given, including the form of the possible, which is to say the alternative as the law of division of the real that immediately assigns my experience to a certain field of possibilities. But that it is not given does not mean that the virtual is elsewhere or for an other: such would be the other sense of the possible as a world expressed by the Other [*autrui*], which is to say as a point of view—perceptual, intellectual, or vital— different from mine; or else the possible under the transcendent form of the necessary or of a ubiquitous totalizing point of view, which we represent to ourselves as being occupied by a God contemplating the actual infinity of eternal truths, as in classical rationalism; or as a perpetual lack and absence, as in structuralism. That the virtual is means first of all that everything is not given, nor can it be given. Next, it means that everything that comes to pass comes only from this world—the clause of immanence and its corresponding belief (to believe in this world "as in the impossible," which is to say in its creative potentialities or in the *creation* of possibilities (C2 170; WP 74–5). The recourse to this category is not explainable by who knows what spiritualist temptation of a world-beyond or a hidden Heaven: the elementary misunderstanding of the virtual consists in seeing it as *another type of actuality*, thereby confusing it with that from which it distinguishes itself by definition—transcendence. Its explanation lies in the effort to equip philosophy with a set of logical tools capable of conferring a consistency on the idea of immanence.

*** This is why we must not approach the virtual solely through the process of actualization, for in this case the reader could be tempted to interpret it as a primitive state of the real from out of which the actual is derived. And even if the mode of explication of Chapter 5 of *Difference and Repetition* can favor such an impression, however contradictory this is to its more explicit thesis (contrary to *A Thousand Plateaus*, which will bring the embryological question back into relation with the question of real experience, and will affirm with more clarity the contemporaneity of the egg with all the ages of a life—cf. 164–5), it remains the case that the virtual is introduced in Chapter 2, explicitly within the purview of a thought of experience, which is to say of the given (DR 96–106). There is no experience of the virtual as such, since it is not given and has no psychological existence; on the other hand, a critical philosophy that refuses to "trace" the form of the transcendental from that of the empirical, assigning the given the form of an *already-given* as universal structure of possible experience, will do justice to the given by constituting the real from both an actual *and* a virtual component. It is in this sense that there is no real—which is to say no *encounter*, and not merely objects recognized in advance as possible—except in the process of actualization; and if the virtual is not itself given, the pure given on the plane of immanence of real experience is all the same connected to it, implicating it intimately. And this is why the process of actualization is logically inseparable from the inverse movement of *crystallization* that restores to the given its irreducible virtual component.

If we now ask why the whole of the world is neither given nor capable of being given, the answer lies in the refutation of the pseudo-originary status of the possible: the history of the world, like that of a life, is marked by redistributions—or events—that pluralize the field of possibilities, or rather, multiply them across fields incompossible with one another. These redistributions are certainly datable, but they cannot be aligned in accordance with the continuity of a permanent present coextensive with the time of the world (on the new meaning of dates, see N 34). There is no sense in calling them successive: spatio-temporal effectuations (or states of affairs) are successive only when they are considered abstractly, on the basis of a dimension "supplementary" to that of experience—which is to say when they are separated from the determinate field of possibilities to which they are connected, their virtual component omitted, so as to appear as pure actualities. The derivative character of the field of possibilities results in the affirmation of a multiple temporality, of a multidimensional time—the revelation of a non-chronological reality of time, one more profound than chronology (see "Crystal of Time"). It is a matter of inserting exteriority into time; but the outside of time is not the supra-historicity of the eternal, even under the seemingly immanentist form of hermeneutics, which maintains at very least the continuity of a human consciousness and, consequently, of common sense; it has become internal to time, manifoldly separating it from itself. Thus the whole can only be thought by means of a synthesis of heterogeneous dimensions of time: hence the fundamentally temporal sense of the virtual. It is this synthesis that makes us *see* the crystal; in other words, it is what is at stake in every *becoming*.

War Machine

* "To the extent that each time a line of flight turns into a line of death, we do not invoke an internal impulse of the 'death instinct' type, we invoke another assemblage of desire which brings into play a machine which is objectively or extrinsically definable. It is therefore not metaphorically that each time someone destroys others and destroys himself he has invented on his line of flight his own war-machine" (D 142). "We define 'war machines' as linear arrangements constructed along lines of flight. Thus understood, the aim of war machines is not war at all but a very special kind of space, *smooth space*, which they establish, occupy, and extend. *Nomadism* is precisely this combination of war machine and smooth space" (N 33).

** This concept involves two levels of difficulty, one related to its content (the war machine is insistently said to not have war as its object) the other to its status (as an assemblage, is it historical, universal, metaphorical?). It starts with a meditation on the relation between war and desire, and on the recurrence of the image of war in the writers swept along by a "line of flight." As always, Deleuze and Guattari dismiss the qualification of metaphor as proceeding from a misinterpretation (D 141). The concept of the war machine responds to the question of the ambiguity of the "line of flight" (which consists less in fleeing a situation than in "putting into flight," in the exploitation of points of deterritorialization): its capacity to convert itself into a line of abolition. Thus just as it would be too simple to consider a love of death or a fascist vertigo to be the opposite of desire, it would be too simple to believe that desire confronts no other danger than that of its reterritorialization. In *Anti-Oedipus*, despite the logic of the "body without organs," the relation that collective desire entertained with death was still related to the interiorization of its own repression: in this context, fascism is distinguished from every other society only by the extreme character of the archaic reterritorialization to which it proceeds in its attempt to the ward off the deterritorialization proper to the capitalist epoch (AO 29–30, 257–9, 366–7). The situation is different in *A Thousand Plateaus*: the "passion of abolition" designates the moment where desire confronts its repression under desperate conditions and finds in the destruction of others and itself the "only object" that remains once it has "lost its power to change." Fascism is therefore this complex moment, which we hesitate to qualify as interiorization, in which desire finds at the heart of defeat the terrible resource of turning the State against itself by "channeling into it a flow of absolute war" (ATP 229–31). This state of desire functioning in a vacuum, so to speak, is not to be confused with the non-desire of the neurotic, since interiorization is precisely what desire wards off by taking war or death as its ultimate object; we are reminded rather of the "repulsive" or "paranoiac" pole of the body without organs (AO 8–9). However, the concept of the war machine is not exhausted in the description of a clinical state, whether individual or collective: for it is what gives a truly problematic content to the critique of the State as form or model (why the "war machine" tends to be identified with desire as such, rather than designating only its critical threshold, will be explained below). The thesis of the *exteriority of the war machine* means at once that the State cannot be conceived without a relation to an outside that it appropriates without having the power to reduce (the institutionalized war machine of an army), and that the war machine has an in-principle and positive relation to a social assemblage that cannot by nature ever enclose itself within a form of interiority. This assemblage is *nomadism*: its form of expression is the war machine, its content—metallurgy; the ensemble is related to a space described as smooth (ATP 380–416). This thesis has a practical significance: instead of maintaining intact an uncritical faith in the revolution, or of abstractly calling for a revolutionary or reformist "third way," it makes it possible to *specify the conditions* of a non-Bolshevik revolutionary politics, without the organization of a party, that would at the same time be in possession of an analytic tool with which to confront the "fascist" drift characteristic of collective lines (D 145–7; ATP 466–73). Deleuze's engagement on the behalf of the Palestinians and their resistance meant this: he saw in the PLO a "war machine" in the precise sense that he had given this word (N 172).

*** To avoid remaining with a first impression of ambivalence or apparent contradiction, the reader must understand in what sense the war machine "does not have war as its object." The ambiguity from which the war machine draws its name stems from the fact that it leaves only a negative trace in history (D 142). This is testified to by the destiny of every resistance: to first be qualified as terrorism or destabilization, then to triumph bitterly—if at all—by passing into the form of the State: this is because it belongs to *becoming*, to a "becoming-revolutionary," and is not inscribed in history (N 152–3;

WP 110–11). Hence it could be said that the "non-organic vitality" of a collectivity, its social inventiveness in terms of original assemblages, sometimes manifests itself only in war, even if it does not have war as its object. It is only when it is appropriated by the State, "separated from what it can do," that it takes war as its object: this then changes its sense or its "regime of signs," since it is no longer the same assemblage; the guerilla becomes a military operation (ATP 416–23). Ultimately, the concept of the war machine condenses the two poles of desire, "paranoiac" and "schizoid," which were brought to light by the logic of the body without organs (AO 366 ff.; ATP 165–6).

Notes

1. A few examples pulled at random: DR 181, 190, 199; AO 2, 36, 41, 84, 141, 293; BS 91; K 22, 35–6, 45; D 3, 112, 117, 140; ATP 198, 200–1, 234–5, 274–5, 453; C2 20, 56, 129, 182, 242; CC 68; etc.
2. The reader may also consult Zourabichvili's article "The Eye of Montage: Dziga Vertov and Bergsonian Materialism," in *The Brain is the Screen: Deleuze and the Philosophy of Cinema*, edited by Greg Flaxman (Minneapolis: University of Minnesota Press, 2000), pp. 141–9—Trans.
3. Cf. *Being and Time*, §61 ff. To the three temporal "ek-stases" presented in §65, one finds a response in Deleuze's three syntheses of time in *Difference and Repetition* (Chapter 2), where the direct relation between the past and the future as well as the temporal status of the possible are equally decisive, yet conceived differently and from an ethico-political perspective incompatible with that of Heidegger. For a brief insight into the divergence that opposes the two thinkers, one may consider among other things their respective concepts of destiny (DR 82–3; *Being and Time*, §74). An understanding of the Deleuzian position presupposes a combined reading of *Difference and Repetition* (the three syntheses of time), of *The Logic of Sense* (the opposition between Chronos and Aion), and of *Cinema 2: The Time Image* (the opposition of Chronos and Cronos, Chapter 4—see "Crystal of Time").
4. The French term "*entre-temps*" can also be translated as "meanwhile." I have opted for "in-between" because it conveys the more philosophical sense of an interval between two chronological series, which Zourabichvili often exploits—Trans.
5. Quotation erroneously cited in the French edition—Trans.
6. I have followed Brian Massumi's decision to preserve the French words *signifiance* and *asignifiance*. See the Translator's Note, ATP xviii—Trans.

7. Alain Badiou rightly speaks of a "movement of two movements"; cf. "Deleuze's Vitalist Ontology," in *Briefings on Existence: A Short Treatise on Transitory Ontology*, trans. and ed. Norman Madarasz (Albany: SUNY Press, 2006), 63–73.

8. On the use of the term "lived body" [*corps propre*] in phenomenology, cf. Maurice Merleau-Ponty, *The Phenomenology of Perception*, trans. C. Smith (New York: Routledge, 1958)—Trans.

9. On the various senses and uses of the term *prélevément* in *Anti-Oedipus*, see the translators' note on p. 36. Cf. also AO 36–41—Trans.

10. A reference to Descartes' "morale par provision." See the *Discourse on Method*, 3rd Part—Trans.

11. It was Félix Guattari who forged the concept of transversality, prior to his collaboration with Deleuze. Cf. *Psychanalyse et transversalité*. The two thinkers constantly borrowed notions from each other, which each understood in his own way, even if these were reworked together in the framework of a common project.

12. This thesis is defended by Alain Badiou, in a book that otherwise must be saluted for the height of its viewpoint and its concern for true controversy: *Deleuze: The Clamor of Being*, trans. L. Burchill (Minneapolis: University of Minnesota Press, 1999). If the pluralism that Deleuze rejects is one of equivocity (p. 24), then we cannot but agree; except that for Deleuze equivocity is precisely a pseudo-pluralism, the most sure guarantee of the transcendence of the One in relation to the multiple. The root of the problem is this: for Deleuze, pluralism can be thought only under the condition of a *primacy of relation*, which is something that Badiou cannot admit, in the name of the void, which is the bearer of a supplement—which for Deleuze would refer to a transcendent miracle and not to creation (the height of the misunderstanding occurs on p. 91, when the virtual past is confused with a simple lived past—see "Crystal of Time"). Consequently, Deleuze does indeed need a "renewed concept of the one" (p. 10), but as the immediate—or disjunctive—synthesis of the multiple (the "univocity of being" has no other meaning). Hence the equation: "pluralism = monism" (ATP 20), which could also be expressed: *internal difference = exteriority of relations*. In this regard, the concept of "simulacra," when applied to beings, is less essential to Deleuzian philosophy than it is to Badiou's interpretation of it; for my part, I would be more inclined to ask why Deleuze definitively abandoned it after *The Logic of Sense*. See "Univocity of Being."

13. There is an error in the English edition, which reads "change" instead of "chance" here. The French word is *hazard*—Trans.

14. In French, "data" is *les données*, which has the same stem as the verb "to give," *donner*. Hence the play on words made possible here (*elles ne "donnent" quoi que ce soit que . . .*)—Trans.

Notes

15. The Latin word *limes* refers to the external frontier marking the boundaries of the Roman Empire—Trans.
16. This would be the place to develop Deleuze's divergence with regard to Heidegger (Husserl renews and radicalizes the exigency of correlating being and experience, which has its origins in Descartes; it is with Heidegger that, for the first time, the experience validating ontological discourse ceases to be related to an originary subject, and simultaneously ceases to be a matter of "evidence").
17. See note 12, above.

Selected Bibliography of
François Zourabichvili's Work

1992
"Spinoza, le vulgus et la psychologie sociale," in *Studia Spinozana*, vol. 8 (1992).

1994
Deleuze: Une philosophie de l'événement (Paris: PUF, in the "Philosophies" collection); 2nd ed., 1997; 3rd ed., 2004, with a new introduction entitled "L'ontologique et le transcendental." The 1997 edition is included in a book entitled *La philosophie de Deleuze* (Paris: PUF, in the "Quadrige," 2004), along with two other studies: Anne Sauvagnargues's *Deleuze, de l'animal à l'art*, and Paola Marrati's *Deleuze, cinéma et philosophie*. Translations: Japanese (trans. Akihiro Ozawa; Tokyo: Kawadeshobo, 1997), Italian (trans. Fabio Agostini; Verona: Ombre Corte Edizioni, 1998), Spanish (trans. Irene Agoff; Buenos Aires: Amorrortu Editores, 2004).

"L'identité individuelle chez Spinoza," in *Spinoza: Puissance et ontologie*, ed. Myriam Revault d'Allonnes et Hadi Rizk (Paris: Kimé, 1994).

1996
"Six Notes on the Percept (on the Relation between the Critical and the Clinical)," in *Deleuze: A Critical Reader*, ed. Paul Patton (Oxford: Blackwell, 1996).

1998
"Deleuze et le possible: De l'involontarisme en politique," in *Deleuze: Une vie philosophique*, ed. Eric Alliez (Paris: Les Empêcheurs de Penser en Rond, 1998).
Translations: Portugese (in *Gilles Deleuze: Um vida filosofica*, São Paulo: Editora 34, 2000); Italien (in *Aut Aut*, no. 276, November–December 1996).

"Le spinozisme spectral d'Anton Tchekhov," in *Actes des journées*, *"Spinoza au XIXe siècle,"* Sorbonne, <http://recherche.univ-montp3.fr/ea738/cher cheurs/zourabichvili/spinozisme.pdf> (accessed February 29, 2012).

2000
"The Eye of Montage: Dziga Vertov and Bergsonian Materialism," in *The Brain is the Screen: Deleuze and the Philosophy of Cinema*, ed. Greg Flaxman (Minneapolis: University of Minnesota Press, 2000).

2002
Spinoza: Une physique de la pensée (Paris: PUF, in the "Philosophie d'aujourd'hui" collection, 2002).

Le conservatisme paradoxal de Spinoza: Enfance et royauté (Paris: PUF, in the "Pratiques théoriques: collection, 2002).

"La langue de l'entendement infini," in *Actes de la Décade*, *"Spinoza aujourd'hui,"* Cerisy-la-Salle, July 2002, <http://recherche.univ-montp3.fr/ea738/chercheurs/zourabichvili/langue.pdf> (accessed February 29, 2012).

"Les deux pensées de Deleuze et Negri: Une richesse et une chance" (interview with Yoshihiko Ichida), in *Multitudes* 9 (May–June 2002), <http://multitudes.samizdat.net/Les-deux-pensees-de-Deleuze-et-de> (accessed February 29, 2012).

2003
Le vocabulaire de Deleuze (Paris: Ellipses, 2003). A partial version of the book appears in *Le vocabulaire des philosophes*, vol. 4 (Paris: Ellipses, 2002).
Translation: Portugese (trans. André Telles; Rio de Janeiro: Relume Dumara, 2004).

"Le pouvoir en devenir: Tarde et l'actualité," Preface to *Gabriel Tarde: Les transformations du pouvoir*, in *Œuvres de Gabriel Tarde*, second series, vol. 2, ed. Eric Alliez (Paris: Les Empêcheurs de penser en rond, 2003).

"La consistenza del concetto di scienza intuitive," in *Sulla scienza intuitiva in Spinoza*, ed. Filippo Del Lucchese and Vittorio Morfino (Milan: Edizioni Ghibli, 2003).

2004
"Chateaubriand, la révolution et son témoin," in *Literarische Fluchtlinien der Revolution nach 1789*, in *Cahiers Lendemains* (Tübingen: Stauffenburg Verlag, 2004), <http://recherche.univ-montp3.fr/ea738/chercheurs/zourabichvili/chateaubriand.pdf> (accessed February 29, 2012).

"L'intime, le temps et le symptom," in *Rue Descartes*, no. 43, *"L'intériorité"* (March 2004).

2005

"Leibniz et la barbarie," in *Les équivoques de la civilisation*, ed. Bertrand Binoche (Seyssel: Champ Vallon, 2005).

"Qu'est-ce qu'une oeuvre interactive?" in *Revue d'esthétique* (2005).

"Géométrie audio-visuelle d'une révolte: Okraïna" (on Boris Barnet), <http://recherche.univ-montp3.fr/ea738/chercheurs/zourabichvili/geometrie.pdf> (accessed February 29, 2012).

2006

"Kant avec Masoch," in *Multitudes* 25 (Summer 2006), <http://multitudes.samizdat.net/Kant-avec-Masoch> (accessed February 29, 2012).

2007

"La Question de la littéralité," in *Klesis: Revue Philosophique, "Autour de François Zourabichvili"* (April 2007), <http://www.philosophie-en-ligne.fr/klesis/F-Zourabichvili.pdf> (accessed February 29, 2012).

2008

"L'Écriture littérale de L'Anti-Oedipe," in *Ateliers de L'Anti-Oedipe*, ed. Nicolas Cornibert and Jean-Christophe Goddard (Paris: Mimesis/MětisPRESSES, 2008), pp. 247–56 <http://www.europhilosophie.eu/recherche/IMG/pdf/Zourabichvili.pdf> (accessed February 29, 2012).

2011

La littéralité et autres essais sur l'art (Paris: PUF, 2011), in the collection "Lignes d'art," directed by Anne Sauvagnargues and Fabienne Brugère, with a preface by Anne Sauvagnargues entitled "Jouer sa pensée." The collection includes the following essays: 1. Event and Literality; 2. The Question of Literality; 3. Are Philosophical Concepts Metaphors? Deleuze and his Problematic of Literality; 4. "What is to Come"; 5. The Game of Art; 6. On Nietzsche's Phrase: "One Should Part from Life as Ulysses Parted From Nausicaa—Blessing it Rather Than in Love with It"; 7. The Vision of Montage (Dziga Vertov and Bergsonian Materialism); 8. Chateaubriand: The Revolution and Its Witness; 9. Audio-Visual Geometry of a Revolt: Barnet's "Okraïna"; 10. What Is an Interactive Work?; 11. Cinema and Transformation: "Others," by Hugo Santiago; 12. "Others," by Hugo Santiago; 13. Aesthetic Difference or Non-Mimetic Recognition; 14. Aesthetic Difference: Play and Non-Mimetic Recognition; 15. The Aesthetic Anchorage of Deleuze's Thought.

Index

abstract machine, abstract motor, 20, 135, 148, 164
abstraction, 129–30
affect
  and forces, 69–70, 70–1, 94
  intensity, 186, 200
  and perception, 115, 141, 195
  and subjectivity, 123–4
  in univocity of being, 3, 10, 14, 39
affirmation, 62–3, 82–3, 186
Aion, 120, 122, 123, 142–5, 148, 159, 160–1, 179
  and Chronos, 107–10, 142–4, 160, 180
animal, 150
anorexic, 169
Aristotle, 153
art, 122, 162, 184
Artaud, Antonin, 86–7, 150, 151, 186
assemblage, 29, 145–8, 164, 170, 181
  and territory, 167–8, 205
  war machine, 217, 218
axiomatic *see* code and axiomatic

Bacon, Francis, 71
Badiou, Alain, 213–14, 220n
Balibar, Étienne, 22
becoming, 23, 148–50, 173–4
  contemplative, 119
  and crystal of time, 157–8
  and difference, 104
  and ethical difference, 119–21, 126
  event as, 40–1
  and individuality, 127
  in literature and cinema, 124
  in nonorganic life, 188

thought in, 85–6
in time, 97, 101, 216
truth as, 112
beginning, relation between thought and truth, 49–52
being
  and becoming, 23, 173
  and categories, 2–3, 36–7
  see also ontology; univocity of being
belief, 39–40, 89, 91–2, 215
Bergson, Henri, 1, 36, 162, 177, 180, 187, 210
  Matter and Memory, 163, 194, 195, 198, 210
  theory of time, 96, 98, 99, 113, 159, 160–1
  on virtual and actual, 162
Blanchot, Maurice, 93n
blocks (of becoming), 21, 149, 188
body, bodies, 17n, 65
  in milieu of living present, 113–14, 114
  and mind, 110
  relation of language to, 129
  representation, 116
  and the virtual, 107, 180
body without organs, 114, 150–2, 168–9, 178, 181, 183, 186, 188, 212
Boundas, Constantin, 16n
break-flow, 152–4, 163

Carroll, Lewis, 151
cartography *see* map, cartography
categories, 2–3
causality, 101–2
chance, 57, 183–4
chaos, 122, 188–91, 192–4

Index

Index

the State, and the war machine, 218–19
Stoics, 109, 142–3, 147–8, 171
strata, 8
structuralism, 179, 215
stubbornness, 86
stupidity, 76, 204
  as structure of thought, 8, 58, 67
style, 27–8, 131, 172
subjectivity
  and becoming-other, 123–4
  and difference, 13, 16n
  in experience as crystal of time, 158
  interiorization of the exterior, 105
  and thinking, 52, 65–6, 68

territory *see* deterritorialization,
    territory
thing, as affirming force, 62, 116
thought
  and beginning in relation with truth,
    49–52
  disappointment and fatigue, 87–9
  effect on subject, 52, 65–6
  and the encounter, 26–7, 56–7, 72,
    85–6, 173, 203
  and experience, 3
  to experimentation, 208–9
  forces in, 72–4
  and necessity, 5–8, 44–5, 48, 61,
    76
  and new appearance of data, 190,
    192–3
  and non-sense, 58–9
  and recognition of truth, 47–9
  stupidity as structure of, 8, 58, 67
  and temporal mode of the future,
    97–8
  and will, 45–7, 86
  see also image of thought
time
  Bergson's conception, 96, 98, 99,
    113, 159, 160–1
  as difference, 101, 102–7, 112
  and the event, 96, 100, 108–10,
    112
  future, 97–8, 108
  heterogeneity, 94, 98–102, 102,
    112

passing of, 96–7, 99–100
present, 94–6, 108
relation to outside, 144
and sense, 112, 143
temporal modes, 94–8, 107–10
truth's essential relation to, 112,
    126–7, 128
see also Aion; crystal of time
transcendence
belief in, 183
distinguished from the virtual, 215
and immanent evaluation, 125
and truth, 47–8
values of, 185, 186
transcendental empiricism, 9, 13, 65,
    170, 207, 209–12, 216
transcendental experience, 3–4, 5, 39
transcendental field, 73–4, 88–9, 199,
    200, 213
  replaced by plane of immanence, 37,
    196–8
transcendental logic, 4
transversality, 178, 179
truth
  as becoming, 112
  and beginning in relation with
    thought, 49–52
  as creation, 185–6, 192
  and the encounter, 56–7
  essential relation with time, 112, 124,
    126–7, 128
  as ethical difference, 124–6, 128
  and falsity, 8–9, 59, 129
  and good will of thinking, 45–7,
    64
  involuntarism and, 1
  and necessity, 5–6, 14, 44–5, 76
  and recognition in thought, 47–9
  voluntarist conception, 1, 4–5

unconscious, 74, 154, 156–7
univocity of being, 2–4, 37, 38–9, 162,
    212–14
  affirming immanence, 104, 107,
    184
  and difference, 169
  and plane of immanence, 188, 195,
    196

231

Index

violence, in thought, 61, 64, 69–70, 73, 87

the virtual, 107
  and the actual, 121–2, 155, 158–9, 161–2, 172, 180, 193–4, 214–16
vitality, 184–8
voluntarism, in conception of truth, 1, 4–5

war machine, 217–19
will
  emergence of, 8–9
  and thinking, 45–6, 64, 86
Wittgenstein, Ludwig, 57
women, femininity, 175
Worms, Frédéric, 19, 23
Worringer, Wilhelm, 186
writing, 29

Zarader, Jean-Pierre, 19
Zourabichvili, François
  approach to Deleuze, 23–4
  article "Kant with Masoch", 23
  claim of "no ontology of Deleuze", 1, 19–20
  Deleuze: A Philosophy of the Event, 19, 23–9
  on fallacies about Deleuze's thought, 25–6
  family, 30n
  life, career and works, 22–3
  Literality and Other Essays on Art, 21
  significance as philosopher, 21
  theme of literality, 20–1
  The Vocabulary of Deleuze, 19–20, 23–9
  work on Spinoza, 22–3, 30–1n